WAKE UP, KOREA!

For Gen. Lesperance,

Sept. 2022

Rocky

WAKE UP, KOREA!
An Essay on Korea's Way Forward

Jung-ki "Rocky" Park

Copyright © 2022 by Jung-Ki "Rocky" Park
All rights reserved
Published Poem&Essay
#170-1, Sangga-dong, 159, Chunghyeon-ro, Jochiwon-eup, Sejong-si, Republic of Korea
phone: 82 (044)863-7652
Printed in the Republic of Korea
ISBN 979-11-91914-25-2 (03300)

Preface

As I approach my 88th year, I realize that I am nearing another milestone in my life. I am a great-grandfather now. *Plain Stories by a Grandpa* was written over 30 some odd years ago, and I am deeply moved by the publication of its sequel.

When I look back through the lens of time, I am grateful for so many things. My parents, my siblings, my friends, the army, this society and this country; I've had the pleasure of countless blessings throughout this life, and for that, I am deeply grateful. I bow my head in gratitude.

With all due respect, I wanted to convey some words of wisdom to the next generation of those that will follow in my footsteps. As one who was born in the Land of the Morning Calm, I think that is my duty.

I pick up my pen. My wording may sound harsh (at times) and the descriptions are sometimes crude. I wanted to rid the narrative of flowery language and obsequiousness. In truth, I wanted this to be an honest conversation between you, the reader, and me. So, bear with me.

I thank our Heavenly Father for my continued health.

October 2021
Han-Nam

Preface 05

Table of Contents

Chapter One A Human Being
  1. Who am I? 10
  2. Embrace your Dreams 12
  3. The Key to Success 19
  4. Never give in 27
  5. Just "do" 32

Chapter Two Gazing away from Korea
  1. Are our neighbors our cousins? 52
  2. What is America? 54
     A. Founding and Ideals 54
     B. The United States and its Morality 61
     C. What is America's Power? 67
     D. The American Civil War 68
     E. Gettysburg 77
     F. Lincoln 96
     G. Jefferson Davis 105
  3. The land we call China 109
     A. China, a grand nation 109
     B. The Daily Life of the Chinese 112
     C. The Ins and Outs of China's Politics 121
        a) Is China a Communist country? 121
        b) The Chinese Communist Party 126

    D. China, formerly the Great and Powerful 153
       a) The Heaven, Earth, and Man 153
       b) The Hundred Schools of Thought 157
       c) Sun-Tzu 169
  4. The nation we call Japan 173
    A. The "real" Japan 173
    B. Spiritualism 179
    C. Harmony 184

Chapter Three What is the Problem?
  1. Korea is disappearing 194
    A. Demographic cliff 194
    B. Super-ageing society and youth unemployment 195
  2. To become a developed nation (A first world nation) 201
  3. Our bare faces 207
  4. National reformation 213

Chapter Four Rise, Young Ladies and Gentlemen
  1. The turning point 222
  2. The Republic of Korea and the 4th Industrial Revolution 227
  3. Artificial Intelligence (AI) and Man 232
  4. Aim High 236
  5. 1988 Seoul Olympics 239

Chapter Five Our Choice
  1. Ceaseless Endeavors 248
  2. Strengthening the ROK-US Alliance 253

  A. Before and After Independence 253
  B. The Korean War and the United States 257
  C. After the Korean War 269
3. Mending our relations with East Asia 274
  A. Chinese conduct 274
  B. Strategic Vision 285
   a) Strategic Paradox 285
   b) Alliances with maritime powers 291
4. Strengthen our cooperation with Japan 293
5. The Reunification of the Korean Peninsula 297
  A. Reunification needs to happen 297
  B. Chun Myung: A Mandate from Heaven 300
  C. How will we achieve reunification? 301

Chapter One

A Human Being

1 Who am I?

I am I. I am not you, and I am not he or she. A unique set of events brought me into this world. Yesterday, I was I, today, I am also I, and by tomorrow, I will still be me. I am a unique being in the universe. I am irreplaceable. When I feel pain, I alone feel pain, and likewise, upon death, only my unique self will die.

Therefore, the life that is once given to me is very precious. I am irreplaceable in this majestic, grand universe. What a precious gift is life! Let us remember that self-confidence makes a person feel superior and makes it appear as though he is only promoting himself. Too much self-confidence crumbles, like a castle in the sand. My self-esteem comes from accepting who I am, exactly as I was born. In this universe, I am unique onto myself; thereby I can take pride in my uniqueness, regardless of whether or not I receive recognition.

Sometimes I may have to bend my own will. But I will not envy others' talents, and I will strive to fill what is lacking in me, while working all the while to hone my talents. This is the description of a noble man by Confucius.[1]

Can anyone become a gentleman? Not even close. One has to shine and

---

[1] Even though others may not acknowledge me, I do not get angry. *Confucius*.

polish stone, day and night. I am a wooden rooster. This idea of a fighting rooster comes from the great Chinese philosopher Zhuang Zhou, also known as Zhuangzi.[2] He who is wise stands firmly and proudly, like a wooden rooster, dispatching his enemies with his unruffled countenance.

A wooden rooster does not flinch or react to other fighting roosters' challenges. But the best fighting rooster in the world cannot best the wooden rooster. It runs away. A wooden rooster does not show off, does not need a piercing stare, and is not arrogant. Just the right amount of self-esteem is the way of becoming a noble man. Not a noble man of Zhuang Zhou's time, but a refined and modern-day nobleman. A true gentleman of the modern world.

Hear ye, the youth of this land, the possibilities are endless! This current life you lead, unique and onto itself, exists only once. Your existence is unique in the whole expansive universe. One's thoughts can transform you into a rat in a sewer, or an eagle, soaring high above. My birth in this land makes my self-worth all the more precious. As I came to be in this world, wouldn't you, like I, rather lead the life of a soaring eagle, flying high above?

---

2) His ideas date back to the 4th century B.C., widely considered to be the pinnacle of Chinese philosophical thought. The legend of the fighting rooster details how a man once brought his rooster to a trainer to become a fighting rooster. But instead of learning how to fight in combat, unlike other roosters, this particular rooster, over time, according to the trainer, won over more aggressive roosters because he unruffled and calm.

2 Embrace your Dreams

Dreams are different from hope. Dreams have a specific architecture and shape, while hope is similar to a flickering light seen from afar. Dreams are individualistic, tailored to the person, while hope is the guide for many individuals. We can live without dreams, but without hope, we despair.

But then again, can we live without dreams, especially during our youth? No. Dreams are the privilege of the youth. If you live without a dream, especially while young, you are essentially throwing your life away. We only live once, so make the most of your dreams.

What is the privilege of the youth? Dream, aspiration, and guts are the privileges of the youth. Its shape, width, and the scope of its ambition matters. Shape your dreams and strive for them; you can and will achieve them.

So, should we dream big? Of course! The bigger, the better. Even absurdist dreams, in my opinion, are better than no dreams at all. The real problem lies with how much effort you put into achieving your goals. Move the heavens with how much care and effort you put into cultivating your dreams. Dreams do come true if you follow this template.

Let me tell you about someone's dream.

If you go to Japan, a Shinto temple exists in the old city of Nara. Called the Kasuga Taisha, it dates back to the 8th century A.D. It is a national heritage site of Japan. Within its walls exists a grove of about 700 Japanese cedar trees. Each tree's circumference is so large that it takes about three grown men to encircle it. These trees are also considered a national treasure of Japan and are thus protected.

In the precinct of Osaka, once lived a carpenter who admired and wanted to own some Japanese cedars. These thousand-year-old trees are very precious, even in Japan. All artisans of a certain class, shall we say, share a similar wish of owning such trees. All craftsmen in Japan take a serious pride in their craftsmanship. The man who lived as a wood craftsman all his life wanted to build a traditional Japanese house using the temple's cedar tree. This was the wood craftsman's dream.

Even if one wishes to own such a tree, how dare he dream of owning a national treasure of Japan? But he could not put away his dream. Even the passage of time did not diminish his dream.

"Maybe I will have a miracle," or so he thought. This was a belief without a base. The time finally came for the carpenter to retire. But what luck! A large advertisement in the city newspaper advertised the sale of a tree from the Kasuga Taisha. The reason for the deal was that the tree was located too close to one of the temple's buildings, and they feared that lightning might strike the tree and damage the nearby temple building.

The Japanese artisan of this tale did not hesitate in spending a small fortune to purchase this particular tree and waged the highest bid. A dream he had nurtured since his youth had finally come true near his retirement. What have I told you all this time? Even an impossible dream, if carefully nurtured over time, does come true. This true story comes from one of the collections of stories by the famous Japanese writer Shiba Ryoutarou.

Take heart, I say, to the generations following mine. A youth without a dream is a corpse.

Now let me share with you another story, this time about a man with an even bigger dream that came true.

Until the 19th century, the German race was divided into small feudal states, including Prussia. General Garibaldi's unification of Italy through difficult challenges stirred the German race that was scattered throughout central Europe. One of them decided to build a unified German nation stemming from the Austrian Empire.

The Austrian Empire, at the time, was a great nation encompassing Eastern Europe, and consisted of many different ethnicities. Seventy-five percent of the empire's people were non-German. On the other hand, Prussia wanted a smaller German state centered around the German people and could not accept the Austrians' idea of a German state encompassing non-Germans. These differences could not be resolved through negotiation.

Two people who resolved this difference and built a unified German state were Otto von Bismarck[3] and Helmuth Karl von Moltke.[4]

Yet, von Moltke's wish of reuniting the German people under a single nation came to pass. At the time, the German people were widely scattered throughout Central Europe, and the unification of these people was unacceptable to countries like Austria, France, and Denmark. But he never gave up on his dream.

If Prussia wanted to unify the German people, it needed the regional powers' approval. How to receive approval from the regional powers? Von Moltke knew very well that such a naïve hope had no hope of success in international politics. He knew the only way was to force the outcome through raw power.

As a young officer, he meticulously started planning. "Let's strengthen our military!" thought he. Develop new tactics, improve weaponry, and improve the transportation system, to wage war against other more powerful countries. One of the problems was national power. Raising a large army

---

3) Otto von Bismarck (1815-1898) was born in the Prussian Empire to nobility in 1815. Against his parents' wishes, he studied law at the University of Gottingen. From his youth, he was very nationalistic and became the Prime Minister of Prussia during a time of political uncertainty and the rise of liberalism in 1862. He believed in strengthening the military might of the Prussian Empire, or a "blood and iron policy," to ensure the reunification of the German people.

4) Helmuth Karl von Moltke (1800-1891), appointed Army Chief of Staff in Prussia in 1857, believed that the uncertainty of war could be overcome through innovation in military organization, unlike Clausewitz (1780-1831), who thought that an army genius like Napoleon could overcome the uncertainty of war. Von Moltke set up a headquarters for the general staff to assist the commander. He strengthened the army's transport and communication capabilities to enhance the effects of concentration and command ability. His views on warfare were able to subdue great powers of the day such as Austria and France.

from a small population base is next impossible. It cannot be done in a short period. It was not possible to wait 10 to 20 years to achieve this result. What could be done?

One of the most critical modern military strategies is the principle of concentration. Although a nation may lack sufficient troops, it can obtain a superior force in a particular battlefield area if it can achieve a concentration of troops at a specific location. In the Austro-Prussian War of 1866, von Moltke turned his eye on the nascent technology of train transportation. Most armies relied on horse or oxen-driven carriages at the time for transportation. No one had thought about using trains for military transport.

The combined Prussian Army was almost 500,000 soldiers against the Austro-Janssen combined army of 600,000. The total number of troops was less, but if one could concentrate force in an area, the army would be able to have a numerical advantage on the battlefield. This strategy of the concentration principle is still used in modern-day warfare. It means gathering more troops than your enemies at a specific time and place. In order to do this, one needs to have better transportation and communication capabilities than the enemy. Raising the number of troops in a short period is impossible but concentrating what you have in an area is possible.

Von Moltke studied railway transportation thoroughly and left several papers on train operations and transportation. He also worked tirelessly on weapons and communications development. European armies used a front-loaded musket rifle that fired a single round per minute, while the breech-loaded Dreyse needle gun fired six rounds per minute. Breech-loaded rifles can be loaded and fired lying down, enabling soldiers to use the weapon in covered positions.

This weapon was developed by Krupp, a weapons manufacturer giant in Germany (the company was acquired in 1999 and is now known as Thyssen Krupp AG). Through a detailed study of topography, Prussians laid more than a single line in a strategic location to enable massive transportation in times of war. When the preparation was almost complete, Prussia engaged Austria first. As von Moltke had predicted, Austrians concentrated its main effort around Königgrätz, 50 miles east of Prague. The Prussians reacted swiftly, mobilizing 280,000 troops, which was a similar number of soldiers as the Austrians.

The Austrians did not expect this many troops to be mobilized in such a short time by Prussia. Austria only had a single rail line to Königgrätz, and Prussia had five lines into Königgrätz from five different directions. With the advent of wireless telecommunications and the Dreyse, the Austrians lost 13,000 men, and 22,000 were taken prisoner of war within a few days. The Austrians used dated tactical maneuvers, such as delivering messages via horseback, while the Prussians used innovation and modern technology to win the war. This is why this war was also known as the "Seven Weeks' War." The Battle of Königgrätz would become a decisive victory for the Prussian Empire.

After their win at Königgrätz, the Prussian army swept through what would eventually become the Northern German Confederation (1867-1870). They advanced to Bratislava, about 60 miles from the Austrian capital of Wein. Nothing could prevent the Prussians from marching into Wein in a day or two. Here Prussia made a critical strategic decision that would be long remembered in military analysis.

Von Moltke stopped the advance on Wien. Bismarck insisted on it to save Austria from humiliation. This decision was unpopular, not only with the Army but with the general public. Even Emperor Wilhelm I insisted on a march to Wien. A weaker Prussia had crushed the mighty Austria. How could it give up such a glorious opportunity?

Sound maneuvers by Bismarck resolved the uproar. In Bismarck's mind there was still the matter of France. Austria was the only country able to influence France's actions. To save Austria's face, Bismarck wanted Austria to stay neutral when the conflict with France happened. Von Moltke calmed the general staff. Professional soldiers of the general staff wanted to march on Wien. Why wouldn't von Moltke himself want to pop champagne in Wien?

Although Prussia won the Austro-Prussian War, it stopped the march into the enemy's capital, a historic move by the victor. As a result of the war, Austria was expelled from the German Federation, and a new Northern German Federation was established, centered around Prussia.

Next, Prussia took on France. It won a decisive battle in Seden by capturing Emperor Napoleon III of France. Austria remained neutral during Prussia's war with France. When Russia wanted to intervene in the war, Austria moved to stop it. Prussia annexed Hanover, Hessen, Frankfurt, the Duchy of Schleswig, the Duchy of Holstein, and the Nassan Federation (also known as the Duchy of Nassan). Its population increased by five million and its landmass by a quarter.

A single man's dream resulted in the unification of the German people into a single nation and changed the course of history.

3 The Key to Success

The brain remains a mysterious domain, with scientific discoveries still waiting to be found. Its influence is so great that it can make the impossible possible through the power of belief. This undercurrent of positive thinking runs deep in the unconscious. Even a taekwondo player with an almost 100 percent chance of breaking the board can sometimes fail to break them. Doubt can cause a misstep while at the attempt. If a taekwondo master or expert wants to succeed, his brain must understand and consciously be aware of splitting the board in two.

This is similar to the placebo effect. The patient doesn't know he is taking a fake pill, but his brain tricks itself into thinking it will cure him. The real problem is how to convince the brain that it can succeed.

In modern sports, a popular type of method exists for athletes wishing to strike gold. It's called the visualization technique (it also exists in other disciplines). This method is something that I myself have seen used in the past. Let me refer back to when I served as the President of the Korea Athletics Federation during the 1986 Asian Games.

An athlete from Korea, Kim Jong-il, won the gold with a record of 7.94 m for the men's long jump. He was known back then as a relatively consistent long jumper whose records until then had been just a little shy of 8 m. But for two weeks before the finals, the future gold medalist had been sidelined by a back injury and couldn't practice. By the day of the match, he was still confined to the bed. So how did he win the gold while not practicing for two weeks? He practiced the visualization technique and imagined clearing the 8m at the event.

On the day of the men's long jump, Kim told his doctor that he wanted to compete. The doctor tried to dissuade him, but Kim would not be swayed. Kim was very convincing.

"For the past year, doctor, I've been preparing for this day. I blame bad luck for this. I won't and can't give up. Just let me go to the qualifying round, at least."

His doctor reluctantly let him go because of his earnest pleas. He received an analgesic intravenously and felt pain-free. He makes it to the finals easily. During the finals, the athlete jumps six times, and the best result out of the six attempts will determine the outcome of the competition; this earns him the gold.

To him, the first four jumps make his body feel a little heavy. But from the fifth jump, he feels like he's getting better, and then it's his turn again. From the approach run, he glides across the sand as if on a magic carpet. He closes his eyes. He flies into the air. It feels so refreshing. He sees the blue sky. Has he really flown?

7.94 meters! It's a win. And best of all, it's a gold medal.

It's a miracle. Kim's been lying in the hospital for 14 consecutive days. When he won, he wasn't even wearing the national Korean team uniform because he came straight to the match from the hospital.

I digress. During the 1986 Asian Games, it was widely predicted by the Korean track and field family at the time that the only gold medalist in the men's 200 m, Jang Jae-keun. But Korea surpassed this modest expectation and earned seven gold medals, outpacing rival Japan. Kim aside, other gold medalists included the triple-crown gold medalist Lim Chun-ae, who won the women's 800 m, 1,500 m, and the 3,000 m, the men's 800 m Kim Bok-joo, and Kim Jong-yoon, who won the men's 5,000 m. Some of them were virtual unknowns like Kim Bok-joo and Kim Jong-yoon. These Korean track-and-field athletes won golds over athletes with better track records like Japan and China. This, I felt at the time, was a miracle.

Another anecdote I would like to mention is the Korean weightlifter Jang Mi-ran. She won the gold at the World Championships in 2005-2007 and 2009. At the 2008 Beijing Summer Olympics she won another gold, becoming a shining beacon of hope for Korean athletics.

Your brain is a mysterious thing. If your brain thinks it can, it can. That's the real miracle. The real problem is how to program your brain to think positively in order to achieve a specific goal or purpose.

First, we have to have positive thinking. Be optimistic. Everything is achievable. There is no try, only do. Why do you have to think positively? Lady luck favors people who are optimistic. By staying positive, Lady Luck will help you seize a golden opportunity. A pessimistic person will not know that Lady Luck has passed him by.

Secondly, write down your goals. I mean this in a literal sense. Write them down and carry them with you everywhere. When you write down your goals, it changes form from the abstract into the concrete. "Thoughts become things." If you write down your goals on paper and carry the piece of paper around with you, luck will line your pockets. This may seem a little tacky. So why do such a thing? I honestly don't know why. But I've seen this technique work for many people. Numbers don't lie.

Let me tell you another short vignette from the United States. In 1953, Yale University recruited 100 soon to be graduates with a specific goal in mind. This longitudinal study measured how successful the study participants would become in the future. Ninety-seven of them did not write down their goals. The three who wrote their goals down, shared the same dream: to become millionaires. After 20 years, the university's researchers found that the three's fortunes exceeded the total combined wealth of the 97 graduates.[5]

What is your consciousness as experienced by the brain? Science has yet to solve this. With the advance of medicine and science in recent years, let us remember the British scientist Francis H. C. Crick. He was the Nobel Prize laureate in 1962, along with James Watson and Maurice Wilkins, and received this highly prestigious prize in Physiology or Medicine. They discovered the double helix structure of deoxyribonucleic acid, now commonly known as DNA, the blueprint that God used to create humans.

According to his theory, a person's "consciousness" is the combination

---

[5] I'm sorry to tell you that during a more recent Yale reunion, this story could not be confirmed by the graduating class of 1953, according to a journalist from the publication "Fast Company," who interviewed some of the class's CEOs in 2007.

of seeing, listening, and feeling. These three senses comprise what he calls "consciousness." According to modern Western philosophy and psychology, one can also call this "qualia," or the "subjective, conscious experience."

According to some medical theorists, this concept of "consciousness" has a physical component in the human brain called the claustrum. The human brain is still poorly understood, but the claustrum, according to current medical theory, is located in the middle of the brain and acts as a transmitter. It combines the three senses of touch, sight, and hearing into one "sensory experience" and comprises of five different types of cells. It's a small part of the brain, but this is where the main "wiring" connects other brain parts. It also acts as a filter so as to not integrate too many extrasensory stimuli; otherwise, you could get overwhelmed. I have a theory of my own. My theory is that if you stimulate this part of the brain, again, and again, then the claustrum will remember and help you execute your goals to the best of your abilities.

Thirdly, talk about it. You have to speak out loud and repeat your goals to yourself. Words can be frightening, and as the old Korean adage goes, words seed your actions and show up in future events. What is the most vital part of the human body? Your fist? Your feet? No. It's your tongue. A tongue can kill a person or start a war.

Bruce H. Lipton, an American developmental biologist who studies the subjective human experience and how it may influence future descendants, wrote *The Biology of Belief* in 2006.[6)] In the book, he talks about the effect

---

6) This book was voted the best science book in 2006 by USA Book News. A Korean translation was also published, *Your Owner is Not Your DNA*. While not a part of mainstream scientific literature, his theory states that the subjective human experience is

that thoughts and words have on the brain. Thoughts and words become actions. Say positive things in all sincerity, and repeat your goals to yourself. Let us swallow harsh and negative words. Let's believe that anything is possible, and achievable. And let us put forth our best efforts into achieving our dreams.

Fourthly, let us pray. Let us pray humbly towards our Heavenly Father. Pray humbly so that God may grant your requests. Praying to God is a form of communication to our Heavenly Father. You seek Him out for help, confess your sins, or express your intent; these are all prayers.

So, if you put these four steps into action, will you succeed in achieving your goals? Nonsense. You must approach everything with "jeong sung." What does this mean? Always do everything with all sincerity, and put forth your best efforts. With pure sincerity and urgency, as if extinguishing the fire on your head, you will quell the desperation of your soul and help you achieve your dreams.

In Chinese characters, when read in Korean, this is called "Jin in sa de chun myung." Do your utmost as a human being, then wait for the will of heaven. It's so easy to say, "jeong sung." People say, "Do your best," or "[You failed] because you didn't give it your all." More actual words cannot have been said. But in reality, this is hard to put into practice.

So what is "jeong sung" again?

Let's take, for example, a metaphor of two expert swordsmen. They face

---

rooted not in DNA but lies in gene expression, or how some genes are switched on and off due to a person's sensory, very subjective experience as they navigate life.

each other in combat. Someone will die. The space between them is called "gan," it's about 1.8 meters or about six steps. In swordsmanship, "gan" is very important.

A flash of the sword. A winner is declared. One man slowly falls to the ground. This happens in a split second. The winner is the one who gave it his all. Awake, asleep, walking, or even while eating, think about winning. "Jeong Sung" decides the difference between life and death.

In the early morning of May 16th, 1961, the then-Major General Park Chung-hee, future President of Korea, arrived with his soldiers at the southern end of a bridge on the Han River. Park was confronted with a surprise, something that he hadn't foreseen. Two trucks blocked the Han River bridge's northern tip. About 100 military police were facing his forces and staring them down. The revolutionary army was momentarily shaken. They had believed they would enter Seoul proper without resistance. The followers of this particular coup détat went to Park to consult him.

"Sir! What should we do?"

Park, at that time, had a cigarette in his mouth. He removes the cigarette from his mouth. His hands are shaking. Major General Park hesitates momentarily. Heavy silence hangs in the air, paralyzing his force. At the time, it wasn't just Park who was anxious. While everyone else seemed paralyzed with fear, Park tossed his cigarette and climbed aboard a Jeep.

"Charge!"

As soon as the ignition is switched on, the jeep gains momentum. It's a narrow bridge on the Han River. They are ignoring the military police's guns at the opposite end. The forces also find their courage and charge. Park's life hangs in the balance because he's at the front of the charge.

But no bullets are coming from the other end. How surprising! They are not firing. But neither side knows when bullets will start flying. Park leads his forces at the head of the column. Not a single shot was fired over a 300-meter-long bridge crossing. Military Police at the northern end flee. What determines who will win in war is determined, in my opinion, by who wants to win more; who is more desperate to win. If you put forth your best efforts, even risking your life to achieve your goals, then no one will be able to stop you.

4 Never give in

On a fall day in October 1941, Winston Churchill, the then prime minister of the United Kingdom, spoke to students at his alma mater, the Harrow School. He was a special guest speaker invited by the school's headmaster. This was approximately two years after the start of World War II, just around the time when the United Kingdom was waiting, with bated breath, for a respite in hostilities. A year prior, at Dunkirk, the British forces had almost lost 300,000 men, and London residents were living in terror night and day due to Germany's bombs. Loyal ally France surrendered on June 22nd. For the United Kingdom, the past year had been an unprecedented terror.

But the British had overcome these past difficulties, which was nothing short of a miracle. At Dunkirk, to save 300,000 troops, the naval forces, boats, and private citizens even used their yachts to rescue the British troops. With bated breath and worried eyes, the entire world looked at Great Britain up until this point in the war. While outnumbered two to one, the Royal Air Force showed great resilience and heroism in defeating the strong Germans. Everything seemed nothing short of a miracle. Britons were proud of their accomplishment, of overcoming what had been a national crisis, and of their unyieldingness in the face of fear. Churchill had been invited to speak at this turning point in the war.

He said, "the past ten months have yielded a great lesson for us. In whichever circumstance, "never give in, never give in. Never, never, never, never—in nothing, great or small, large or petty—never give in." No matter how qualified you are, if you give in, it's over. No matter how brilliantly talented you are, if you yield, you lose. When I am faced with difficulties and can't keep up for much longer, my opponent is also exhausted and is close to death. If you really want to win, endure. If you really want to succeed, don't give up, no matter what the cost.

Let me tell you another little story, this time from the Talmud. You may remember this story from the first *Plain Stories*.

Once upon a time, long ago, there lived a man who had been sentenced to death by a king for some transgression or other. This man petitioned the king and implored him for one more year to live.

"O Great King, please give me a year of freedom. I will then make your favorite horse fly."
"What did you just say? You're going to make my horse fly?"
"Yes, fly indeed."
"What if he can't?"
"Then I will die."
"Look at this upstart young fool. Fine. I'll give you a year."

The king gave him his permission to delay his death sentence. A year? Surely he could wait a year. A man who shared the same cell as the prisoner who had just been conditionally pardoned said to him, "Make a horse fly? It doesn't even make sense!"

The pardoned prisoner said sagely:

"In a year, the king could die. Or the opposite may occur, and I may die. Or, his horse may die. Who knows what can happen in a year?"

Like I said before, this is a story from the Talmud. This is what the Jewish teach their children.

At this point, I would like to mention a celebrated war general as well as a Communist statesman, this time, from Vietnam. His name is Vo Ngyuen Giap. His nickname is "the Red Napoleon." Giap was born in 1911 and left this world at the age of 102 in 2013. He was born to wealthy farmers. He studied history, loved Chopin, and in his native village, also worked for a while as a teacher. Giap is widely regarded as one of the most brilliant military strategists of the 20th century due to his win over the French in the 1950s, the Americans in the 1960s, and the Chinese in the 1970s.

Years have passed since the end of the Vietnam War. As far as I can recall, it appears to have been about 1995. In a Japanese monthly magazine, Giap was interviewed for the 20th anniversary of the Vietnam War. The Vietnam War had ended in 1975. When asked by the reporter about his most cherished thoughts on war, he said:

"The U.S. military is a formidable one. But any formidable opponent has a weakness. The American forces as a whole have no weakness. So, I made one. They have the best weapons in the world, and the soldiers are one of the most elite forces in the world. Unless you make a weakness [in them], you cannot win.

In other words, you fight the battle where you want, when you want, your way. I developed a type of guerilla warfare where the American forces could not use their advanced weaponry. In guerilla warfare, you strike, then retreat. You use the jungle to your advantage. And dig underground trenches, to appear like a ghost, then disappear again like the wind. In the jungle, tanks and gunships are useless. It's the same as entering a small room with a long spear, a lance of about four meters. In a small space, a dagger or a short knife is preferable.

The American forces would have been exhausted. They could not exert their great military might, so they must have been drained. This tiredness becomes the weak point. Do only the opponent's forces get tired? No. The American people tire of the war, the politicians get tired of the war, and this results in a most unpopular war. In a democracy, the power of the press is mighty. This is another weakness. The tired Americans don't stay silent. Stop the war, say the American media. The American President also caves into these demands. I bet this angered the armed forces. But when the President issues the command to stop, what could they do?"

And he added another crucial point to his story:

"But to be sure, we were also very, very exhausted. It wasn't just the Americans who were tired. Had the Americans endured war for just another six months, we would have surrendered and waved the white flag of defeat. Our national power and resources were about to be depleted as well."

Endurance in the face of defeat; this is the lesson that is taught to us by General Giap. The American press played a pivotal role in ending the war because it tired the American people of the war, and the politicians could not withstand the wave of public disapproval of an unpopular war. But in Giap's words, had they just endured for six months more, North Vietnam would have waved the white flag of surrender.

The stubbornness of General Giap changes the course of history again. "Never give in. Never, never, never, never!" I say to today's youth, let us remember Churchill's words.

5 Just "do"

Just "do." Take action. It's easy to say. But it's not easy to put this into practice.

Some things are impossible. But I say to you now, "Make the impossible possible." Was this not the motto of our R.O.K. Army Special Forces?

If you wish to succeed, you must first prepare, make an environment conducive to achieving this goal, sharpen your skills, and win over the hearts of people.

Let me recount to you a story, this time, from my own life. It's from when I was the President of the Korea Athletics Federation (1983-1996), and when I helped inject new life into the sport of long-distance running, or marathons.

Since the 1936 Berlin Olympics, when Sohn Kee-chung became the first ethnic Korean to win the gold in the marathon event, other Koreans swept the world stage with their achievements in long-distance running. Other than Sohn, they include Nam Sung-yong, the bronze medalist at the same Olympics mentioned above, Suh Yun-bok, the medalist at the 1947 Boston Marathon, and Ham Kee-yong, the Boston Marathon champion of 1950.

But when I became President of the Korea Athletics Federation (KAF) in the 1980s, the achievements in this particular sport had waned for the Korean people. Our athletes couldn't even make the qualifiers to compete at an international level. We were losing face at this particular sport, traditionally considered a very "Korean" sport. Back then, our athletes were clocking in best times around 2 hours and twenty something minutes, while world champions were winning around the 2 hour and 7 minutes mark. Just 13 minutes shy of qualifying. But 13 minutes translates into about 5 km. At this rate, they couldn't even compete.

As soon as I was appointed President of KAF, I made a 10-year plan to spruce up long-distance running. My reasoning was this: if our past venerable athletes had, like I said before, swept the world stage with their achievements in this sport, then surely we could do this again. Another piece of information gave me hope for Korean athletics: Japan was making the qualifiers with athletes matching other world champion long-distance runners at around 2 hours and 7 minutes. As soon as I had made my plans for revitalizing the marathon for Korean athletes, I was met with resistance in the form of many different theories. "Today's marathons are the stuff of speed. You have to train in terms of speed." "No! For marathons, it's all about endurance."

I couldn't figure out at first which side was right. As some said, speed is essential, but then again, so is endurance. So what was right? When you are unsure, ask an expert. So this is exactly what I did. I met with the then-President of the Japanese Association of Athletics Federation (1975-1999), Aoki Hanji.[7] Aside from holding this title, he was a revered sports advocate

---

7) Aoki Hanji (1915-2010) A graduate of Waseda University, he was the shot put champion of 1938. Aside from being the former President of the Japanese Association of Athletics

and official. He was 20 years my senior.

Whenever I met with President Aoki, I would make a deep bow by lowering myself onto the ground, and he would always respond by returning this deep bow the same way. Koreans and Japanese share this custom of a deep bow. This deep bow where you kneel and lower yourself onto the ground so that your forehead meets the floor is a beautiful testament to both of our cultures.

"Honorable sensei, please refer a marathon expert to me."

About a month later, he introduced me to Takahashi Susumu.[8] At the time, a man in his sixties was off, how shall I say this, of noble mien. I was only 51-year-old at the time. He coached Japan's first silver medalist at the Olympics and also helped a Korean win a gold at the 1992 Barcelona Summer Olympics. He is a benefactor to us.

His theory went like this:

"Speed is important. Endurance, you can't do without it. You have to work on both. This is what I call competence." This is his maxim on "skill" for runners.

"Skill also encompasses comparing oneself to others and finding an

---

Federation, he was the President of the Japanese International Olympic Committee (IOC), and the Vice President of the International Amateur Athletics Federation (IAAF) from 1991 to 1999.

8) Takahashi Susumu (1920-2001) A secondary school graduate attached to the University of Tokyo. Middle-distance 800 meters, 1,500 meters, Japanese champion. 3,000 meters hurdle champion seven times for Japan, setting a new record for Japan every time.

advantage. Prior records are important, but winning is even more important. Life is an endless battlefield; so winning is the be-all and end-all. Winning takes skill. The real trick lies in catching two birds with one stone. This is hard. But it can be done. Here is my method."

He took a piece of paper out of his pocket, about twice the size of a standard A4 sheet of paper, and put it on my desk. The training regime for 365 days for one whole year was written tidily on it. I am sorry to say that I had, until that point, never seen the likes of such preparation in Korean experts. My mouth fell open. This is how the Japanese runners were able to qualify by clocking in at least two hours and 7 minutes! For a second, I felt myself getting quite befuddled.

Takahashi's vital point behind the training was this:

"A good athlete is born with the ability. But this ability goes to waste if it isn't honed. So to use an old metaphor, as a master artisan, you must find the right tree and carefully shape it. Again and again, you have to bring out the beautiful grain of the tree. This training plan is the method. The sticking point behind the training is how to pick the right tree or athlete, so you will, and how to bring out the best in him [while training]. This method is written here."

We agreed to meet again in a week, and I bid him goodbye. I resolved to ask Sensei Takahashi to become the national marathon coach for Korea and started preparing for this happy event. But I ran into some difficulties, chiefly, in this: all our Korean experts voiced disapproval. I was surprised. I got angry. How could they disapprove when I had put such effort into advancing this sport by getting introduced to and speaking with such a master? What was the problem? Oh, heavens!

The Korean chorus of disapproval spoke to how we were a "birthplace" of running and how we could hire a Japanese to coach the national team. Ok. Fine. You have to learn to pick your fights, anyway. I canceled plans for Sensei Takahashi to become the national coach and instead appointed him as Korea Electric Power Corporation (KEPCO) team's coach. I felt awful. But what could I do but apologize? I went to Japan. With other business to attend to, as well. I respectfully asked for Mr. Aoki's and Mr. Takahashi's forgiveness.

"Sensei Park, I decided to help because of you. What is comfortable for you is comfortable for me, too." These are the words of the great former IAAF Vice President Aoki.

As soon as I returned to Korea, I immediately set up a training camp for KEPCO runners. Along these same lines, I set aside two apartments for these runners. This was because, at the time, travel to Jeju Island didn't require visas, so Sensei Takahashi could travel freely to this region. Sensei would visit the island about twice a month to coach the athletes. The runner he favored during that time now works as the official coach for team KEPCO[9] and also for the national team of Korea. His name is Kim Jae-ryong. Sensei looked at then-athlete Kim and said to me, "This athlete is one to watch. He'll [easily] come within the two-hour and 10-minute mark." That meant he would have to shave five minutes off his record.

Kim, in the future, would compete at the 1992 Barcelona Summer Olympics with another teammate, Hwang Young-cho. And guess what. Kim

---

9) In Korea, professional teams for sports, such as basketball, are backed by a conglomerate or company, and are named after them. This is one such example.

placed 10th overall, a significant achievement again for Korean athletics. As Sensei Takahashi had predicted, he had become a world-class athlete.

But what luck! His teammate, Hwang won the marathon at Barcelona and earned himself a gold. With skill combined with a chance. Had fate been kinder to Kim, he would also have become a medalist.

Sensei Takahashi's "killing two birds with one stone" method is outlined below: First, you have to search for innate talent. To do this, pool the athletes and make them compete within a given time for a given distance. In this scenario, for example, running 30 km within 100 minutes, or an hour and 40 minutes. After a few tries, the coach makes a judgment call. So sorry, if you don't make it, you are out.

This is a combined skills test. Both speed and endurance are tested and evaluated quickly through this method. If you cannot finish within 100 minutes (speed), then you're out, and if you cannot complete the 30 km distance (endurance), you're also out. Once you pluck the players from the pool who have qualified under this basic skills test, the next part, hard training, comes into play.

This is a hardcore training method called "Dam Geum Jil" in Korean. Sensei Takahashi's method is rational and somewhat harsh. You train until your body is about to give out until you almost gasp your last breath. If you cannot endure this draconian training, then you are out. The stage for the competition is a harsh one. You're doing all of this to win, and if you can't win, then it's goodbye.

What if all of them fail under this type of training? Then you quit. Luck is not your friend. Live as an enslaved person, or live as an underling. If you don't like it, then find another route. All in all, decisions shape our lives, and each individual makes his very own choice in the end. We Koreans integrated and spread Sensei Takahashi's method to our long-distance running.

In the late 1980s, Korean athletics were blessed with two different fortunes. The first came in the form of Lee Dong-chan,[10] the then chairman of the KOLON Group in Korea. The second came in the form of coach Chung Bong-su. If it weren't for Chairman Lee, we would never have won gold in a marathon. Lee spared no expense in furthering South Korea's ambitions in this sport.

Coach Chung's nickname used to be "poisonous snake, or viper." Now he was a real "monster." He was initially not a long-distance runner. In the past, he had garnered no praise during his short-lived career as a runner. But as a coach, he was ferocious in making the athletes on his team suffer to the point of (nervous) exhaustion. One such example is when Hwang Young-cho was running in a 90 km practice run and felt like he was going to die. He couldn't run anymore, glared at Coach Chung, who was trailing him while riding a bike, and uttered an expletive.

Even for someone as talented as Hwang, this training method was brutal, almost beyond the limit of human ability. Coach Viper's training, though, would pay off in the long run.

---

10) Lee Dong-chan (1922-2014) was the President of Kolon Corporation in Daegu from 1957 and became a major player in the Korean textile industry. From 1985 onwards, he initiated and promoted the KOLON Marathon Tournament to advance running, or marathons, in Korea. In 2002, he was invited to become the chairperson of the 2012 Korea-Japan World Cup by FIFA.

While we're still on this subject, do you know who was blessed with the perfect "instrument" of a body that is built for running? The athletes I mentioned above: Sohn Kee-chung, who won gold at the 1936 Berlin Summer Olympics, Choi Yun-chil (bronze medalist at the 1950 Boston Marathon), and Hwang Young-cho, who came in first at the 1992 Summer Olympics.

Let me refer back to Choi Yun-chil. At the 1948 London Summer Olympics, he was in the lead starting from the 20 km mark for the marathon event. He outpaced the fastest runners and was headed for victory when much to everyone's dismay, he withdrew from the competition with just 4 km left to go. According to an Olympics official, Choi had been predicted to win, and broadcasters had unofficially declared him an early victor.

One of the worst-case scenarios had happened. Choi's luck ran out because he suffered from such severe dehydration that he developed temporary muscle paralysis. He was suffering from severe dehydration because he hadn't drunk any water. This used to be a common practice for Korean marathoners while training and competing. This was what Korean coaches used to do back in the day while training their athletes to run the full course (42.195 km) without any water.

On average, a marathon runner loses about three liter of water through sweat, and severe dehydration can sometimes lead to death. Nowadays, at every 5 km, there is a water station for athletes who wish to drink. I've been observing track and field athletes for about 50 years, and there is something that I have realized time and time again. Winning or losing is determined by a difference in ability. Of course, the one with the most extraordinary power wins.

But let me also say this: no matter how physically and genetically blessed you are or how much preparation you go through, you can't win over the luckiest athlete. I still believe in this. Isn't this absurd?

Let me introduce the following equation for success:

Competence ≠ Body type + Training
Competence = Body type + Training + Luck

Let me recount another story, this time about a celebrated Japanese marathoner named Toshihiko Seiko. Born in 1956, his best personal time to date is 2 hours 8 minutes and 27 seconds. During the 1970s and 1980s, he won every single competition he entered at the national and international levels and was widely regarded as a world-class, number one athlete by many. Ahead of the 1980 Moscow Summer Olympics, the Japanese track and field family was very excited. They had a dear wish. Gold for the men's marathon. Why? Because like Korea's female golfers of today (win after win after win), in the seventies and eighties, several Japanese marathoners were ranked and included in "The World's Best 10." The Japanese wanted a gold medal for the men's marathon during the upcoming Olympics.

In 1976, Toshihiko couldn't compete at the Summer Olympics in Montreal. Other Japanese athletes entered the competition instead, finishing 20th and 21st. During four years, Toshihiko's talents and abilities came to fruition right before the next Olympics. Japanese sentiments were running high again ahead of the 1980 Moscow Summer Olympics. It was widely predicted that he would win the gold medal. But alas, a horrible set of circumstances came hurtling through. The Soviet Union had invaded

Afghanistan, and the free world responded to this by a boycott of the Olympic Games. Japan, also a democratic nation, could not but follow the actions of its allies. Dreams of Japanese gold disappeared into thin air. This was Japan's bad luck, and Toshihiko's lousy luck.[11]

Hwang Young-cho's 1992 Barcelona Summer Olympics cannot be left out of this story. As I went to the games, I expected Hwang to place 6th at least. If luck favored him the day of the competition, he would win at least a bronze. As the IAAF delegate for Korea, I didn't even dare wish for gold. Even a bronze would do…I don't know how others feel about this, but for the Olympics, becoming a medalist at the Olympiad is an extraordinary feat. The color of the medal does not matter. Even a bronze is scary good.

If you remember the event (it's still available on YouTube, I believe), you can see a strange thing happening. For marathons, there is something called "a marathon's wall." It's within the 30 to 35 km mark. This separates the wheat from the chaff, so you will, and where you spot the best athletes. According to most experts in this field, the consensus is that this mark is the upper limit, and anything beyond that is beyond the limit of human ability. Or so they say…

So as soon as you reach this "marathon's wall," most runners are exhausted. About 15 elite runners then remain within reach of the medal; almost always, victors are declared from this elite group. At the 35 km mark, the group splits into smaller groups of about four to five, and by the 40 km mark, about two to three athletes remain, still in the running for a medal.

---

11) Afterwards, during the 1984 Los Angeles Summer Olympics, due to a coach's miscalculation, he arrived two days before the match and only was able to rank in 14th place.

But that day, the athletes hit the "marathon wall" at around 20 km. Some dropped out of the race, and only four to five runners remained. At the 22 km mark, the strongest of the runners, Japan's Taniguchi Hiromi, stopped at a water station and tripped over another runner after being stepped on. A year ago, with his best of 2 hours, 7 minutes, and 40 seconds, he overcame extreme humidity and high temperatures to win the 1991 World Championships in Athletics in Tokyo. So, for Japan's star athlete to falter and get disqualified must have been a tremendous loss and disappointment for Japan.

Let us return to the race in Barcelona.

After the 25 km mark, only three athletes remain. Hwang Young-cho, Kim Wan-gi, and Japan's Morishita Koichi. It is a sight to see, something different from most other races. What usually happens before and after the 40 km mark occurs at the 25 km mark. At 35 km, Kim starts lagging, and only Hwang and Morishita are running towards the gold. You'd be hard-pressed to see such an unusual sight. The most challenging part of Barcelona's course starts at the 35 km mark. Runners have to run uphill. It's a "marathon wall" for just about anyone and hilly besides being at an incline. It's like running through Hell: just awful.

Morishita's nickname is "Tortoise," and like his nickname, his will to live as well as his desire to win is unmatched. Here, Morishita starts putting the pedal to the medal by increasing his speed. He is certain of his stamina. Five kilometers of a gradually hilly incline plus adding speed is paramount to anyone falling behind "Tortoise." I am watching the screen and losing hope. I also have been privy to rumors that Turtle has an unflinching, strong heart.

This is the sure fire way to win for Tortoise, and this is a calculated move on the part of the Japanese coach. I, as the Korean representative for the International Association of Athletics Federations (IAAF), start worrying for Hwang, wondering if he can keep up with Tortoise. Japan's Tortoise versus the athlete coached by the Korean Viper. Morishita's still in the lead. Hwang is a finely tuned instrument, but is he a match for the Tortoise?

Morishita's in the lead, Hwang increases his speed. They're neck and neck. 2 km past the 35 km mark, and Hwang is still about two paces behind. I realize that is a calculated move on the part of Viper's athlete. They're well matched. So the question remains: when is Hwang going to increase his speed, if ever, to overcome the Tortoise?

Until they reach the pinnacle of Montjuic Hill, the two runners keep their current pace. Then at the end of the Hill, the vista looks flat again. Then Hwang increases his speed like a bullet. He sprints past the Tortoise. The Tortoise cannot keep up. The distance between them increases. Hwang crosses the finish line and breaks the finishing tape about 200 meters ahead of Tortoise to win the gold.

For the first time in 100 years of Korean marathons, I watched the Korean flag being raised while a live orchestra played Korea's national anthem. This was history in the making on that day: August 9th, 1992. Imagine that, our national anthem is playing in the foreign land of Barcelona, Spain. Our victory that day was an honor to Korean athletics. Hwang was able to achieve victory because of incredible luck, the chance of competing against another able competitor from Japan, and our two countries engaging in a neck-to-neck race against each other. That day, a relative unknown from

Korea dispatched all the strong athletes from Africa, such as Kenya's Ibrahim Hussein and Tanzania's Juma Ikangaa, along with Mexico's Dionicio Ceron and Salvador Garcia. Let us also remember Japan's Taniguchi Hiromi who was used to competing in hot temperatures. If Taniguchi had survived the 35 km mark to compete with Hwang, then the results may have been very different.

Why did the African athletes not do so well at Barcelona and fail relatively early during the competition (about 20 km into the race)?

Let me tell you a little bit about the course itself. The men's marathon at Barcelona that year was about 20 km of coastal road, followed by 15 km of roads within city limits, finishing with 7 km within Montjuic Stadium's hilly roads. Montjuic's Hill lies about 200 meters above sea level.

That day, the marathon started at six thirty in the evening. Barcelona is known for its heat. The temperature that day was around 30 degrees Celsius, with a humidity of 80 percent. But luckily, for the Korean athletes, right before the start of the race, there was a sudden rain shower, making the asphalt steam. It was already humid that day, but when the humidity in the air hit the steamy asphalt, all the athletes would have already been depleted of their strength, leaving them limp. But this rain shower from the heavens above helped Korea win. Africans are used to the heat, but not humidity. But right before and after the marathon's steaming roads, along with the natural humidity from the coastal roads, was brutal on the well-qualified African athletes, ending their dreams of medaling.

Our last training camp was at Yamaguchi Prefecture in Japan. Korea chose this location to train the athletes because it's remarkably similar to the course in Barcelona. About 20 km of coastal roads at sea level, then 7 km of an uphill climb; in other words, an excellent substitute for Barcelona. We ran and ran for our lives there. The humidity in Japan is deadly in the summers. Barcelona's heat and humidity? We could handle it. We had done it before in Japan. Why did Japan not use this course? They are better off than Korea. They usually used training courses in the States. We did not have the financial means, but we were blessed with training at a similar course at Yamaguchi. Great luck, or "Dae Un," in Korean, was in our favor that year.

So how to make Luck your leading lady? I really don't know. In hindsight, I think luck accompanied me all the way here. Everyone who said it couldn't be done, even those many events untangled themselves quite naturally and what more could I have asked for? That is why I am always grateful, and I pray. You will remember after you, dear reader, finish reading this book. Let us always be thankful. Let us always be in prayer. On an international stage, a competitive relationship doesn't exist just politically or economically. Cutting-edge technologies or sports are also fields with fierce competition. In sports, Japan and Korea are competitors.

After the 1936 Berlin Summer Olympics and Sohn Kee-chung's win, the Japanese probably knew that Koreans made better runners (back then). Vice President of the IAAF, Aoki Hanji, probably knew this. But why did he help Korea by handing down secrets from Japanese marathoners through Sensei Takahashi? He helped me out of the goodness of his heart. Because he cared for me. But why?

Where does the practice of bowing deeply and kneeling on the ground in this modern era exist? This practice is disappearing in Japan, so why do we receive this ancient tradition from a foreigner? I don't know, but this spirit of giving and receiving makes you interested in the other person. You want to help. You want to do something for that person. This stems from genuine interest. As I said, a spirit of concession can win a person over. This is not about just winning hearts over, but making relationships between people beautiful and society brighter and pleasant. Concessions or keeping the rules of etiquette makes everyone more amiable towards each other. We help each other and cooperate.

Look at the Americans. They, in my opinion, always yield first and greet you warmly. In this way, they surpass Koreans. Most developed countries are like this. As far as work goes, just do. Of course, there are things that are undoable. What do I mean by this? Actions that surpass human ability. So what do I mean by this? I mean literally, all things are doable if it is not literally plucking a star from the sky. If you do your utmost, as far as human ability can take you, then anything is possible. Think, work hard, receive help, and sincerely do your utmost, then the possibilities become endless. If you want to receive support, please cultivate an air of gratitude for friends and invaluable friendships.

While we're on the topic of track and field athletics, I would like to boast a little about my personal achievement. Other than the Summer Olympics and the FIFA World Cup, the third crown of international athletics is called the World Championships in Athletics. In August of 2011, it was held in Daegu, Korea. Two hundred and four nations competed with a total of 1,945 athletes, a mammoth event.

In order to secure the bid for this venue, Daegu had to compete with distinguished cities, including Brisbane, Australia, Moscow, Russia, Gothenburg, Sweden, and Barcelona, Spain. Regarding track and field events, Daegu, Korea, lagged in popularity, infrastructure, and public awareness of this biannual event. Even Seoul lags. Public opinion from the world athletics family was initially lukewarm towards Daegu for the reasons I mentioned above. But it would be unprecedented to hold the World Championships in a city and a country where track and field are not very popular. The council members of the IAAF Congress wouldn't even consider it.

But in March of 2007, the Congress held in Mombasa, Kenya, the 13th World Championships in World Athletics decided on Daegu. Everyone there had predicted there would be at least three rounds of voting, surpassing even two rounds, to pick the final venue for the upcoming championships. Why? Because except for Daegu, the other cities were formidable. So the voting starts and the ballots are counted. But what to make of this? During the first round of voting, relatively unknown Daegu, Korea, intakes more than half the votes, securing its solid status as the future venue for the World Championships.

"Election results: Daegu to host World Championships over Goliaths Moscow and Brisbane." This is a translated headline from a leading Korean newspaper, *The Chosun Ilbo*.[12]

How did Korea achieve this extraordinary feat? The ones with voting power, the council members, voted for Daegu. Of course, the city of Daegu and the organizing committee had done their part well. But all in all, it was because I had done my personal best to sincerely win over my colleagues during my 16-year-run as an IAAF council member, starting from 1991. I

---

12) *The Chosun Ilbo*, April 2, 2017.

sincerely did my best: this is called "jeong sung," in Korean.

"We picked Daegu for Rocky's sake,"[13] they said. This was also the headline for a daily newspaper belonging to Doha, Qatar. One of the IAAF council members had said this to a journalist who had used this as the headline.

In reality, the very idea that the World Championships could be held in Korea was unfathomable. The IAAF had a long-standing unofficial policy in place: where track and field events and all things running are not popular, not to pick that city as the host. It's an unwritten policy.

So if I wanted to host the event in my hometown of Daegu, Korea, I had to make track and field and related events popular. But this feat would take eons.

Is there any other method? The council members of the IAAF can make it happen. But unless they are fools, they would not vote for Daegu. Do you see what I mean? So I had to convince the council members that they were making a wise and not foolish decision by picking Daegu. So I deliberated over how to turn the logic of giving the event to a country where athletics events are popular.

"This argument that the IAAF council members made holds true. But if we choose host cities based on how popular our sport is in a particular country, then will we give up on places where our sport is unpopular? In other words, we need to develop the sport in an unpopular place so that the

---

13) Rocky is my nickname

spectators in the stands get excited. They will fall under the mysterious spell of watching the athletes compete. They will develop an interest in track and field athletics, and when the number of spectators increase, then the host city, as well as the country, will become a popular place for our sport."

This was my main argument: inspire excitement about our sport in unpopular cities and have it spread like a grassroots movement in the host country. Thankfully, my colleagues agreed with my argument and justification for the possibility of holding the championships in a previously unknown Daegu. Two months later, they picked it as the host city.

Daegu achieved something extraordinary during the Championships and became the second "World Athletics City" after Stuttgart, Germany. So do rational arguments and justifications move people? No!

People are essentially social creatures, moved by emotions. Feelings always win over rational thinking. If you want your rational argument to stick, then you have to win over people's hearts. No matter how perfect and logical the argument, if the other party does not like its counterpart, they do not take action. Try to win over the other sincerely.

What moves another person. The truth.
How do you move another person's heart? With genuine sincerity.

Let us remember that no matter what, just think positively and believe that it is achievable. Then win over people's hearts. In all things, genuine sincerity is the key.

Chapter Two

Gazing away from Korea

1 Are our neighbors our cousins?

To the younger generation, I say to you, turn your eyes to the wide, wide, world. If you are caught unawares of the harsh realities of life, you will suffer. If you close your eyes, you will undoubtedly be eaten, and if you live your life as a simpleton, you will be consumed, whether or not your eyes are open. A hundred years ago, our ancestors had our country snatched away from them because we were hermits, hence our Western nickname back then, the "Hermit Kingdom." Harnessing national strength is paramount to success as a nation. Let us not curse at our neighbors. If we are weak, then they will strike.

Are our neighbors our cousins? No, they are not. Neighbors are potential threats. In matters of international politics, this holds true. Look at the world around you. What do you see? China and Japan? The neighboring countries that you can see are your competitors and potential threats. Let us always face reality with steely eyes.

But here, we must lay aside falsehoods, lies, and pretenses. Let us always speak the truth. My wife and I, our beloved son and daughter, grandchildren, and you, dear reader, and your families: this is a safe space. They say that neighbors are like cousins. In times of trouble, they can be our support system. But neighboring countries always seek to gain an advantage by catching us unawares or knocking us out. That is what a neighboring country is. If you want to befriend another country, seek one from far away.

Even the United States eyes its closest neighbors as potential threats. There's no need to speak further about this matter. Are we not still growling over the disputed island of Dokdo with Japan?

Then, let us now turn our eyes to the country afar, the United States of America.

2 What is America?

A. Founding and Ideals

"The land was ours before we were the land's.
She was our land more than a hundred years
Before we were her people.
(omitted)
Such as we were we gave ourselves outright
(omitted)
To the land vaguely realizing westward,
But still unstoried, artless, unenhanced,
Such as she was such as she would become."

American poet Robert Frost (1874-1963), recited this poem at the presidential inauguration of then President-elect John F. Kennedy on January 20th, 1961.[14] He would become the 35th president in office.

"The United States foundations rely on the inherited ideals of the ancient Romans, based on Christian beliefs, with the protections of the dignity of the individual for and by a free and democratic society," Frost said.

---

14) Frost had written a new poem for the inauguration, but the glare from the sun glinting off of the snow, made him resort to reciting a poem from memory. This poem was written in 1942, and is titled, "The Gift Outright."

Frost, at that time, was 87-years-old. He would leave this Earth two years hence. Frost's short speech would highlight ideals of the land of the free, and his hopes for a golden era for the American people that started with the first British settlement at Plymouth colony. The eventual writing of the Declaration of Independence and the development of the theory of "Manifest Destiny,"[15] allows the poem to celebrate the future of the American people, even today.

After the end of World War II, the age of Post Americana opened. While brilliant and mighty, the Soviet Union's eventual dismantling was due to several factors: the United States military, its economic strength and the democratic ideals of a democracy. These strengths brought the Soviets to their knees. That long ago day, when that poem was recited, would prognosticate the rise of a nation blessed beyond measure: the United States of America.

What created today's United States of America? A Christian mindset. Christianity lies at the core of American politics and government. From its establishment in 1776, it was a nation to be reckoned with.

On November 21, 1620, in search of religious freedom, 102 Puritans[16] from Great Britain lowered the anchor at what is now Cape Cod, Mass., to establish a colony there. The new immigrants' welcome by the weather was

---

15) Manifest Destiny is a slogan for expansion westward, that the "American people had the right to spread the Christian as well as their democratic ideals, and this was their calling from God. They had to aggressively pursue their influence towards the Western part [of the North American continent]."

16) The Puritans were Protestants from Great Britain, who believed firmly in the evangelistic and chaste elements derived from the Anglican Church.

very grim. It was extremely cold. They had to start from scratch, withstand the terrible cold, and seed the crops during the spring. When the seasons changed to fall, finally, they could harvest. They thanked God. The United States Thanksgiving holiday originates from the first official shared meal between the Native Americans and the pilgrims. The tables were laden with food from the harvest. The first Thanksgiving was celebrated to thank God for his bounty and goodness and is still one of the most important annual national holidays in the United States today.

Let me tell you about one of the first written agreements made by the first Pilgrims. There is a document called the Mayflower Compact. Before disembarking the ship, 41 men aboard the ship (coincidentally named the Mayflower), wrote and signed the agreement mentioned above. "For the universal goodness of the colony, we always agree to concede and obey each other." In all, this agreement was to provide that at their new colony, they would live in harmony and peace by abiding by society's laws and regulations. A man named John Carver was established as the first governor of their new colony. Thereby, starting with America's first immigrants, the society they established has roots in the high democratic ideals of the Mayflower Compact.

Ten years later in 1630, a man named John Winthrop brought hundreds of new immigrants to the New World and created the colony of Massachusetts. And for the good of the rest of the colonies, he worked tirelessly for 12 years. The reason why historians regard him as a luminary is due to his vision and his writings. Already famous in his native Great Britain, from the onset, he worked to improve the immigrants' economic conditions and spread the Good Word. His sermon, "City upon a Hill," alludes to the promise or a covenant that Man must make with God.

Here is an excerpt from his sermon:

"For we must consider that we shall be as a city upon a hill. The eyes of all people are upon us. So that if we shall deal falsely with our God in this work we have undertaken, and so cause Him to withdraw His present help from us, we shall be made a story and a by-word through the world."

Winthrop's devotion to his faith (Christian/Puritan) still influences the mindset and breathed life into the modern American psyche. His "City upon a Hill" sermon has expanded and emphasized what political scientists today call, "American Exceptionalism."[17]

In truth, the North American continent was originally the land of the Native Americans who lived there. Before the forefathers of the modern-day United States of America, Christopher Columbus had discovered the New World in 1492. Though he ended up not on the North American continent and at the Bahamas instead, after his discovery, three countries would fight over predominance in the new world: Great Britain, France, and Spain, with some presence from other European countries. For about 300 years, it was an outpost of European colonization. After the passage of time uneasy, the United States of America was born.

Because the British colonized the new continent's eastern coast, the contemporary colonials saw a rise in their numbers, and as the business

---

17) American Exceptionalism stands for the unique establishment and historical growth of the United States of America, and how it doesn't fit into the mold of other nations during their nascence. In other words, it is "unique" unto itself. Americans' pride is also alluded to in these terms, and, in other countries, it is sometimes frowned upon as "American supremacy."

developed, they became permanent settlers. But rebellion occurred in the colonies over issues such as taxation without representation, and their growing calls for independence eventually led to the American Revolution and the establishment of a new government in 1776.

The American Revolution lasted approximately seven years, from 1775 to 1783. The thirteen original British colonies took on the great British Empire and won. What's remarkable is that they also declared independence during the short-lived revolution. After their independence, the settlers kept on heading West for about 200 years, hence the word, "Moving Frontier."

This gradual movement westward would have a profound impact on the American mindset. The reclamation of this land was always wrought with dangerous and harsh conditions. The rugged landscape, continual fighting with the Native Americans, and the vast land that they conquered were only possible via mutual aid between the pioneers and their tolerance of these harsh conditions.

Bravery, independence, a tough mentality, a burning desire to work, and an iron will all contributed to the American psyche of today, along with their willingness to lay aside complaints. The American mindset of progressiveness, coupled with idealism points to and furthers this idea of American exceptionalism. The "American cowboy" of many Westerns is the gift that stems from this westward expansion.

In my opinion, the true character of the Americans is the "American cowboy." Brave, progressive and tough as nails, unable to be a bystander of injustices, but still chivalrous to the ladies and generous towards his neighbors: this is the American cowboy.

Self-governance and self-reliance were something that the Americans had to abide by on their own, because the-then fledgling federal government was unable to exert control over the expansion of the American West. After all, it was too vast. Therefore, the American West was a potential wide expanse of lawlessness and had not the Americans abided by societal and other rules by keeping themselves accountable. They would not have succeeded in making the United States of America a great nation.

To the early European settlers of America, your neighbor was your friend, not your enemy, and a friendly spirit of optimism and goodwill helped them harvest the fruits of their labor. Here, they learn the true meaning of cooperation and duty, along with the personal, yet law-abiding freedom that stemmed from within.

"We hold these truths to be self-evident, that all men are created equal, that they are endowed by their Creator with certain unalienable Rights, that among these are Life, Liberty and the pursuit of Happiness."

This is a short excerpt from the American Declaration of Independence. This is a remarkable declaration. Why? Back then, even in civilized countries like France, King Louis XIV had said, "I am the State" (l'etat c'est a moi)." And it was a time when the powers were exerting and using their ability to lead their country as they pleased, like an absolute monarch. The thinkers like Jean-Jacques Rousseau and Jeanne d'Arc expressed these ideals, such as "freedom," and "equality," but only said these things in books. But the Founding Fathers took these ideals, untested in a country, and put them into practice.

Suppose you think about this in 5,000 years of human history. In that case, it becomes even more significant because, in the entire world's past, such a political test had never been done, except in the United States of America.

At this time, anyone could immigrate to this country and become an American citizen, making it a world-class attraction for would-be immigrants. As Ralph W. Emerson (1803-1882) so eloquently put it, America was the "land of opportunity, of freedom and a futuristic country for a worldly gentleman."

When we talk about the America of today, we cannot do so without mentioning American Republicanism. This is the tradition handed down by the Founding Fathers of the 18th century. Each state and federal constitution in the United States reflects tri-cameral republicanism that has roots in ancient Rome. In a republican government, life, liberty, equality, and the pursuit of happiness prevents society from becoming rotten, and the trilateral government becomes a restraining influence on constitutional rights.[18]

One of the core constructs of the Founding Fathers also lies in the political freedom of the individual. Every citizen is guaranteed certain unalienable rights, and these are outlined in the constitutional law. If the citizens' freedoms are obstructed, then the republican government becomes threatened. One Founding Father, John Adams, Jr., who later became the second president of the United States, said in a letter to a friend:

"If private rights are violated, then public virtues cannot exist. And in a republic, only public virtues exist."

---

18) Bae Yong, *Neo Roman Empire* (Seoul: Book and People, 2020), p. 179.

This speaks to the very point of what a republican form of government should be. A republican government is a government for the people by the people through the powers of electing their public officials. Unlike dictatorships, one's citizenship is protected by a charter and a constitution and cannot be taken away. China, Russia, and North Korea are essentially dictatorships that use the word "republic" or "democratic." This concept of a "republic" or "democracy" is so beautiful that even dictatorships borrow this term. But in terms of these respective countries, it's fake. It's nonsensical.

The United States may have some contradictions today; but the Founding Fathers' ideas have stood the test of time. Regardless of some of these contradictions, the Founding Fathers' firm traditions and their wish to create a republic birthed the United States of America today.

B. The United States and its Morality

Sometimes, when someone says the United States of America is a moral country, he is met with censure. But we must also remember that from a balanced standpoint, the United States' basic fundamental spirit can be boiled down to ideals espoused during the French Revolution: liberty, equality, and freedom from (religious) persecution. These roots date back over 200 years ago when the Puritans first landed at Plymouth in November 1620; these ideals are also alluded to in the Mayflower Contract. Even during the American Revolution, when they led the nascent country to victory, these ideals are mentioned continuously; their puritanical spirit, coupled with a burning desire for freedom, are still at the core of the American spirit of today.

In these pages, I do not wish to delve into the convoluted arena of political science. For the purposes of this book, I hope that the average reader will understand the fundamental spirit driving the Americans of today. Countless Americans have felt these core values in their blood, and as such, these are reflected in their day-to-day lives; this requires no more input from complicated theories or ideologies.

Though, I do have a personal theory that when discussing political systems such as communism, you cannot leave out the ideologies behind the framework. Forgive me, but I personally believe that communism, in practice, is amoral at best. There's no need to outline why it is such, other than to say that communist systems always gasp their last breath and expire early compared to other political systems. I am not condemning the ideology but rather the practice of it, for it is inefficient and can lead to human greed. So let us speak of beautiful democratic ideals instead. What's of importance is whether that society under a certain type of governance is fair or not. This is the essential question that need not be debated over with complicated arguments.

Another important point that needs to be made regards the people and their government: are the people law-abiding, are the lawmakers and others who work for the government just, and are the people honest. In truth, does society also allow for equal opportunities for everyone?

There's a sizable Korean-American presence in the United States, and I've had the opportunity to talk to several Korean-American civilians over the course of my lifetime. Their consensus was that Americans still have a very healthy society. Ethical values still dominate the average American culture, which means actions such as donations and charitable works. These virtues are still reflected in America. They also told me that being positive was paramount to co-existing with white Americans.

Equal opportunity is also still alive and well. Of course, you have to work, but hard work and sweat is still justly rewarded and rewarding on a personal level — this is why many Korean immigrants have been successful in the States.

I am going to tell you about one of my close friends. He loves golfing, and once, he applied to a very famous country club in America. This club, whose name I cannot disclose, is so exclusive that even the elite are not admitted sometimes. He was sitting in front of the board of directors, and fielding questions right and left until he mentioned that he had also served in the Vietnam War in the 1960s. Immediately, the questions ceased. He had just achieved the impossible: he was in! A society, which recognizes and values the military officer, is proof that the United States is a meritocracy. Wherever you travel in America, many cities and schools honor those who sacrificed for their country. They erect statues and monuments to commemorate them and their charitable deeds.

One of the upper class's signs of health, in my opinion, is noblesse oblige. During the Korean War, 142 of upper-class American sons served in the armed forces, and of that number, 36 of them were wounded or were killed. Out of the upper classes, a son of a high-ranking army officer, James A. Van Fleet (1892-1992), was one of the Americans who met an unfortunate fate. Van Fleet was Commander of the U.S. 8th Army. [19)]

---

19) On September 16th, 2020, Van Fleet's grandson, Joe McChristian, Jr., said during a consulate general online seminar that Van Fleet, Jr., may have been captured by North Korean forces and held captive as a prisoner of war. Afterward, he was transferred to

Van Fleet was called "the father of the modern Korean forces." To advance the Korean Army, he modernized it, and during the war, in 1951, he established the Korea Military Academy, a four-year institution for would-be army officers. During his military career, his only son, James "Jimmy" Van Fleet, Jr., was a part of the U.S. Air Force fighting during the Korean War, and he went missing in action on April 2, 1952, after an enemy downed his B-26 plane somewhere around Pyeongannam Province. After Captain Van Fleet, Jr. went missing, a request for an extensive search and rescue operation was denied by his father, the then-Commander of the U.S. Eighth Army. This decision was because Van Fleet worried about losing more men during a potential search and rescue mission.

Van Fleet, Jr., whose nickname was Jimmy, had seen active duty in Greece, but still chose to serve with his father during the Korean War. He was a newlywed and his wife had recently just given birth. As I said, he went missing in action (MIA) during a routine bombing operation. General Van Fleet established in 1957, the first non-profit organization between Koreans and Americans called the "Korea Society" to foster friendly relations between the United States and the Republic of Korea. The Korea Society, to this day, confers an annual "Van Fleet Award."

These virtues are not limited to the U.S. Army but are reflected in today's American society. There is something called a "Giving Pledge." This organization was created by some very wealthy Americans who pledged

---

China and the former Soviet Union and is believed to have died in a forced labor camp in Siberia. While the findings have proven inconclusive, Joe A. McChristian, Jr.'s father (1914-2005), son-in-law of Van Fleet, told him this story while still alive, so there may be some truth to this unfortunate tale. Joe A. McChristian Sr. was Deputy Chief of Staff, Intelligence, Department of the Army, U.S.A. as a two-star general.

to gift some money towards the betterment of society. As of 2019, the organization counts among its 200 plus strong members, Bill Gates and Warren Buffett.

American leaders have and constantly are worrying about the country's moral values. For example, at West Point, one of the textbooks chosen by the faculty includes a book called *Just and Unjust Wars* (1977).[20] A Vietnam War protestor named Michael Walzer wrote the book. It explores the unethical and immoral events during the war and criticizes the army and the past presidential administrations. The book concludes that the commander-in-chief needed to demilitarize the civilians, and the military needed to face and aggressively the dangers ahead of them, no matter the cost. This, according to Walzer, is bravery.

So save the civilians by sacrificing their own army subordinates? Upon graduation, the alumni would serve as platoon leaders and company commanders. Do they have to put the civilians' lives ahead of their men's lives? This question led to some heated debates in the classroom. Sometimes people run into pitfalls that lead to confusion. But the U.S. military still enforces this code of military conduct.

Next, I would like to examine an incident that occurred in Afghanistan in June of 2005. Four Navy Seals led a covert operation. Their mission: to capture Afghan rebel militant leaders. To keep the operation top-secret, they tried to infiltrate the village where the leaders were hiding with only a few men. If more men had been involved, then the mission's purpose would have been revealed, resulting in the rebel leaders' evacuation from the said

---

20) Michael Walzer, *Just and Unjust Wars: A Moral Argument with Historical Illustrations* (1977), Translated in Korean by Kim Duk-hyun (2007).

village. Unfortunately, as they were approaching the village, three Afghani shepherds discovered the team. At first, they held the shepherds as hostages. Then the Navy Seals had to make a decision as to what to do with them. Should they let them go or dispose of them? Michael P. Murphy (1976-2005), who was leading the operation as a commanding officer, made the executive decision to let them go. This was a brave decision. But the cost was too great. One hour later, the Taliban militants were back. The shepherds had become informants.

The militants numbered around two hundred. Though very talented and elite, four Navy Seals were no match for them; they were pushed back. Three of them died, and one was near death when finally rescued. This military operation is recorded as one in which the U.S. military lost 19 men. There were two helicopters involved in the rescue mission. Unfortunately, one of the helicopters crashed, leading to a higher number of casualties.[21] This event was regarded as a tragedy and made into a movie called "Lone Survivor." Besides this tragedy, a similar situation occurred in Iraq for a U.S. Special Forces unit (ODA-525), which amounted to another incalculable cost.

I myself respect the U.S. military officers' bullheadedness. And I am astonished by the junior grade officers' bravery. But I don't agree with the military ideology behind what is called in Korean "Byung bul yum sa," or "In war nothing is too deceitful."[22] If the war wasn't waged to begin with, then I would have a different opinion, but once a war is waged, I personally believe that "the war should be waged with ideology specific to it."

---

21) James Suh (1977-2005), a Korean-American soldier, was also involved in this rescue operation and lost his life.

22) Sun-Tzu, *The Art of War*, "Warfare consists of lies. All warfare is based on deception."

C. What is America's Power?

Americans, in my opinion, are blessed. They, in part, owe this to their excellent forefathers. The nation known now as the United States of America started with the Founding Fathers, who were influenced by ideas from the Enlightenment and put them into practice, a remarkable achievement during that particular era in history. And their political successors' achievement in building an elaborate yet efficient system of an American-style of republican governance is something that I hold in high esteem, even today.

I want to introduce a new topic that has its origins in science but can be applied to many other systems: entropy. Entropy is the second law of physics. It basically means that all systems, as time passes, go from good to bad. This even applies to the universe; order turns into chaos. So it follows that systems or organizations created by humans eventually, over time, become flawed and change into something far from the ideal. This concept, when applied to companies, for example, can be averted via shuffling the staff and replacing the CEO; otherwise, without change and innovation, the law of entropy will make any company worse and worse until it decays.

A constitutional monarchy or a great country, after 200 to 300 years, also enters a state of entropy (without changes or innovations to fix the original system). The United States of America is over 250 years old. But how does it keep on advancing to avoid a state of entropy?

The answer, in my opinion, is this: most Americans intrinsically have a high self-esteem and a moral sense of duty. This is their cultural heritage handed down by their first settlers' ethical beliefs rooted in Christianity, along with the Puritanical mindset[23] that spread universal ideas of equality and freedom not just to the continental United States but eventually throughout the world.

This attitude of equality for all encouraged and continues to encourage Americans today. Even though the reclamation of the West has ended, their need to spread the American spirit and values all over the world runs deep in their unconscious. In other words, the spirit of Manifest Destiny still persists. The American mindset can be seen elsewhere across the West, the Pacific, and even beyond.

The United States of America was born out of a revolution on a new continent. It was founded on ideologies such as freedom, equality, social justice, and entrepreneurship. I want to call this Americanism. If you read former U.S. President Abraham Lincoln's Gettysburg Address, the United States of America was founded upon noble and honorable ideologies. Americans have a sense of duty that they hold dear to themselves. Thus, America's founding and sense of duty run pervasive through the American mindset of today. I believe that Americanism is another term for American exceptionalism, which is embedded in the pride of the Americans.

D. The American Civil War

Today's United States of America would not have been possible without the American Civil War (1861-1865). Why did one nation, indivisible, under God suddenly try to split into two countries? Especially when they

---

23) The Puritanical mindset holds fast to some ideals: the first, freedom, and second, a fair society governed by an honest government, and third, a pioneering spirit.

are brothers? America is a vast country. The divide between the North and South exists along several axes of identity: climate, economics, and ethos. The North had industrialized very quickly, while in the South agriculture was king.

The North had morphed into a version of modern-day Europe: industrialized, with a stronger economy and championing equality for most. In contrast, in the South, agriculture dominated its economy, and like agriculture-driven systems, tended to be more conservative and valued hard work (labor). In the American South, as evidenced by Sir Walter Scott's historical novel *Ivanhoe*, the image of Southern gentility was also taking hold. So the archetype of the "Southern gentleman," who was honorable, mannerly and chivalrous to the ladies, and hospitable to guests, harkened back to the days of old Europe. This genteel ethos had produced many distinguished military men, including generals, and until the start of the American Civil War, most of the military leaders had been from the South. When President Lincoln picked a general to lead the Union Army, he turned to the South, but was turned down by General Lee, who eventually would lead the Confederate Army.

But why wage war based on differences in ideology? Let us examine the what and the why behind the American Civil War. The main reason was the difference in the justification of two very different economic systems; one had industrialized with modern Europe, while the South was held back by what some would call an outmoded economic system, which relied heavily on agriculture. The problem with the South's workforce was that it was driven by slave labor. The two sides also fought because they were not homogenous, and their sense of identity was being threatened by each other.

America was constantly changing and advancing, unbeknownst to itself, thereby preventing entropy. Let us remember the Louisiana Purchase, the ideology of Manifest Destiny, and the pioneers who went West and pushed the boundaries of the land west of the Mississippi. The third President of the United States, Thomas Jefferson, who served from 1800 to 1808, along with the 14th President of the United States, Franklin Pierce, increased the total landmass of the nation. The first purchase was the Louisiana Purchase of 1803. The Louisiana Purchase increased federal land west of the Mississippi River by 828,000 km squared and was purchased from France for about $15 million U.S. dollars. President Pierce, likewise, purchased from Mexico, after a series of wars with its neighbor, about $10 million U.S. dollars for land near modern-day Texas, where a railroad would eventually be built towards California; this was called the Gadsden Purchase, which was named after the ambassador of Mexico. This took place in 1853.

Another problem lay with adding more land and more states and whether they would embrace the ideology of the North or the South; in other words, which would become slave states or free states. Let me introduce how cotton became King in the South. In the late 18th century, a man named Eli Whitney (1765-1825) invented the machine called the "cotton gin." As a graduate of Yale University, he was visiting a friend in Georgia when he came upon a cotton field. He got an idea to make a machine to separate cottonseeds from cotton. Before he came up with and designed this machine, the "cotton gin," enslaved people from Africa would have to pick the cotton and then manually separate the seeds, which would result in only about a pound's worth of cotton per person. The invention of the cotton gin made it possible to harvest 2,000 pounds of cotton per day, which required about two horsepower engines worth of power.

This resulted in 100,000 tons of cotton production being increased to 1,600,000 tons per annum. The cotton was then exported, mostly to Great Britain. This is how cotton became the mainstay of the South's economy. The problem with the cotton trade was that it relied heavily on slaves from Africa. On the other hand, the North was industrialized and used paid workers, so they had no need for slaves and no reason to support slavery. Most Northerners regarded slavery as a "grave sin." In the North, meanwhile, I would like to introduce a man named William Garrison (1805-1879), a staunch abolitionist who ran a newspaper called *The Liberator*. Garrison was one of the first abolitionists to actively support the end of slavery and disseminate this ethos to his readers.

When his newsletter was criticized for being too sensationalist and liberal, Garrison responded thus: "If my house was on fire, would I heed your advice to stay calm? If your wife was being raped before your eyes, would you agree with someone if they said, please leave the premises in a calm manner? If a baby was trapped in a room on fire, would you tell his mother that she shouldn't hurry [to save her baby]?" Garrison's abolitionist movement began to have a huge impact on society. And the media of that day began to agree wholeheartedly with him. While the ethos had merit, there was a backlash to the abolitionist movement because *The Liberator* came to be blamed for a violent uprising in the American South by a slave named Nat Turner in 1820, which led to the murder of 60 white people.

The backlash to the Nat Turner uprising upset many living in the South. They became depressed, upset, and shuddered with anger. Until then, Southern gentility had believed that they were honorable and traditionalist. They lost their humanity after this point, and bloodshed and rage ran rampant for a while in the American South.

Fifteen states were pro-slavery and supported its legalization. They included: Virginia, South Carolina, Georgia, and Alabama. The North, on the other hand, had 15 states where slavery was illegal. The divide between free and slave states worsened over time over ideologies.

In 1848, gold nuggets were discovered in what is now the state of California, triggering a wave of rumors all over the world that the tributaries in that state were full of gold. For the next fifty years, about 2 billion dollars worth of gold would be discovered in California. People rushed to the area, resulting in the California Gold Rush. From 1849 to 1850, the population of California would increase from 6,000 to 85,000. In a few years, the small fishing town of San Francisco would become a large city of 200,000 people. As the population grew in California, legislators had to figure out whether to admit the newly populous land as a state and also decide whether it would be a free state or a slave state.

A decision was reached, and a compromise was struck. Henry Clay, the former Whig party presidential candidate from 1832, struck a deal in what would become known as "The Compromise of 1850." California would join the nation as a free state. At the same time, the newly conquered territory won from the Mexican War would decide later for themselves whether to join once they declared statehood. But the American South was very angry over this decision. One state legislator from Georgia said, "We shed blood and helped win California [from Mexico], and if you drive us out, we are going to secede from the Union."

Another point of contention arose with the publication of *Uncle Tom's Cabin* in 1852. Written by Harriet B. Stowe, the novel details how slaves from Africa were sold like livestock to the highest bidder and the inhumane treatment they receive at the hands of some slave owners. She wrote the tale to expose some atrocities of the slave plantations that were far from the ideal Christian community. Her minister father heavily influenced Stowe. Even the-then queen of what is now Great Britain and Northern Ireland is said to have cried over the book. Upon its publication, the book was an instant success and sold 1.5 million copies. It was also translated into 23 different languages, turning Stowe into a famous author worldwide. But more importantly, the novel helped the abolitionist movement move across the continents. The Southerners responded to the publication's success with anger. They were angered by being vilified and portrayed as bad, and were also angry at being demonized by the world at large. During this time, yet again, differences in ideology would lead to political problems.

A former slave and later freeman Frederick Douglass also ran an abolitionist newspaper, which influenced what would happen to the territories of Kansas and Nebraska. Whether to admit them as free states or slave states became heated, but the federal government decided to leave that to the new territories to decide for themselves. As soon as this news spread, the Southerners rushed to Kansas. They needed more anti-abolitionist Southerners to vote en masse so that Kansas would be admitted as a slave state. In neighboring Alabama, one plantation owner sold all his slaves, then armed and dispatched 300 white men to Kansas Territory.

The North could not ignore what was happening in Kansas. One church in Connecticut decided to collect donations for Northerners who would use the funds to buy firearms to fight the pro-slavery activists in Kansas Territory. Kansas' farmers armed themselves and sowed the fields. The two sides fought fiercely with one another. Skirmishes resulting in deaths became common; for example, in Lawrenceville, anti-slavery activists attacked the pro-slavery activists and set a fire, which resulted in 200 deaths. This incident would spiral into a series of events of what is now known as "Bloody Kansas." During this bloody time in U.S. history, a man named John Brown emerged. He believed that the emancipation of enslaved Africans was his calling, and the reason why he was born. He, along with his five sons, committed murder and killed any pro-slave or slave owners who crossed his path.

Another incident of monumental proportions emerged from the Harpers Ferry raid. John Brown headed to Virginia in 1859 with his supporters to incite rebellion amongst the enslaved Africans. He wanted to build an army to attack Southerners and destroy slavery. But the Southern militias fought back and captured Brown alive. The one who was pivotal in capturing Brown was the future Commanding General of the Confederate Army, Colonel Robert E. Lee. When Brown was being sentenced at a trial, he said, "This court of law, [I believe], believes in fairness and acknowledges it. I am only following God's commandments and [for] the suffering slaves that are being robbed of their [basic human rights], I am prepared to die, and my sons will shed blood [in my place]."

This testimony solidified the Southerners' belief that their world was vastly different from the Northerners. They were tired of being vilified as demons, and the abolitionists' coverage of slavery focused on and emphasized the inhumane treatment of African slaves, when most Southerners did not engage in such inhumane treatment of them. The anti-abolitionist movement also resulted in the pendulum swinging in the opposite direction to the point that white Southerners became afraid of African slave uprisings. When they looked to others for help, they were met with challenges. The free states in Congress would soon outnumber slave states, and since the president always appointed them in office, the Supreme Court would be partial to the Northerners' cause. Who would help them? Aha! A president who would support their cause and not attack the Southern gentility.

A presidential run was coming up in 1860, and the outcome would affect the slave states' livelihood in a profound way. But the Southerners' way of life was struck with lightning when Abraham Lincoln, a senator from the free state of Illinois (1809-1865) was elected as the 16th President of the United States. He was a small-town lawyer and was largely unknown in politics, yet he had staunchly disapproved of slavery even before his election. The Southerners' hopes were dashed.

The white American South's hopes turned into grief, and desperation turned to rage. Demonstrators protested President Lincoln's appointment on the day of Lincoln's inauguration. *The Whig* Party wrote in a Richmond, Virginia newspaper, The Whig, that "The election of Lincoln to the presidential seat [of the United States of America], is paramount to one of the worst sins in our nation's history. But this sin has already started. Our [Southern] American way of life is being threatened, and our rights are being curtailed. [His election] will cause a storm of epic proportions."

The nation fissured and split. On a December day in 1860, South Carolina seceded from the Union. Others followed: Texas, Georgia, Alabama, and eventually 11 in total. They formed a new government called the Confederate States of America and elected a new president, Jefferson Davis (1808-1889). In the early morning hours of April 12, 1861, Fort Sumter in Charleston, South Carolina, fired a cannon. This signaled the start to the war that would be fought between brother and brother, cousin and cousin, for four long years.

How did this tragedy occur? How did this tragedy come to pass in a brave country with excellent forefathers and many talented citizens?

Let us examine the facts. Political and economic systems determine the trajectory of any country, but human bullheadedness, coupled with prejudice, can result in a country veering off the path that God intended. Anti-slavery newspaper publishers, coupled with religious extremists, created a divide so deep that it caused a rupture in the nation. Events like Bloody Kansas, and killing slave owners in the name of God and righteousness, along with people like John Brown creating massacres, caused a backlash in the South. The South became more racist because the North kept on inciting rebellion and dehumanizing them.

As I have stated before, the South responded in kind. "South Carolina will immediately secede from the Union," was the repeated mantra of former vice president John C. Calhoun. A leading abolitionist newspaper's publisher, *The Liberator's* Garrison, used a moral argument to say that slavery was against God's will. Northerners took action that went to extremes, inciting the South to rebellion. A peaceful settlement could have been reached between slave and free states, but extremists caused the divided nation to veer off into bloodshed for a while.

Some Southerners even burned dolls that looked like the newly elected President Lincoln. This stubbornness between the North and the South resulted in catastrophe for the newly divided nation. The North's extremists kept on justifying their actions as that of acting in "God's will," while the South insisted on justifying their actions via the law. In the South, the law reigned supreme, and what the North did, by inciting rebellion and printing extremist abolitionist newspapers, made them angry.

In the North, for example, a Boston lawyer named Wendell Phillips called for the end of slavery by saying inflammatory things, such as, "The one on God's side is a majority." To the majority of the South, however, they kept on insisting on the illegality of the North's decisions. They responded, again and again, with rising anger. Any society is bound to, at some point in time, produce treasonous or perhaps fringe groups. But when these groups take center stage, then a desperate struggle ensues in a nation.

In short, these paradoxical stereotypes, anger, religious extremism, and political divides resulted in four years of bloodshed that would later be called "The American Civil War."

E. Gettysburg

When talking about the United States of America, I cannot leave out Abraham Lincoln or the Battle of Gettysburg. Nor can I not speak about the eloquent speech the former 16th President of the United States gave there and the brave boys who died at Gettysburg. About twenty-some-odd years ago, I wrote a book about the American Civil War. It took me five years to write. If I may say so, I was a bit daunted and frightened whilst writing the book. It was a difficult book to write. I stopped writing at parts because it was tough going. Sometimes I would stare at the ceiling while the unfinished manuscript was before me for hours, then get up and go do something else. I suffered from severe writer's block. I was no historian, nor was it the topic about my home country. Then I had an epiphany of sorts. "Let's go there, to the place [where battles were fought], let's go to America."

So, I boarded a plane. Aboard the plane, I made a plan. I would visit Virginia, Maryland, and Pennsylvania twice in a month. I planned to visit Manassas, Antietam, Chancellorsville, and other important battle sites, and I did just that. I visited Gettysburg five times. I was surprised. Every battle site I visited was peaceful and beautiful. One hundred fifty years ago, these sites were where battles were fought and waged. During the day, both sides, the Union versus the Confederates, would battle, and at night, the soldiers would dream of home and their parents, and shed tears. So how could these places look and be so peaceful? How could these sites have so much beauty?

I sat on the grass and turned to imagination, which transported me to those long-ago days, more than 150 years ago. The fear that the soldiers felt, the anguish of the commanding officers—all these I felt down to my very bones. Suddenly, I am surrounded by a whirlwind of Imagination. The soldiers charging at the other side while shouting, the commanding officers' hoarse shouts while brandishing swords, I can hear them all—both armies charging at each other. There's no hometown. No parents. Only the fight to the death! Man turns into beast. My head spins. I open my eyes. I see the face of men, turned into beasts. I shake my head. I try to return to the present. I close my eyes again. I can still hear the yells, screams, and shouts in my head.

Gettysburg, Pennsylvania, lies about 40 miles north of Washington, D.C., and is a small city. When I first visited Gettysburg, it looked like a bustling one, due to the tourists. But the exact battlefield where the civil war was waged was quiet. It was nearing sunset, and the plain looked so beautifully tranquil. But this was the very site where the American Civil War reached a turning point, and also a deadly site where 50,000 men on both sides died or were wounded.

Let us examine the circumstances leading up to the battle. Vicksburg, Virginia, was the South's lifeline, and it fell under danger. General Ulysses S. Grant, of the Union, had surrounded the city with his soldiers. The Confederacy's President, Davis, held a cabinet meeting, in part, to deal with this new situation. After much discussion, he decided to deploy General James Longstreet's Corps to the site, to save Vicksburg from danger. But after he made this decision, General Robert E. Lee opposed this move and believed that attacking the North would be the only way to save Vicksburg. Lee planned to send Confederate soldiers to the north, and Gettysburg, Pennsylvania, would become the battlefield that would mark a turning point in the American Civil War.

The battlefield where the Union troops would achieve decisive victory was located on a low hill with two graveyards. Between the two graveyards situated there, the Union and Confederate soldiers fought for three days. The distance between the two armies was about a mile or about 1,500 meters. Neither side, initially, had believed that the battlefront's lines would become redrawn at Gettysburg. General Lee thought that if they struck Pennsylvania first, they could target the Union's capital of Washington, D.C., draw the majority of the Union soldiers away from Vicksburg, and put the other side on the defensive. So the Confederates were going to direct troops towards Gettysburg first.

The Union knew that the Confederate soldiers were moving to the north. It so followed that the Union then also started transporting their troops to meet the Confederates. But the Union Army's Cavalry Brigade commander John Buford realized Gettysburg's importance and dispatched troops near the two neighborhood graveyards. It was June 30, 1863. Gettysburg was like an artery of sorts, where, including the railroad, nine road networks converged. He was certain that the Confederate soldiers advancing up North would pass through Gettysburg.

Another Confederate Commander of the Third Corps, A.P. Hill, arrived at Gettysburg, Pennsylvania on the first of July, with his troops from Virginia. At that point, the North was wealthier, and General Hill strolled through the small town's streets to see if he could find some boots for his soldiers. Many of the Confederate soldiers were without shoes. Two years into the war, the Southern army couldn't supply essential shoes for their soldiers. He and his troops, surveying the area, were met with a shower of bullets from Union troops. They escaped to warn the others.

The Commander of the Third Corps of the Confederate Army, A.P. Hill, arrived first with his troops. Then Cavalry Commander John Buford's brigade troops arrived, and they were pushed back. Luckily, nearby, Commander of the Union Army's First Corps, John F. Reynolds, was there with his troops and barely blocked the brunt of the battle. Around noon, they were joined by the Union Army's 11th Corps led by Oliver O. Howard. Around the same time, Richard Ewell's Confederate 2nd Corps also arrived. This conflagration of troops at Gettysburg met its fate at Gettysburg. Without fail, and much to everyone's surprise, the Battle of Gettysburg would become a turning point for the Union Army in the American Civil War. At this point in the battle, however, the Commanding General of Union Army George E. Meade had yet not arrived with his soldiers, likewise his counterpart General Robert E. Lee and his troops hadn't, either.

Let us pause here and examine the causes and the broader themes governing the American Civil War. In truth, the war should never have happened. The North and the South were not well matched, for the North had 22 million people compared to the South's combined 12.5 million (including slaves). Additionally, the Union's GDP was about 20 times that of the Confederacy; you could even call the war a fight between an adult parent and a son that was still not of age.

So how did the Confederacy endure? For the first two years, it did not just endure; it prevailed and displayed its military might against the North. This was partly due to the South's history of producing excellent military men and commanders. In truth, the Confederacy's military officers, such as General Robert E. Lee and General "Stonewall" Jackson, were brilliant commanders. Unfortunately, for both sides, this led to pain for the North and also a bruised legacy for the South. Had the South not had brilliant commanders, the war could have been shortened to just one to two years, but because of the South's military and tactical brilliance, the war lasted for four long years.

One of the people most affected by the war was the North's President, Abraham Lincoln. To him, the war was waged over the issue of slavery. He wanted to emancipate the slaves throughout the divided nation, but the war roared on a year into his presidency. Additionally, while the North had better weapons, more men, and more supplies, they kept on losing battle after battle. Lincoln was also worried about losing face at home and abroad. The United Kingdom, for example, was an economic rival of the North, but to the agricultural South, it was a trading partner. Additionally, France was looking to expand its territory on the North American continent through Mexico, and was even thinking of sending soldiers to aid the South during wartime.

Lincoln's wish was to crush the Confederacy's spirit whilst displaying military might against the opponent, to show the United Kingdom and France that the remaining Union was a force to be reckoned with. He wanted to push his abolitionist agenda too, after the Union won some battles. Between September 16th and 17th, 1862, the Battle of Antietam was waged in Sharpsburg, Maryland. General Robert E. Lee's troops went on the offensive. While the battle lasted only a day or two, both sides lost 22,000 men. It was the deadliest battle yet between the two sides. Both sides also lost 18 generals during this battle, or nine on both sides.

So, who won the Battle of Antietam? It's hard to say. Neither side won per se, although the North fared a bit better after it ended.

"In the year of our Lord one thousand eight hundred and sixty-three, all persons held as slaves within any State or designated part of State, the people whereof shall then be in rebellion against the United States, shall be then, thenceforward, and forever free..."

On September 22, 1862, several days after the Battle of Antietam, the 16th President of the United States, Abraham "Honest Abe" Lincoln, issued the Emancipation Proclamation, which would, in broad terms, free the African slaves from bondage. He couldn't wait any longer. But the real emancipation of slaves would take place a year after the start of the American Civil War.

President Lincoln and General Lee were able to read the British and French diplomacy with the newly divided United States. These two leaders would also devise their politics and strategic positions concerning foreign policy. As such, General Lee thought that the South's strategy would be to win via battlefields, to show that the Confederacy was a force to be reckoned with. Then diplomatic channels could be established with other countries, and the Confederacy would really become, in the eyes of the world, a newly created country. In short, the Confederacy wanted to flatten the nose of the United States, which they had seceded from.

General Lee was riddled with anxiety. Up until this point, the war was in General Lee's favor, but they had failed to reach a decisive victory over the Union forces. If they could strike and bring the Union troops to their knees with at least one triumphant victory, he believed the dream of the Confederacy would be preserved. But the Union forces did not move in the way in which he anticipated or wanted. He did not want the war to drag on forever because it would deplete the South of its resources. He wanted to win the battles so that the nascent Confederate States of America would be recognized as a nation and exercise its national power internationally. It needed to move quickly while the United Kingdom and France were in their favor.

General Lee appeared at Gettysburg for these reasons. In early June 1863, General Lee mobilized three corps of 75,000 men to fight the Union army. It was composed of three different army corps. General Longstreet, who Lee liked to call "My Old War Horse," led the First Corps. General Longstreet was regarded as Lee's "right hand," as he was indispensable to him. The Second Corps was led by General Ewell, also known as "Old Bald Head." He had been a division commander under General "Stonewall" Jackson[24] who had been killed at the Battle of Chancellorsville two months

---

24) Thomas J. "Stonewall" Jackson (1824-1863), an artillery officer, was a graduate of West Point (Class of 1846), and at the Battle of Manassas (in Virginia), he withstood, proud and still, a shot of enemy bullets heading his way, hence earning him the nickname of

prior. The Third Corps was led by General A.P. Hill, who had also served as a divisional commander under Stonewall Jackson. General Lee needed an early win to weaken the Union morale, and as he had hoped, the Union Army quickly assembled near Gettysburg, Pennsylvania. Now was the time to strike, he thought.

This is my analysis, but I wonder if General Lee had thought that the Battle of Gettysburg may be the last battle of the American Civil War; in other words, the final battle to end all battles and the war. It was vitally important for the South to win this particular battle, as they, two years into the war, were running out of resources and potentially impacting the Confederacy's morale. This must have proved to be a sticking point for General Lee, and would remain his obsession during this particular battle. To show not just the Union but to display to the entire world the Confederate States of America's military prowess, he would launch an unprecedented bayonet charge on the North at Gettysburg. When you examine his military tactics, they are overwhelming and unparalleled, yet when one examines them, they all have some reason or logic behind them. Two months ago, at Chancellorsville, a military man of might had used new tactics on the world's stage.[25]

Back to the Battle of Gettysburg. At this battle, three divisions

---

"Stonewall." He was a vitally important General for the Confederate Army.

25) On May 1, 1863, at the Battle of Chancellorsville, Virginia, despite being outnumbered 2:1 (Union troops: 130,000, Confederate troops: 60,000), there were four main attacks by the Confederate Army. What is remarkable is that the Confederate Army withstood and sometimes even surpassed the Union Army. If an army of 60,000 prevailed against an army of 130,000, then it means that some extraordinary tactical measures emphasizing concentration must have been used. To summarize, it means an electric seizing of deception and maneuverings, speed, and cooperation; all these things must have worked to the South's advantage. Only a "military god" is capable of leading troops and seeing victory like this.

were deployed. To use such a number in a staged attack is somewhat unprecedented. To this day, whether this was an excellent strategy or not is up for debate. An attack that also involves charging across a mile-long open terrain is decidedly a type of plan that would draw critics. But still, General Lee insisted on it. Even his "right arm," General Longstreet, opposed the idea. Lee ignored his right-hand man three times.

In my opinion, I agree with Lee. While this offensive was unsuccessful, and a lot of people may disagree with me, I think General Lee's bullheadedness at the Battle of Gettysburg was correct. In theory, this charge may be incorrect. However, if the Confederate Army had not amassed all their strength and all their might into defeating the Union Army at this particular battle, I believe that all would have been lost. An agreement to end the war or keep the French and the British on the side of the Confederates, would have been lost if they lost at the Battle of Gettysburg. So General Lee could not lose this chance. He needed to end the war at this particular battle, at this specific time. An attack, a launched and planned offensive, was pivotal in deciding the victor in battle. This was the only way to win.

So they charged. Not a normal one, but a massive charge of three divisions. It involved Pickett, Trumbell, and Pettigrew's army divisions. If they are able to break through the defenses of the Union Army, then they also cannot fix the momentum; then the South would emerge victorious. This was their thinking, anyway. Three army divisions, consisting of at least 15,000 soldiers, would be enough. Even if they lost at least half these men, about seven to eight thousand soldiers would still be able to charge and stage an attack on the North. At the very least, even if they lost two-thirds of their men, about 5,000 men would still be able to attack the North. Good! Let's end the war, right here, on Pennsylvania soil.

Around noon on July 3, 1863, the Confederate artillerymen fire a round of bullets. They are ready to attack. The Artillery unit consisting of about 150 men open fire. The peaceful field is suddenly awash in a spray of bullets and gunfire. There is mass confusion. The North fires back. It is artillery against artillery, yet the union artillery rounds are outnumbered. The Confederates fire three times, to one from the North. The North is saving their bullets and their cannons. This is a planned move. Two hours into battle, the battlefield is engulfed with smoke. It's so dark and smoky that the Confederate soldiers use this to their advantage and change ranks.

As soon as the smoke clears from the field, you can see the remnants of the Confederate Army's charge. A 15,000 human wall of soldiers was made from the combined nine units. The Confederate Flag flutters in the wind along with the Union's flag for over a mile. The hot July sun bears down on the soldiers from both sides of the divided nation as they fight, raining bullets on the other. The human wall of Confederate soldiers marched ahead to meet the Union soldiers. From the Union Army came a shout.

"Ah! What do I see here? This is a sight for sore eyes! Look at their majestic forward march. What a lovely sight to behold!" said an astonished Union officer. He was awestruck by the Confederate soldiers marching into battle.

Thirty minutes in, the human Confederate wall broke. The majestic march into battle disappeared. These lofty ideals of human bravery, defending one's country, fighting to keep the family safe, all these lofty ideals that made men brave enough to possibly die on the front, dissolved into thin air under the hot July sun. In the face of the Union artillery's rain of fire, these brave men lost their nerve, and so it follows that they did not stand a chance. When the Confederate Army was about 300 yards away from the Union Army, the Union soldiers began throwing canister grenades. These rudimentary canister grenades were full of iron and would blow into fragments. A single canister could wipe out 30 men at a time. They threw them without abandon. Soon, the battlefield was littered with the bodies of horses and men. How gruesome. Two thirds of the 15,000 Confederate soldiers fell. This brave charge would be remembered later in history as "Pickett's Charge."[26] Unfortunately for the Confederacy, Pickett's Charge was unsuccessful, and would eventually lead to the unraveling of the Confederate States of America.

Why did this fail? How could a celebrated general such as General Robert E. Lee's plan of attack fail? In my opinion, I agree with General Lee's tactics used during the battle. But as I said before, the results he was expecting did not come to pass. Throughout history, whenever someone faulted him for the Confederacy's failure at Gettysburg, he would only say, "It was all my fault." That was his only response. He did not fault his subordinates. Everything, to him, in terms of what ended up happening at the Battle of Gettysburg, was his fault, and his alone. But to a few close confidants, he did say one last thing, "If we had had a coordinated attack, then the charge would have been successful."

The reason why I'm dwelling so long on the topic of the Battle of Gettysburg is that it encapsulates, in my opinion, the psyche of the American public. Not just soldiers or military men, but even civilians. For instance, it explores human successes down to the minutiae, along with leadership

---

26) George R. Stewart, *Pickett's Charge: A Microhistory of the Final Attack at Gettysburg*, July 3, 1863.

and man's psychology during wartime. Strategically speaking, from a military viewpoint, Pickett's Charge is also fascinating to study. That is why according to a historian, George R. Stewart, "The United States' history's climax is the American Civil War, and the American Civil War's climax is Gettysburg, and Gettysburg's climax is Pickett's Charge."

After the Battle of Gettysburg, four months later on November 19, 1863, a dedication ceremony for a national cemetery was made. It was made for all the brave men who gave their lives for their country. This dedication was originally not supposed to be attended by the president. Initially, the idea for the cemetery came from the residents of Gettysburg, and the site was supposed to be consecrated as a public cemetery. But the people of the town did not have enough money to do this, so they decided to ask for donations from the families of those who passed. But a young judge named David Wills managed to convince the then-governor to allocate some money, or about $2,400 U.S. dollars, to build the cemetery on about 17 acres of land.

The orator who was chosen to speak at the dedication of a public cemetery was Edward Everett, who had served as the governor of Massachusetts as well as the Secretary of State in previous years. As Everett was picked as the main speaker, President Lincoln was asked to simply recite a dedication. On November 18, President Lincoln arrives at Gettysburg and resides at the house of a judge named Walls. He examines the speech he has prepared. He's been writing and rewriting this document from the White House, and tonight was no different. I don't agree with the historians who say that he wrote what would become known as the Gettysburg Address on the train on the back of an envelope. The cemetery's dedication was to be attended by many neighboring states, such as the home state of Pennsylvania (where Gettysburg was located), Maryland, and New Jersey; in total, about six states' governors, and 15,000 others. T. H. Stockton, a minister, started the ceremony with a prayer, and Everett's two-hour speech then began.

"Standing beneath this serene sky, overlooking these broad fields now reposing from the labors of the waning year, the mighty Alleghenies dimly towering before us, the graves of our brethren beneath our feet, it is with hesitation that I raise my poor voice to break the eloquent silence of God and Nature."

This is an excellent speech. And the two-hour speech soon concludes after these words.

"...But they, I am sure, will join us in saying, as we bid farewell to the dust of these martyr-heroes, that the accounts of this great warfare are read throughout the civilized world. Down to the latest period of recorded time, in the glorious annals of our common country, there will be no brighter page than that which relates THE BATTLES OF GETTYSBURG."

The speech was met with thunderous applause. Those who fell into a trance while listening to the address also woke up, as if from a dream. It's an excellent speech, one for the ages. The audience continues clapping. They are deeply moved.

President Lincoln advances to the podium. He is tall. I digress, but he cuts a gangly figure. Lincoln gets up and adjusts his glasses awkwardly. Then he starts reading from the speech, rarely straying from the page, in a slightly high-pitched voice.

"Four score and seven years ago, our father brought forth on this continent, a new nation, conceived in Liberty, dedicated to the proposition that all men are created equal.

Now we are engaged in a great civil war, testing whether that nation, or any nation so conceived and so dedicated, can long endure. We are met on a great battle-field of that war. We have come to dedicate a portion of that field, as a final resting place for those who here gave their lives that that nation might live. It is altogether fitting and proper that we should do this.

But, in a larger sense, we cannot dedicate—we cannot consecrate—we cannot hallow—this ground. The brave men, living and dead, who struggled here, have consecrated it, far above our poor power to add or detract. The world will little note, nor long remember what we say here, but it can never forget what they did here. It is for us the living, rather, to be dedicated here to the unfinished work which they who fought here have thus far so nobly advanced. It is rather for us to be from these honored dead we take increased devotion to that course for which they gave the last full measure of devotion—that we here highly resolve that these dead shall not have died in vain—that this nation, under God, shall have a new birth of freedom—and that government of the people, by the people, for the people, shall not perish from the earth."

His short speech was initially met with silence. This silence was the type of solemn silence that sometimes is found during mass. The press of the day was divided on what to say about President Lincoln's speech. *The Chicago Times*, which usually supported the Democratic Party, said that President Lincoln's speech before foreign dignitaries was somewhat messy and said it burdened Americans with shame. However, the main speaker at the dedication of the cemetery, Everett, praised President Lincoln's two-minute speech as being much better than his own two-hour speech.

History now tells us that President Lincoln's speech would live on as one of the best speeches of all time. It is now known as "The Gettysburg Address." Referring to the ideals of the Founding Fathers when they established the nation 87 years ago and the dedication of the fallen soldiers who had sacrificed for "a new birth of freedom," Lincoln stressed that Americans should follow in their footsteps to defend the democracy of their nation. The address also reaffirmed the concepts of "American Exceptionalism" and "Manifest Destiny," which defined the American ideals and mission.

I am not going to translate the Gettysburg Address. The English and Korean languages are too different, in this instance. I am afraid that President Lincoln's profound and lofty language may become distorted if I try to translate his speech that long ago day. I hope that you read it in the original English.[27] If you read it over and over 100 times, it becomes better and better as you read it. Why don't you try translating it, just for practice? There are many good translations.

President Lincoln is truly a magnificent historical figure. The more you study him, the more frightening his achievements become. Without President Lincoln, the American Civil War would have resulted in either a loss for the Union or a ceasefire and a forever-divided nation. I believe that the Confederacy would have divided upon itself too, eventually, with separate nation-states like Texas, a people's republic of Georgia, a constitutional monarchy in South Carolina, in short, several nation-states instead of a united Confederate States of America. President Lincoln is truly

---

27) The keyword in the address is "dedicate." The United States of America's ideals and its democratic foundations, for the people, by the people, a nation of immigrants will never perish, these ideals are grounded in the very politics of the nation.

a great president, as well as a monumental figure in American history.[28]

In 1993, I visited Appomattox, Virginia. I was visiting this town to write my book on the American Civil War. I believed (back then, anyway), that learning about the reconciliation between the Union and the Confederate forces would lead to perhaps a blueprint or model for the reunification of the two Koreas. This is where General Robert E. Lee, Commanding General of the Confederate Army, surrendered to General Ulysses S. Grant. This is where the four-year war came to an end. Much blood was spilled up until this point during the American Civil War, with 620,000 men losing their lives for their country. Back then, this represented about 2.5 percent of the total population of the United States of America.

But what is this? There is nothing to be found here. I couldn't find any monuments or memorials to commemorate the end of the war. There was a little house there,[29] and on the second floor, two desks, with some paintings on the walls. There was no mention of the Union and Confederate commanders meeting here to end the war. The desks there were not the original desks that General Robert E. Lee used to sign papers of surrender. Philip Sheridan, a Union Cavalry General, snapped up the real desks. He

---

28) According to four polls by C-SPAN (Cable-Satellite Public Affairs Network), out of 41 presidents after 2000, President Lincoln was rated the best president of all time (June 30, 2021).

29) The war ended in a little house belonging to Wilmer McLean. This is near the site where the Union and the Confederate armies fought for the first time, in Manassas, located near Washington, D.C. Back then, a Confederate Army commander Pierre G. T. Beauregard used McLean's house as his army's headquarters. Three years later, when McLean fled his home after Virginia fell to Union forces, the house was used again as a place for the Confederates to surrender to Union forces. In later years, McLean would say half-jokingly to his close friends and family, "The American Civil War started in my backyard and ended in my living room." How curious.

was also talented in battle and very quick, or so they said. After visiting this little house, I wondered if there was something outside. I found nothing. Perhaps I could find a monument there for the brave boys who died in battle? Or a memorial perhaps, to commemorate them? Still nothing. Really. Small town Virginia is still small-town Virginia.

Are the townspeople trying to deny what happened here? I started doubting them. I tracked down a person from the place to find some bearings. I almost started to think that I shouldn't have come here.

"You might find something if you go to the nearby hamburger joint. There is something there that you might find," he said.

I found a little tombstone there.

"This is the site where the Confederate and Union soldiers agreed to a ceasefire."

This was engraved onto a little tombstone. It really is a little tombstone. I closed my eyes for a little while. Oh, these people! Look at these Americans! I became a little dizzy. I remembered the words of a dear friend of mine from Korea, General Kim Jun-bong, who had visited the place a year prior. He is a brilliant historian and military strategist. People in his field of work know of him.

"I went to Appomattox, and tears poured from my eyes."

This is the first thing he said to me after visiting the States on that particular trip. He must have thought of General Robert E. Lee's brilliance in warfare, and his wisdom, his humanity, and even more, his leadership back then.

The Confederate Army was hungry. They had no more cannons. For two weeks, they had fought for over 120 miles, ran away, and reached Appomattox. They were supposed to get supplies and food from this Virginia town, but General Sheridan seized the train before the Confederates got there. General Sheridan had recently been promoted to commander of the Army of the Potomac's Cavalry Corps. The Confederate Army reached exhaustion. Their one, last aim was to reach Appomattox, to fill their stomachs, but their food was stolen from them. Their one last hope disappeared. This is when General Lee finally considered surrendering to the Union Army. General Kim must have thought of General Robert E. Lee's sentiments when he spoke those words to me. As a fellow high-ranking military officer, there is anguish in his understanding of Lee.

My American friends deliberately seem to wish to evade the historical significance of Appomattox. In fact, history makes it seem like they are distorting the facts. But why? This is the site where the Union Army prevailed over the Confederate forces. It's a site imbued with historical significance. To commemorate it only with a little house when there's potentially money waiting to be raked in by making it a booming tourist attraction? They can, but they choose not to. They are intentionally erasing this painful fissure in their shared history. And so it goes that they leave behind a little house and a little commemorative tombstone. Americans are deep. They are wise. They are not people who reach immediately for a gun when the going gets tough.

If I think about it, the American Civil War was a tragedy for the United

States of America. Many young men, or about 600,000, gave their lives in battle. Between themselves, brother against brother, father against son. In hindsight, regret settles in. It still hurts, even today. They feel heartbroken. Let bygones be bygones. Let's not even think of it. Let's forget about it all! The hurt runs too deep. Don't touch it. It may fester. You must forget about it. Erase it from the heart. The North and the South must never talk of the civil war. Don't even bring it up. This therapeutic method of the Americans is something I regard highly. You cannot erase the past, but you do not have to dwell on it. The past is the past. Burying it is the best answer. Forgetting is the best answer. If you stay in the past, then it will, to use a Korean saying, "grab your ankles," thereby preventing you from advancing any further. You will never be able to wade out of a quagmire.

The United States of America would not exist today had they tried the South and treated them as rebels. They would have gone bust. All the Confederate men are rebels. It is an undeniable fact. They pointed their guns at the Union. A total of thirteen states seceded from the United States of America. They conspired together and challenged their original government. They elected a new president, formed a new government and started a civil war. Had they been faulting the other side, then they would have had a whole list of criminals to punish, starting from the very top, the former president of the Confederacy, Jefferson Douglas.

Had the Union punished the Confederates as criminals, thousands would have been executed or put in prison, or shot with bullets. Yesterday's comings and goings, there is no need to speak of them. Instead of worrying about the past, let us worry about tomorrow and speak about tomorrow. The logic behind this is simple. Completing today's tasks is tough enough, but why stay chained to the past when we don't even have enough time to contemplate tomorrow? Look behind your shoulder, fall ill. What do you earn from this? It's mere stupidity to investigate the past. If you keep on excavating the past, you will become trapped in it. You become trapped in a quagmire. There's no redemption in it. Why?

People don't change. Execute a few (evil) men, and other (evil men) will pop up. It's an eventuality. Punish evil, and evil will emerge again. Don't we all know that people don't change? History, for example, repeats itself over and over. Hundreds of years can attest to this. Fix the past a little bit, and hang on tight to the future. Teach, and cultivate defensive tactics. Worry about tomorrow; that is the correct answer. If you keep dwelling on the past, you need to examine why you don't understand the fundamental human psyche. If you focus on the past, you go bust. This is the harsh reality of life. No need to wax lyrical about this fact. We all saw the method by which the Americans mended their nation after the American Civil War. Let us "forget" the past. This is the wisdom we glean from the Americans.

F. Lincoln

Let us return, momentarily, to President Abraham "Honest Abe" Lincoln. About six months prior to the end of the civil war, General Ulysses S. Grant, who was Commanding General of the Union Army since March 1864, met with President Lincoln. They met near the Potomac River.

"Sir, I believe the war is almost at an end. What should we do with 'those people'?"

General Grant did not call the Confederates the enemy forces. Usually, army battalions in this type of situation call the other side "rebel forces." But General Grant refused to call the Confederate Army "rebels," even when discussing them with his subordinates. Instead, he called them, "those people." He was no less different when talking with President Lincoln.

President Lincoln never pointed out General Grant's word "those people." His face is grave. The chief commanding officer of the Union Army has just called the Confederate Army "those people." President Lincoln looks at General Grant. He towers above him. Then President Lincoln says something that shakes the world to its very core.

"Those people, just let them go."
"You just told me to let them go."
"Just?"
"I told you to just let them go."
"Then, are you saying that I should send them home?"

Lincoln pauses again. General Grant's face hardens for a minute. So really. These are President Lincoln's thoughts? But General Grant then says gravely,

"Sir, there are strict military laws in the Army."
"I just told you to let them go."

But General Grant's reply is even more astounding.

"Yes, sir."

What does General Grant mean by this? The Confederate Army consisted of rebel forces and traitors to the United States of America. Even so, does that mean he will forgive them all? How can the Commanding General of the Union Army say such a thing! These two giants were sincere. Even at Appomattox, when General Robert E. Lee met with General Ulysses S. Grant, while they were a bit awkward, it was not a meeting between loser and victor. It was more of a meeting of gentlemen, a solemn meeting. That is how it is recorded in history. They respect each other, and are very much the gentlemen who respect each other's characters as one signs papers of surrender. This may be hard for us to understand, but at Appomattox, this was so. And thus came to be.

Let me digress for a little while. If you read Churchill's memoirs, you will come to understand the two generals' reunion of a once divided America, rewritten in beautiful words. The generosity of the winner, coupled with the dignity of the losing party, and their beautiful way of ending a civil war speaks not only to the two generals' noble spirit, but it is also a victory for the human race as a whole, according to Churchill.

The head of the Confederate Forces, General Robert E. Lee, is actually a rebel leader. The head of the rebel leaders is usually subject to strict military laws. Had it not been for General Robert E. Lee, then the Civil War would have been only two years long, at the most. But because of his brilliant military genius, the war lasted four long years. Would not have the brave boys who went into battle and lost their lives, would not have at least half of them been still alive had they not dragged the war on for four years?

In many respects, General Robert E. Lee cannot be absolved of his many sins. In another country, he may have been executed. However, he returns home, without any legal repercussions. It's not as if a friendly match has ended. The Confederate Army has fought as rebels against the Union Army for four years. Lee has sacrificed, in a sense, the young lives of 600,000 men. But Lee becomes a university president in the years to come. Until his death. In the South, he becomes and is regarded as a hero. If you visit Lexington, Virginia, you can see the university where he served: Washington and Lee University. The college's name was changed upon his appointment.[30]

His subordinates were also allowed to return home without any ramifications. Cavalry was allowed to keep their horses, and they also went home. On the day of surrender, General Grant shows a generosity of spirit. The men returned home to help with the spring planting. This was a request made by Lee to Grant, and it was granted. Lincoln and Grant: what peculiar men! Even while writing my book, *The American Civil War*, I remember trying to reimagine and describe the scene of surrender by the Confederate Army, and I fell into confusion. I couldn't understand the psychology behind these two men. How could two victors treat the losers of the war as such?

The officers were allowed to go home with their weapons, the soldiers were allowed to keep their horses—this is not an end of a friendly athletics match. It was a horrendous war that took four years to end. Moreover, 600,000 young men sacrificed their lives for their country. How could the Union ask for their horses, their guns? In a state of confusion, I could only write this: "Grant was kind-hearted because he met a good person in Lee." I couldn't say it otherwise, as there were no other roads to take when re-explaining this scene. That chapter in my book is titled "Good People."

---

30) Washington and Lee University also houses a mausoleum for General Robert E. Lee, calling it, "Lee's Shrine." The Confederate States of America's former President, Jefferson Davis, serves two years in jail after the Confederate Army's surrender but doesn't serve other sentences and is not convicted of anything else. This is surprising to all of us.

When these good-natured men met, I think they deliberately spoke vaguely.

Lee was an excellent military general; moreover, he was a good and down-to-earth, person. He valued his subordinates and deeply loved his hometown. While he himself disagreed with the institution of slavery, he could not abandon Virginia, his home state, where slavery was legal. For this reason alone, he resisted then-President Lincoln's invitation to lead the Union Army during the start of the American Civil War. He was not the type of man who found justification in everything, nor was he quick to defend his actions with ideology. He seemingly evades the hero's laws. Instead, he was a genuine and pure person, and a genuine and pure military officer. While they made a myth and a legend out of General Robert E. Lee, this was because of his kind nature, who cared for the ordinary people.

So what kind of man was Grant? If you delve into a detailed description of him, you will find something like this: "He was, by character, a quiet and modest man of repute. But when he spoke, his subordinates listened to him intently, and would take notes. He spoke plainly, but could penetrate and understand the other person's inner world, and see into the heart of the problem, as if he could grasp it with his hand and clarify it. His decisions were simple and swift." His wife Julia, who knew him better than anyone, had this to say about him. Let me paraphrase the quote here: "He never mentions war [to me]. Even when they captured Vicksburg, he didn't even mention it in the letter [he sent to me]. He always thought compassionately of the Confederate Army." He also was a man who knew how to empathize with the South's pain, as he was a pure and honorable man. His wife Julia was the younger sister of one of his West Point classmates, Fred Dent.

"My brother would always praise Ulysses (Grant's name) as a man of great distinction. Even to family, my brother never was short in his praise of him. And to me, my brother would always say, 'Ulysses is the best man out of all of my friends. He's like a man made of pure gold.'" A man made of pure gold? Why the comparison to pure gold? Through Julia's words, we know that Grant was indeed a man of considerable purity.

Two Americans who loved the young men they led to battle, and were of excellent moral character, fought ferociously, and as heroically as they could. But they had a task before them: finish the bloody war the only way they could without more warfare. To them, naming the victor and the defeated was unimportant. Justifications were unimportant. General Grant showed compassion to the rebellious Confederate Army, and General Lee could only keep the laws of the ordinary people and sigh in consternation. These two men, as pure as pure gold, and upon meeting each other, their kindred souls commiserated. It was neither the time nor the place to cast blame or revenge, or lay down the law. The two American generals, according to historians, would set the gold standard on how to gracefully end a war.

Lee was not the only one who was forgiven that day. The President of the Confederate States of America, Jefferson Davis, was also spared from being executed for treason. The only one who was executed in the American Civil War was the prison camp commander of the Confederacy, Major Henry Wirz. He had overstepped military laws and received the death sentence. He had abused prisoners of war. Civil rights were championed that day over treasonous acts. This is the American way of dealing with painful history. While writing about this topic, I felt a lot of hardship. I couldn't recreate the feelings of the two generals and, likewise, their officers. People's hearts, especially that of the Americans during the Civil War, I still do not fully comprehend.

On April 14, 1865, in Washington D. C.'s Ford Theater, located on 10th Street, a gunshot rang out. The theater that evening was staging the British comedy "Our American Cousin." President Lincoln was in attendance with the first lady on the second floor of the theater. He was also accompanied by his friend Senator Ira Harris's daughter, along with her fiance, lieutenant commander Henry Rathone. When the theatergoers were shaking the foundations of the building with their laughter, a man named John W. Booth slipped through a door almost silently.

There were no guards at the entryway, or within the theater. Lincoln was about two meters away from his assassin, Booth. He held a pistol in his right hand and a dagger in his left. He aimed towards the back of Lincoln's head, then pulled the trigger. The first lady started screaming then grabbed her husband. Major Rathone stood up immediately and ran to the assassin. Booth started waving the dagger at him. The assassin jumped four meters down to the theater's stage.

"Get him!" Rathone screamed.

Booth held the dagger high then started screaming nonsensically at the theater crowd. Then he darted to the back of the stage and disappeared. The actress who played the lead that day, Laura Keene, jumped into the royal box. Harris was trying to calm down the hysterical first lady, while Keene put the President's head on her lap. A doctor ran in. He had also been a spectator in the theater that day. He examined the wound. The bullet had pierced through President Lincoln's left ear, damaging the brain before becoming stuck beneath his right eye. It's a fatal wound. President Lincoln had lost consciousness by that point. The military men moved President

Lincoln to a hotel across the street. Cabinet ministers swarmed his bed. They stayed the night, guarding Lincoln's last hours.

On April 15, 1865, at 7:22 A.M., President Lincoln passed away. A giant in many respects had passed on.

"O Captain! My Captain! Our fearful trip is done; …the port is near…. O the bleeding drops of red, where on the deck my Captain lies…" wrote Walt Whitman, a famed poet of the day in response to President Lincoln's assassination.

When I read about the assassination, I cannot help but think that President Lincoln, whilst he lay dying, may have thought that Booth or someone from the American South had made Booth assassinate him. Lincoln's security team was sorely lacking. Lincoln himself should have known this as well. The war had dragged on for four long years. After the American Civil War's end, only rage and bitter resentment would have been in their hearts for the average former Confederate citizen. Their houses burned, their husbands and sons dead, how would the Southern women's grief be assuaged? How could they alleviate their pain? President Lincoln was a martyr. His last drops of blood were the very last ones spilled during the war. His death may have assuaged the grief of the South. Could he not have prognosticated himself that he may become a lamb for the slaughter? We have to admire his noble sacrifice.

It was an open secret that President Lincoln would be at the Ford Theater that day. On the night of April 14, the entrance, as well as the royal box, did not have security agents. This was the presidential procession of the United States of America. But the wave of hatred rising against President Lincoln was growing. If God wanted the nascent United States of America to come to fruition and sent George Washington there, then the newly (would-be) integrated United States of America was reborn after the dispatch of Abraham Lincoln. President Lincoln was a seasoned captain. Brother fighting brother divided a united nation and became a civil war. President Lincoln had weathered the storm and saved them all from shipwreck, only to die himself.

President Lincoln was a man with many dreams. He wanted to preserve the Founding Fathers' ideals and preserve their ideas of human liberty and dignity of the person. To put his ideals into practice, he had to attack the institution of slavery but still preserve the Union. So President Lincoln held the Union in high regard, and his first and second objectives were to keep the Union secure, and thereby, he had to bear the brunt of the Civil War.

Now here was a man who painted a vision for the new America to come. Lincoln's ability to see the big picture, and General Grant's vision of America, and his successor, Andrew Johnson, received inspiration from him. Most politicians would have said that the states that seceded should be punished after the civil war ended. However, President Lincoln strongly disagreed with them and forgave all.

Any death, no matter whose death it may be, is a tragedy. A man from the former Confederacy assassinated the President of the United States of America. His death may have created ripples in the American South, where resentment was running high. Had Abraham Lincoln not sacrificed himself, then would the United States of America have been able to reintegrate the South into the country? A giant of a man, by living, saved the Union, and by dying, assured that the seceded states would indeed be included again into the United States of America.

G. Jefferson Davis

While writing my book, *The American Civil War*, the one person I felt a lot of regret for was Jefferson Davis, the former President of the Confederate States of America. A graduate of West Point, he even served as a Senator and the Secretary of Defense for the U.S.A. before the Civil War. He was highly regarded as a man of ability. Moreover, he was loyal to himself, his family, and he was dedicated to a life of public service, so determined was he to put forth his best efforts into being a hard-working, honorable man. Surprisingly enough, after the defeat of the Confederate States of America, he staunchly supported the former "lost cause" and refused to say that he had been in the wrong.

As a former military man myself, I really wish to understand the tragedy he brought upon the American people by becoming President of a rogue nation of seceded states. I also wish to understand his reasoning behind going to war and his worries as the head of the Confederacy. But after September 1862, when the Battle of Antietam was waged, he should have ended the war there. He should have seen beforehand the trajectory of the Confederacy of the future. The Battle of Antietam forever dashed the Confederacy's hopes that some European powers, sympathetic to their cause, would eventually intervene to help them.

Additionally, there were a few Northerners who had secretly held the Southerners' cause in their hearts, but their few supporters in the North also disappeared into thin air after the Republican primaries; he should have been privy to this knowledge, yet he hadn't been wise enough to look ahead to the future. As the head of a newly formed government, the first objective is always to defend national security, then make his citizens comfortable. A country, compared to a ship, should have smooth sailing and weather storms as they come, with the captain being a metaphor for the head of state. But Davis failed to do this by all accounts.

The other mistake was his myopic vision. Instead of looking forward, and moving towards a new age, as the Union was doing, he was not innovative. The South, from the first, had not embraced the North's freedoms and ideas regarding equality. Davis also largely ignored industry, which relied on competition. He should have looked toward what would eventually become the Industrial Revolution. The Founding Fathers also stressed democratic ideals, such as freedom and equality, which the Confederacy failed to do. The American South instead considered the North's experiment a low-class, ungentlemanly thing to do. As most of the European powers during that time were composed of governments with a monarch at the head, the Confederacy did not realize that they were supporting an outdated, outmoded institution with agrarian roots.

In July 1863, as General Robert E. Lee conceded at Gettysburg, Davis insisted on invading the North, leaving commoner Southerners to endure two more years of war. When viewed as an individual, he was a man to admire. Yet as a leader, he was unable to put these fine individual traits to good use, causing damage to not just the Confederacy, but to the United States of America as a whole.

In conclusion, Jefferson Davis did not live up to the ideals of the Founding Fathers, and was unable to figure out when to go forth and when to concede.

He had terrible timing, and even more, his ability to look at the big picture as well as the minute details was sorely lacking. Davis could not look at the forest for the trees, and he could not look at the trees for the forest, causing the Confederacy to ultimately fall.

In the *I Ching*, also known as *The Book of Changes*, there is a saying that I would like to recount to you. "Heed the signs in your work in order to successfully complete Heaven's mission." In other words, you must heed the signs (omens) to be even in the midst of work; the timing must be right. What is exposed, and what is still hidden; the middle ground between these points can be translated to "gi" or "gae." When I talk about "si-joong," I am referring to perfect timing. "Gi-mi" means to know what is hidden between what exists and what doesn't exist, but how can one do this as an ordinary person?

"Si-joong," means the right time, but how can an ordinary person have the perfect timing in keeping with the mysterious ways of the universe? This path is hidden from most ordinary people. To put it mildly, it may be impossible. So is there no method?

In the *I Ching*, there is another saying. "A man must observe the strictest self-restraint and reserve in dangerous times." In other words, "Be fearful at all times and don't be lazy or give up and make sure that (in your work) there are no flaws, even a small amount." In even easier words, "With fearful hearts seek the Heavens, care for the people and the land, and stay humble." Now, can you see what I mean? In the easiest words possible, I say to you, stay humble. And pray.

Gentlemen, how do you feel? If you are humble and pray, there is nothing that you cannot achieve. In everything, know that you are capable and can achieve anything. Have confidence. Even though someone may not know the particulars or even be in that particular situation, we say in Korea to not talk of specifics. I may have overstepped my bounds a little. In the previous passages, I, myself, may not have been humble. I hope you understand that everyone must learn this lesson.

3 The land we call China

A. China, a grand nation

China is large, populous, with a long history, complicated, a little bit of a braggart, and a nation that is very difficult to understand. "Americans count seconds and minutes. We, [the] Chinese, count decades and centuries," a Chinese-American instructor said at the U.S. Army Public Affairs Center on the first day of class.

A Chinese person breathes deeply and everything is "Man man di." In other words, they embrace the slow life, practice largesse in everything because of their long-standing history and vast and expansive land mass. For the Chinese, there is no need to be in a hurry. If you can't finish something today, finish it tomorrow. They know how to stop to smell the roses. Compared to Koreans' "Bbal-ri-bbalri," or "Hurry, hurry," they are different. So how large is their country? The land covers about 9.6 million km squared, about a hundred times that of Korea, and is comparable to the size of the continental United States or all of Europe. As for its history, it is largely divided into three dynasties, "Ha," "Sang," and "Joo," which lasted for 5,000 years. China is the birthplace of the Hwanghe ancient civilization (Yellow River Civilization).

In many respects, "China" is not the official name of the country. The Chinese always regard themselves as the cradle of civilization, thus their nickname, "The Middle Kingdom." Culturally speaking, the Chinese consider themselves a cut above the rest of Asia, as one to be revered due to their history from ancient times. Even during the "Ha, Sang, Joo," periods, their empire was called the Qin Dynasty, the Han Dynasty, the Qing Dynasty, and they did not use the name "China" to call their vast country.

The first time they were referred to as "China" was in 1911, during the Xinhai Revolution when the head of the government renamed the country as "Joong Hwa Min Guk (Zhōnghuá Mínguó)." Shortened, this became the name Koreans call China today: "Joong Guk." So what is China to Koreans? It is many things: scary yet a country to be thankful for, feel a lot of regret for, hate, regard as a teacher, a master, and for hundreds of years, pay homage to, in the form of (very expensive) gifts, or taxes.

About a century ago, Koreans finally emerged from China's influence. Until then, we Koreans were unable to stand with our backs straight to China, but were always kowtowing. What kind of karma did Koreans owe to the Chinese that this kind of relationship came to pass? It is a strange twist of fate, and China defies understanding, yet it is a country that has a deep and meaningful history with Korea.

On September 28th, 1992, at Tiananmen Square, the Korean anthem was played while our flag was hoisted to the flagstaff. It warmed my heart. It was a historic day. The then-Korean President Noh Tae-woo, along with the then-President of China, Yang Shangkun, had just been elected, and he established diplomatic ties with Korea first. In Korea's history, this was the first time that we were wealthier than China, and were in a position to help

China and were their equal. This was a celebration held in honor of our new partnership in the future.

Even thirty years ago, China had 11 billion people, with a GDP of $44 billion U.S. dollars and a GDP per capita of $ 370 U.S. dollars. Korea's GDP was about $50 billion U.S. dollars, with a GDP per capita of $9,000, about 23 times that of China. My "pull-yourself-up-by-your-bootstraps" generation had finally done it! We had achieved the impossible. Secretly, that day, we hid our tears. Our ancestors had never been able to hold their heads up high around China, and what we had suffered under the soldiers of the Ming Dynasty, and when our King In-jo of Joseon Dynasty had to kowtow to the emperor of the Qing Dynasty at the Sam-Jeon-Do, after losing in war. Yuan Shih-kai's violence and CPC's intervention in the Korean War, and prevented the reunification of the Korean Peninsula—how can we recount all these insults and sorrow? How are we supposed to forget? You will not understand how moved we were that day. There's no need to know. Our fathers and our grandfathers must mark this historic significance. Dear reader, our youth must always look forward. Don't look backward. Too many bitter events may bind your feet to the past.

Before the 1990 Asian Games held in Beijing, China, my friend Liu Dao Peng came to visit me. As the Vice President of the Chinese Athletics Federation, and the International Association of Athletics Federations (IAAF) Vice President, he was a gentleman in every sense of the word, for he had been educated abroad in Great Britain. In my personal and professional life, I have only been acquainted with two very wise men, and he is one of them. I would also like to add that he is incredibly disciplined and hardworking.

Whenever I think of the gentlemanly IAAF Vice President Liu, I think of a character from *Sam Guk Ji*, also known in English as *The Romance of the Three Kingdoms*. The character I speak of is "Zhuge-liang." At every meeting we attended at the IAAF, I can say with certainty that every time he spoke, everyone would listen solemnly to what he had to say. His perfect English and perfectly logical arguments would keep us fellow non-native speakers of English, in awe of him. I admire him to this day. His comments were always on-point. It seems that Beijing wasn't cordial to him because of his "bourgeois" background, which included studying at a London boarding school.

The reason behind his seeking me out was that in preparing Beijing for the upcoming Asian Games, he needed the Korean Athletics Federation's help. China must have been in much more dire straits than we had known then. As a proud member of the IAAF family, the KAF donated about $350,000 to purchase much-needed items such as the hurdle, high jump, pole vault, and so forth. My generation of Koreans did what we could to help China, the giantess.

Dear youth, if my generation could do it, I am sure that your generation will surpass us, for what is out of your reach? Do not be so self-effacing. Don't be frightened! Go forth! I did the same.

B. The Daily Life of the Chinese

China's strong point, without a doubt, is its population. When Deng Xiaoping started his reforms in 1992, the population was around 1.15 billion people, or about 21 percent of Earth's total population (out of a total of 5.4 billion people). Now, their population is around 1.5 billion people, so they are neck and neck with India. According to common knowledge, if the entire population of China walked as the column of four towards the Gate of Heavenly Peace (Tiananmen), they would continue marching until the end of days (the apocalypse).

One billion is a scary number to behold. Everyone always says life is a precious thing, but imagine if you had a billion (of something). If everyone out of the billion donates a single dollar, then you would have a billion dollars within a short time frame. But according to Chinese scientists, the Chinese population cannot exceed 1.6 billion. The land mass is large, but the land cannot be put to good use once they exceed this point, and they predict that there will be a water shortage if the population exceeds this number. Rugged mountain terrain along with desert areas make up a vast majority of the country, so only about 34 percent of the remaining land remains usable. The yearly waterfall is around 650 mm. The government cannot support more than about 1.6 billion people.

When talking about China, one cannot leave out their Sinocentrism; otherwise, it is difficult to fully understand the Chinese. Sinocentrism refers to China being at the center of the world and they are the cradle of civilization and ancient peoples that deserve to be looked up to; in other words, they are a proud nation. Chinese civilization falls under one of the four most ancient civilizations, including Mesopotamia, Egypt, and India. This is called, "Joong Hwa Sa Sang," in Korean. The Chinese began to take immense pride in their nation during the "Suh Joo" period, in the 11th century, by comparing themselves with the nations around them. They started becoming increasingly proud of their cultural heritage.

"Joong," means, in this instance, "center," and signifies their geographical and cultural center, and "Hwa" refers, in this instance, to their heightened cultural legacy. The problem with Sinocentrism is its inherent racism. Other nations or peoples around them were looked down upon in a strategy called "Hwa Yi Sa Sang." To them, the Koreans are "Dong-i," Vietnam is "Nam-man," Uighurs are "Suh-yoong," and the Mongolians are "Book-juk." This is how much they used to demean their neighbors of other races. When they encounter their neighbors, they look down on them immediately if they are not the Han people. There is no love for thy neighbor as thy neighbor philosophy, and they fail to realize that others around them are just as valued and important as they are. They are full of pride and self-confidence, but as for their self-worth, I fail to understand why they would not treat others as they wish to be treated.

Additionally, when talking about China, we cannot fail to leave out "Hwa-gyo," the Chinese expatriates and their descendants outside the mainland. Eighteen sixty was when the Chinese first became expatriates by immigrating to other countries. This happened during the Qing Dynasty. This was after the signing of the Beijing Treaty between the U.K. and the Qing Dynasty in 1860. "If the waters of the sea meet land, then wherever you go, there will be 'hwa-gyo.'" The Chinese of yesteryear set sail for Southeast Asia and were hugely successful there. Almost all of them made great strides in their new settlements to the point that they took over the commercial districts for many of them.

Let's examine South East Asia's Chinese expatriate community. We can find people of notable worth like the Philippines' founding father, Jose Rizal, Vietnam's founder, Ho Chi Minh, former Vietnam's Ngo Dinh Diem and former President Nguyen Van Thieu, Singapore's former Prime Minister Lee Kuan Yew, and Myanmar's former Prime Minister Ne Win. The overseas Chinese were able to succeed on foreign soil because of their strong sense of national identity, their cohesiveness as blood relatives, patience, diligence, and a tendency towards excellent financial literacy along with assiduousness. They use an aphorism to describe this phenomenon, and it is as follows: "Even a gentleman loves wealth, but there are moral laws behind the business." Another wise saying that the Chinese like to repeat is, "Do not deceive children or a man who does not have anyone to rely on."

Chinese expatriates' power comes from their country of residence as well as their ancestors' home country. Chinese abroad represent about 160 countries in total by 2020 estimates, or about 40 million. This is not a small number. China is a large country by landmass, and many different peoples actually live there. About 92 percent are Han Chinese. The rest consist of about 55 other ethnic minorities. Out of the 55 ethnic minorities, about 19 of the number over a million each. Chuang are about 16 million, followed by "Man-jok," with 10 million, Hui about 9 million, then Uighurs and Tibetans. Korean-Chinese rank 13th, at about 1.3 million. The majority of the ethnic minorities have autonomous rights.

The country of China houses many languages, because of the size and girth of its land and the different ethnicities that live there. Even the Han people have different regional dialects, and sometimes communication problems occur. So it follows that a common language must arise out of necessity. The common language becomes the "Putonghua (or Mandarin)," spoken in Beijing. In television, radio, schools, and the field of education, Mandarin is the norm.

Common spoken and written Chinese can be divided into two main categories: written, or literal Mandarin, known in Korean as "Mun-un," and

"Baek-hwa," or spoken Chinese. "Mun-un," is usually not used but is found in classical literature, history, and philosophy.

Nowadays, "Putonghua (or Mandarin)" is the common spoken language. It was largely used after the Six Dynasties era and became today's colloquial language. The Chinese government ensured that the standard Mandarin was the dialect spoken in Beijing. Throughout China, if you receive an education, you can communicate via standard Mandarin spoken and written by Beijingers. But even as recently as 20 years ago, a Beijinger would have trouble communicating with someone from Shanghai, and it was impossible to communicate with someone from Guangdong. In 1991, in the *Shin-si Ilbo*, there was an article about two men from Shandong who went to a farm in Wuhan and got into a dispute because they could not communicate with each other, which gave way to a disagreement. Eventually, one person died and the other person was gravely wounded.[31]

The Chinese are fond of the colors red and yellow. Red signifies wealth and honor, while yellow was exclusively used to decorate the King's quarters. The origins of red and yellow were inspired by ancient times when they worshiped the Sun god and the Earth god. The Sun god was associated with the color red, while the Earth god was associated with the color yellow. The earth was seen as the fundamental origin of everything. According to the Five Elements philosophy, the earth is always in the center of the five elements, which are as follows: wood, fire, earth, metal, and water. As the emperor was seen as the center of it all, the color yellow became the standard

---

31) "Why are you going to Wuhan?" (qù Wǔhàn shā) was misinterpreted as "I'm going to Wuhan to murder" (qù Wǔhàn shā). The word "sa," in Chinese characters, signified "what," but was confused with "sal (to kill)" due to the differences in intonation. Unfortunately, the word is the same, but it was pronounced differently (February 11, 1991).

decorative color of the Chinese imperial family.

Culturally speaking, Confucianism has deep roots in China, but as they moved towards a communist framework, many of the old ways, the customs as well as the cultural traditions have been lost. The Cultural Revolution especially did away with some cultural practices rooted in Confucianism. But due to their long history as an ancient culture, vestiges of the old ways, and manners, still remain in the blood of the Chinese. These ways still weigh heavily on them. The Chinese are deep, unlike the Koreans, who like joking around. Once you befriend the Chinese, they are faithful and loyal. Like the Koreans, they are also generous and warm-hearted. The Chinese and the Koreans share some traditions. One example is refilling an alcoholic beverage once a guest drinks from the glass. Koreans fill it partially, but the Chinese pour generously. This may be the difference between a country of plenty and Korea.

In drawings and other pieces of art, Koreans like leaving some of the canvas blank or embracing the beauty of space, whereas the Chinese prefer to fill the entire canvas, to use a metaphor. The Chinese character pronounced "Chae-ul man," applies in these instances. Translated, it means "to fill [to the brim]."

In everyday life, the Chinese place a strong emphasis on human relationships. The Chinese call this "Guan-shi." Explained simply, if you somehow make an official request that seems a bit excessive, if you find the proper "unofficial" way, then the request may be granted unexpectedly. "Guan-shi" simply doesn't apply to the relationship with another person but to relatives as well, and taking care of relatives seems to be regarded as a virtue there.

"If a distant relative rises to a high-ranking position, then the rooster or dog you have been raising at home also sees a positive change in their present circumstances." Another aphorism says, "If a person reaches spiritual enlightenment, then the dog or the rooster that you have been raising also ascends." In recent times, however, these tendencies are not accepted today. The regulation by authorities may play a factor, but the other difference is the difference in how public authorities are viewed in China.

Let us return momentarily to another short tale I heard from the venerable President Aoki of the Japanese Athletics Association. His mentor was Yasuoka Masahiro,[32] a famous Japanese historian. During the Sino-Japanese War (1894-1895), Masahiro visited the occupied territory where the descendants of Yelu Chucai[33] lived. During his lifetime, Mashiro was regarded as the most outstanding Japanese scholar of the day. He believed that Yelu Chucai's Manchurian/Mongolian descendants would move Japanese sentiment to action through him.

---

32) When POSCO (formerly Posco Iron and Steel Co., Ltd.) was being established, the United States, Germany, the United Kingdom, and Italy repeatedly rejected appeals for help regarding steel technology. The then-President of POSCO, Park Tae-jun, went to Japan and met with President Yasuoka. He was nicknamed "the invisible hand" for his influence on politics and in business, and was a giant in his own right. President Yasuoka believed, "Being contrite about past misdeeds [towards the former colony of Korea in the early to mid 20th century] and helping Korea was in Japan's national interest." He had this type of mentality toward Korea, and with his help, Park was able to meet with the Steel Association of Japan's President and former Prime Minister. The initially lukewarm Japanese government's response to Korea's request for help turned into a real partnership, and POSCO was born (*The Chosun Ilbo*, 'Japan as seen by Park Tae-jun," (March 5, 2015).

33) Yelu Chucai (1190-1244), was a Manchurian astronomer, geographer, mathematician, and scholar of Buddhism and was selected by Genghis Khan as the most renowned scholar of his time.

"We, the Chinese, since the beginning of history, have not been at war, so we have dealt pretty well with the aftermath of warfare. But after being defeated by the Imperial Japanese Army, there was a major shift. We lost not only our face. Our 'Nyu-gyu' was destroyed. 'Nyu-gyu,' is the antonym to 'Chung-gyu,' and 'Chung-gyu' refers to the rule of the ruling class. The ruling class also intermingles with the scholar-gentry class, the intellectual class. But 'Nyu-gyu' refers to the rule of pickpockets, thieves, the lower classes, and backstreet dealings.

We Chinese have always had manners, and even thieves and gang members have had manners. But what I really want to say is that when Japan occupied us, the "nyu-gyu" actually disintegrated. This is a fact. Why this is a problem is because of the intellectual class, and the ruling classes' demise, we can correct with a revolution, but once 'nyu-gyu,' once it falls, can never be put together. And that is a problem.

The most sensitive part of 'nyu-gyu' is bribes. China, since ancient times, is socially accustomed to giving and receiving bribes. In large families, however, China shows grace by helping their more needy relatives. For example, those who work government jobs help those who don't have the means of making a living, and this is called a virtue in China. This is an example of the Chinese way of 'nyu-gyu.'

But after the Japanese Imperial Army occupied our land, bribery became the norm and increased so much in number that the distribution of goods sank into confusion. China, for the first time since its establishment as a country, fell into disrepair. This is because 'nyu-gyu' disintegrated."

I think his worry is reasonable. China, once established, was a world power once upon a time. For many years and centuries, China could keep its long-storied traditions, keep the great empire, and maintain order.

After the Industrial Revolution, a new world order came to power. And along with it, new forms of political order and structure. But in terms of social mobility or rank, there was not much reform. The lower classes were still viewed as the lower classes. This principle was evident in both the East and the West. After the 3rd Industrial Revolution, the 4th Industrial Revolution followed, and now the COVID-19 virus epidemic is shaking the world to its core foundations. Where do we head next?

Korea is still a developing country, yet we have reached a standstill at the apex. Upon reaching the summit, there is nowhere to go but down. Where are we supposed to go from this point onwards? There is no need to ask, we just have to jump over this hurdle. We have to jump over the obstacle that defines us as a developing country in order to achieve a new goal. The goal should be to strive toward becoming a developed country and conquering a new mountain. The rise of China may actually be a boon for Korea. It puts us on our guard and makes us try harder. Korea does not have a history as a developed nation. But we know how to jump over this hurdle. When we pass from being a developing nation and join the ranks of the developed nations, we have a fortuitous aspect on our side; we have already experienced the idea and excitement of having passed from a less developed country to a developing one.

Dear youth! Let us try. There is nothing you can't do. A new stage awaits you. Just wait. Opportunity will come. China's current rise to power in the future will have geopolitical consequences in East Asia. The change in geopolitical structures in the years to come, however, will not leave us at a disadvantage.

C. The Ins and Outs of China's Politics

a) Is China a Communist country?

Is China a socialist country? No. You cannot say that it is a socialist country. Economic theory is the starting point for socialism, yet China has veered from this long ago. They shifted from the economic theory behind socialism to embrace one of a capitalist market economy, and named this economy with a flourish. Their economy, translated into English, is, "socialist market economy."[34] China is not a communist country. In fact, according to their wording, they are "a socialist market economy nation." So just where does my thinking end and theirs begin?

Deng Xiaoping is a great man. For China, he is. Due to his greatness, the world has suffered. Let me digress a little bit and tell you a story. Deng went on a factory inspection. Pointing to a computer, he asked a question to one of the workers.

"Is this [product a product of] a free market economy or a socialist market economy?"

---

34) Jiang Zemin coined the term "Socialist market economy" in 1992. It refers to a communist state like China that combines socialist politics with aspects of a free market economy. China introduced a free market economy back in 1992, when it reformed some parts of its economic structure.

The worker looked confused.

Then Deng said, "When it was abroad, it was [the product of a] free market economy, but within Chinese borders it's [the product of a] socialist market economy."

This is analogous to a metaphor for a black or white cat. It doesn't matter what you name it. The fact that it introduced a product or an aspect of a free market economy means that they are no longer purely a communist nation and points to a fierce denial that a communist nation can flourish. But suppose you keep arguing that such a "socialist market economy" can exist. In that case, they contradict the Chinese venerable philosopher, Confucius' teachings about determinism, or a preordained fate. Confucius used to argue that if a political system were to be on the straight and narrow, then it should first be named correctly.[35]

One of the most basic communist ideologies is controlling the economy, not letting loose a free market economy.[36] Have I gone too far as a former military officer? I'll leave it at this. I did not pick a fight as to whether China

---

35) Chung Yu Ja, also known as Zaro, was a disciple of Confucius. He once asked Confucius, "If the emperor of the Wei kingdom put you in charge of politics, what would be the first thing you would do?" Confucius replied, "I would first correct the name." Another disciple asked him about politics and Confucius said, "A king must be like a king, and a gentleman must behave like a gentleman." This basically means that the name has to be the right fit for whatever it is describing.

36) In 1840, after the Qing Dynasty lost the Opium War, they decided to "not change the original qi of something, but change the packaging." They integrated the superior technology of the West, and enhanced the country's prosperity and defense via the Chinese Westernized Reform. Changing from a controlled economy to a market economy and changing the name of the type of economics governing the country contradicts the long-storied tradition of what it means to be China and what it means to be Chinese.

is a communist nation or not. What you have to emphasize is China's emergence and its future trajectory. It's not precisely an emergence. It's more of a "China Rising," according to them. They stand tall. Just because I prattle doesn't mean that China will stop. In 2019, China's gross domestic product (GDP) stood at over 14 trillion dollars, about 67 percent of the United States' GDP. China's catching up. In 2027-28, China is projected to become the first nation to surpass the United States, and become the world's biggest economy, and finally become a developed country.

The China of today didn't belabor the issue of whether the cat is black or white; they just raked in the money. While the entire world is in a recession (or seems to be) in 2020, China boasted growth of 2.3 percent, one of the few economies that saw growth during that year. The IMF projected that in 2021, China's economic growth will be 8.7 percent. I'm scared. Aren't you?

History is the product of "yeon-gi."[37] This is my own theory. History cannot be understood with mere human wisdom. Rather, history is the product of a tangled network of connections between people, their vocations, and their karma. Whether the zeitgeist creates the hero or the hero opens the zeitgeist is unknowable. This is the influence of God at work. There is no need to traverse and climb from the far off Three Sovereigns and Five Emperors to Qinshihuangdi. Without Mao Zedong, then the People's Republic of China would not exist. Would today's China exist without Zhou Enlai and Deng Xiaoping?

On October 1, 1949, Mao Zedong proclaimed the establishment of the

---

37) This is my theory that I postulated in one of my previous books, *Story of Civilization: Civilization and Energy*, stating that history is the process of many connections and relationships all tangled up.

People's Republic of China at Tiananmen Square. Could Jiang Jieshi have taken his place? Is Mao Zedong's emergence the work of fate or chance?

This is all "yeon-gi" at work. "Yeon-gi" is also God's predetermination at work. A "socialist market economy," can this term even exist? No, it cannot. But China is rising to power based on this strange ideology. I say to you now, dear youth, don't get tangled up in ideology. Don't get buried by facts and figures (knowledge consists of more than that). Open your hearts. Open your minds. Knowledge and logic sometimes render us fools.

Columbus leveled the bottom of an egg and made it stand upright. He was asked to make the egg stand, so he cut the bottom and made it stand. No one prohibited him from leveling the bottom of the egg. Deng Xiaoping seized the chance to create a socialist market economy. And he saved the Chinese people. Communism didn't work by itself; communism couldn't feed the people, so they threw away a purist form of communism. But they couldn't actually say that they trashed it, so instead, a hybrid form of economic structure was born, called the "socialist market economy." Doesn't it sound fancy? But does anyone protest a market economy in the first place?

Deng Xiaoping's greatest strength was in discarding what didn't work. He threw away communism. If he hadn't thrown it away, the idea of a socialist market economy would not have come to pass. A socialist nation's "closed market economy," has no "market economy" anywhere. Because they threw away their ancestral tablet, to use a metaphor, they were able to fully embrace a socialist market economy.[38] The empirical tradition says that

---

38) A new idea is born when one throws away what doesn't work. Yelu Chucai's wise saying says, "It's better to abandon something than add to it [if it doesn't work]." When Steve Jobs retook the helm at Apple, the first thing he did was focus on new product development. He removed many products, leaving only four main products in place. Chuang-tzu says, "Hold a funeral for yourself first." This is the harsh reality.

starving to death in a communist country is worse than the full belly that a market economy promises. He just followed the great cause. Can anyone become a Deng Xiaoping? No, of course not. An open heart, stubbornness, and bravery are needed, and you also have to risk your life on it. To say it plainly, jumping over a "wall" is very difficult, and not everyone can do it.

China is changing these days, though. In 2012, when Xi Jinping became the head of state, the country returned to its communist roots. He has already done away with the electoral process that may see another leader rise to power. In 2022, at the national convention, he will be inaugurated again for a third consecutive term. A journalist said in an editorial that President Xi Jinping has, during his first 10 years in office, charted a course for the People's Republic of China that is reminiscent of China 60 years ago, which harkens back to the Cultural Revolution.

Xi Jinping, has of late, been promoting "Gong dong byu yoo," or "Let's live well together." Along with this new unofficial slogan, his administration has been cementing their grip on the economy, education, and even the entertainment sector, and censorship has been getting even more vigilant.

Due to these changes, the educated elite has protested. For example, a professor at the country's most prestigious university, Peking University, has voiced concerns over these reforms that harken back to the past. Professor of Economics Chang Wei-ying (who has a doctorate from the University of Oxford, by the way), said in September 2021, that if the government takes control of the "CE50," which are the top 50 public and private firms, then "[The people] will lose confidence in the strength of [China's] economy, and if the government seizes control of the economy again, then instead of an economic boom, they will become fixtures for, 'Let's all be poor together.'"

As a person who cares about China, this worries me too.

To the young men and women of today, I say that there are so many walls to scale ahead of us. To usher in a new era, we must wisely discard what no longer serves us. Let us greet tomorrow with an open mind and full hearts.

b) The Chinese Communist Party

The Beginnings

On May 4, 1919, at Tiananmen Square, about 3,000 students assembled. It would come to be called the May 4th Movement.[39] After the First World War, China wanted Germany to return Shantung Province and some 21 agreements made with Japan to be rendered void. Chinese students and citizens alike had pinned their hopes on the Paris Peace Conference, but with its collapse during negotiations for China, anger displaced their hopes. Nowadays, we can say that many trials and errors have rendered the May 4th Movement as a success. Not just students, but later, even the citizens and blue-collar workers gathered to assist the cause. The May 4th Movement opened Chinese citizens' eyes as it was one of the first public movements of dissent in the country. By protesting imperialism and feudalism, it became the birth of and the starting point of a new, modern China.

The May 4th Movement created national solidarity amongst students, ordinary citizens, and the proletariat. This gave way to Chen Duxin,[40] and

---

39) The May 4th Movement is similar to the March 1st Movement in Korea (the March 1st Movement refers to resistance against Japanese colonialism in Korea). It was an independence movement by the Chinese against Russian influence in the country. It was anti-imperialism, anti-federalist, and in essence, a revolutionary movement of great importance in history.

40) Chen Duxin (1879-1942) was a Chinese communist, a member of the Comintern (The

the influence of Marxism, which eventually led to the creation and the rise of the Chinese Worker's Party, and the first time the working class in China actively participated in politics. Mao Zedong's leadership in 1921 also was born as a result of this movement.

About ten years prior, on that very soil, the Xinhai Revolution happened, which ended Chinese imperialism in the country and the death of the Qing Dynasty. A man named Sun Wen (also known as Sun Yat-sen) established the first Democratic Republic on January 1st, 1912. Sun Wen stressed three things in this republic: the people, their civil rights, and the livelihood of the people. This doctrine, based on these three things, became known as the "Three Principles of the People." The first republic on the continent of Asia was born.

On July 31, 1921, Mao Zedong, along with 11 others, put Chen Duxiu as the figurehead of the newly formed Chinese Communist Party.[41] This gathering took place in Shanghai. With the death of Yuan Shikai, the world saw again proponents of the warlords struggling with yet another potential civil war. In 1922, Sun Wen, who had anticipated a civil war, joined hands with the Comintern. He wanted to quell the warlords who would divide and occupy the country. A year later, in 1923, the foreign head of China's Comintern, Mikhail M. Borodin, struck a deal with the key figures of the Chinese Communist Party and allowed them entry as individual members into the Nationalist Party.

Third International), as well as a journalist and revolutionary.

41) The Chinese Communist Party, after French oppression, was pushed out of the French settlement of Shanghai and only 12 representatives were able to hold a conference. On the last day of the conference, they formally established a new party and placed Chen Duxin as the chairperson.

Against the wishes of Sun Wen, Borodin tried to insert members of the Comintern into the Nationalist Party. Borodin wanted the Nationalist Party to be heavily influenced by the Soviet Union, or, in essence, become an affiliate organization. Up until this point, the Communist Party in China and their activities were, at best, weak. In 1921, the members of the said party were only about 300. Even in 1925, they numbered around 1,500. On the other hand, by 1922, the Chinese Nationalist Party boasted 50,000 members.

In 1924, at the Chinese National Convention held in Guangzhou, the first Kuomintang (National Party)-Communist Collaboration ascended to its nascency. It came to be called the First United Front. In early 1923, Sun Wen sent Jiang Jieshi (also known as Chiang Kai-shek) to the Soviet Union to learn military strategies and tactics. In late 1923, when Jiang returned from abroad, he established the Whampoa Military Academy and became its superintendent. The political head that was inaugurated during this time at the academy was Zhou Enlai. Zhou was well equipped to teach and lead the next generation of elite students, and forged a strong bond with them as their leader and mentor as he understood their mentality. Lin Biao,[42] along with many other prominent compatriots, would become, along with Jiang Jieshi, important during wartime and a pivotal leader of the eventual communism-driven China (although he was later exiled and labeled a traitor).

On March 3, 1925, Sun Wen died, leaving a void in the political vacuum until the emergence of Jiang Jieshi as his successor. In March of 1926,

---

42) Lin Bao would eventually become the vice premier, vice chairman, and the Minister of Defense of the People's Republic of China for many years. He served in various posts until a failed coup d'etat and was exiled as a result. He died in a plane crash in September 1971.

the Soviet advisory committee was expelled by the Kuomintang. The Kuomintang then tried to oust its communist members in a purge. In response, the Comintern grew alarmed at Chiang Kai-shek's political purges and tried to adjust to the changes but ultimately failed. Thereby, the First United Front was unsuccessful and led to a two-party divide in 1927.

China, for a while, split into two governments, each claiming sovereignty. One was the Kuomintang in Nanjing, and the other, a hybrid government composed of both the Kuomintang and the Chinese Communist Party (CCP) based in Wuhan. But this two-government system did not last for long. In the following year, Jiang Jieshi attacked the Wuhan government, purged the communists, and then absorbed the right-wing coalition so that his government would be recognized abroad as the real, authentic one.

In 1926, Jiang Jieshi started an attack on the North to quell the powerful warlords' influence in the region. This event was also known as the Northern Expedition. He was met with success; in two years' time, by 1928, he had united the northeast regions of Mukden, Kirin, and Hielong Jiang, of which there were two castles. Jiang Jieshi created, for a while, a unified China. When unified China came to be, Jiang decided to root out communism, launching an extensive series of measures between 1930 and 1934. During four waves of a large-scale suppression operation, he failed to achieve a decisive victory. But in October 1934, to prove his competence once again, he assembled a counterforce army consisting of 700,000 men to the south of China, where there was pro-communist sympathy. Jiangxi, Ruijin, was under siege, and the Communist Party of China (CPC) faced total destruction for a while.[43]

---
43) Ruijin was established by Mao Zedong and Chu Teh, as the capital of the Chinese Communist Party in 1931. It was created with the help of the Soviet Republic. After the

The Red Army, in the face of a purge, broke out of the region where the counterforce encircled them and fled to Shanxi Province. They needed to find a new base and deliberately chose one with rugged topography. Additionally, by moving to this land-locked southern region, they could more easily obtain help from the Soviet Union. The move was strategically sound.

Within the main unit of the Red Army were future communist luminaries such as Mao Zedong and Zhou Enlai. Mao, who shared leadership with Zhou, once lost power for a while because of pressure from the Soviets. However, after the Soviets believed the Chinese Red Army could recoup their losses later by engaging in guerilla warfare with a far superior enemy, Mao was selected as the successor by the USSR, thereby cementing his leadership and position in the CPC by January 1935.

The Long March by the Red Army began in 1934 and ended almost exactly a year later. On a superficial level, the Long March was a retreat by the Red Army escaping from the Kuomintang (Chiang Kai-shek's army). Yet, in many respects, it would encourage the growth and resilience of the Communist Party of China. For 368 days, the Red Army unit, consisting of 86,000 men, marched 12,500 km. It was a terribly difficult, arduous period in Chinese history. But it speaks volumes about the Chinese.

Strong steel must be tempered in order to become strong. Without a trial by fire to make something stronger, you cannot be born anew. This applies just not to people but to organizations as well. Mao Zedong was able to

---

attack led by Jiang Jieshi, the CCP capital was moved to Zhidan County.

achieve victory over his formidable opponent, Chiang Kai-shek, because of this analogy. These are my personal thoughts.

Most people, once they walk 40 km, develop blisters. At the 100 km mark, their blisters break open. Over 200 km, their feet start bleeding, and their feet and toes start malfunctioning. Once they reach the 300 km mark, their bodies start sustaining injuries. The Red Army marched over 12,000 km, while fighting the Kuomintang. They barely had anything to eat during this time. It was cold, and diseases had to be dealt with, with nothing but fortitude and mettle. This is similar to what happened in the American West a few centuries ago when the new settlers had to move elsewhere. The Red Army, upon reaching their destination of Ya'an, had shrunk to just about 7,000 men. They had started with 86,000 men. Less than a tenth of them made it; the rest perished under immense peril.

Their journey to escape from the Kuomintang took them over 18 mountains, 24 large rivers, and 11 provinces. All the while, they had to fight not just the Kuomintang but the warlords who controlled parts of China. For over a year, their retreat was under the most brutal of weather conditions (it was freezing), and they lacked rest or care for the diseases which plagued them. And yet they marched on. The survivors of this long retreat marched 12,000 km. They had achieved the impossible. The Long March was long and arduous. The road taken brought them into contact with many farmers. Unlike the Army of Jiang Jieshi or local warlords, who plundered and pillaged, the Red Army protected them and helped them when they could. Over a year, they came into contact with about two million farmers.

This would prove to be strategically important for the farmers' later support for the Communist Party of China over the Kuomintang government headed by Jiang Jieshi. The surviving 7,000 would become the elite party members of the CPC. Their first step may have been a retreat (or even seen as a defeat). Still, through overcoming innumerable hardships, the road led to the eventual solidification of the CPC's control over China.

This trial by fire, and much like the tempering of steel to make it even stronger, morphed the survivors, who supported communism to withstand and overcome national crises. Just as "Manifest Destiny" became the driving force for the United States of America, China's Long March would prove, again and again, the steely mindset of the modern day Chinese and why China would become a powerhouse, and a country to be reckoned with once again in the years to come.

The Chinese Civil War

"Guk gong nae jun," refers to the Kuomintang and the Communist Party of China's struggle to wrest control of the government; in essence, it was a civil war resulting from ideological differences. Generally speaking, it is divided into two phases, from 1927 to 1936 and 1936 to 1949. The war ended in 1949, with Mao Zedong proclaiming the birth of a new nation called the People's Republic of China. He made the announcement at Tiananmen Square (the Gate of Heavenly Peace).

With the death of Sun Wen in 1925, Mao Zedong and Jiang Jieshi fought for over 30 years to wrest control of the country. In my view, this spectacle between the Kuomintang and the Chinese Communist Party is unparalleled in history. Some might compare this fight with the fight between Liu Pang and Hsiang Yu back in the 8th century B.C.E., but both can't be at the same table, thinking of the enormous resources that had been used during this civil war.

My lads, shall we start unpacking the drama that unfolded during the Chinese Civil War? The important point is not just to read what I have written on these pages. You have to grasp the background, read between the pages. A historian's description are just words. In Buddhism, there is something called "bul rip mun ja." It means that sometimes, words are insufficient, and that all the truths cannot be neatly translated to words. So the scene that I describe in the following pages, you must read not just with your mind but with your heart. When reading history, you have to let the wings of Imagination transport you to a different place. Don't be swayed by my words only. The actual events I discuss in the next pages may be slightly different from how I wrote them. If you read about the events that unfolded with these guidelines in mind, then you will learn important life lessons. My wish for you is that you will be both moved and inspired.

On April 12, 1927, the Shanghai Massacre occurred. This was Chiang Kai-shek's influential Kuomintang-friendly forces attempting to stamp out communism once and for all. CPC leaders such as Li Dazhao were arrested, and many communist party members were tracked down and came close to being destroyed. This resulted in a bloody purge. This is also known as the "Shanghai coup d'état." The uneasy alliance between the Kuomintang and Communists fractured permanently as a result. Mao Zedong realized at this point that the CPC needed a stand-alone, armed group of men. This resulted in the Nanchang Uprising, which was a direct result of the Shanghai Massacre, but this time, on CPC terms. More importantly, on August 1st, 1927, in retaliation for Chiang Kai-shek's purges several months prior, Mao Zedong created what would become the People's Liberation Army (PLA).

The Nanchang Uprising resulted in another retreat by Mao Zedong's forces, so Jiang Jieshi became recklessly audacious. He thought he had mostly swept away communism in the country, and the Kuomintang's influence was growing day by day. Concentrated power and prosperity always give birth to new problems. He grew arrogant, and poisonous mushrooms began growing on the top as well as the bottom. These are a metaphor for corruption. Jiang Jieshi's Kuomintang was no different.

At first, corruption starts small. It grows in strength and power over time. If not caught in time, it grows like cancer. The monster that it births has been documented countless times in history. So many corrupt people and organizations have brought many nations to their demise. As corruption grew within the Kuomintang, public discontent grew widespread, especially for the proletariat and farmers. But Mao Zedong was different. Strict discipline was his unofficial motto. Even a food thief, who stole a chicken, was executed. He tightened discipline, and severe punishments were doled out in areas where he exerted control. Yet he always helped farmers, on a large scale, when he could.

Let's take a closer look at these two leaders, Chiang Kai-shek and Mao Zedong. It certainly is worth the trouble. One person unites China and becomes its leader, while the other escapes to Taiwan. Surely there must be a reason as to why this happened.

Chiang Kai-shek is a military officer turned politician. Mao Zedong is a thinker as well as a schemer. While he himself is not a military man by trade, he was well versed in the tactics of a mercenary. Chiang Kai-shek commanded four waves of a war, determined to purge the country of communists. However, he failed every single time. Chiang Kai-shek had about five to ten times the men as well as superior military equipment compared to Mao Zedong's loosely called "Red Army." However, Chiang Kai-shek never emerges victorious. Mao Zedong, during three out of four waves of attack, expertly commands his troops to conduct guerilla warfare. His victories over Chiang Kai-shek's Kuomintang indicate that Mao Zedong's tactics indicate a man who is naturally talented as a commander.

Mao Zedong's talents did not stop there. Even during the Korean War, he was a brilliant military strategist. He was behind Operation "Chromite," and after the Chinese army joined the Korean War, troops from China were directly commanded by Mao, not Peng Duhai. After experiencing successive defeats, Chiang Kai-shek assembled a new formation of men and gathered 700,000 men to fight in the fifth wave of the civil war. In October 1934, Jiang Jieshi finally took Ruijin, one of the Soviet Liberation Zones. At this point, Mao Zedong was suffering from a chronic disease, so he could not command the troops this time. But Li Lisan, Zhang Guotao, and 28 Bolshevists led in his stead.

Chiang Kai-shek appointed a German military advisor named Johannes F. "Hans" von Seeckt and used an encirclement strategy to close in on his enemy forces. Then, he decided to use the military strategy of attrition to gradually weaken the Red Army. This was only possible for the Kuomintang because they had numerically overwhelming troops. Guerilla warfare could not be used at this point to attack and retreat multiple times. In the end, the Red Army again reached the point of destruction and started its retreat, the aforementioned Long March.

What is the difference between Chiang Kai-shek and Mao Zedong?

In my opinion, an excellent leader knows the virtue of balance. Balance refers to staying aware of what the center is and where it is. The center must know from the left to right and from the front to back. If you are unaware of the center, then it leans to one side. If you are too bull-headed, driven by greed, and or only know the facade but not its innermost workings, then troubles will definitely lie ahead.

Mao Zedong knew the two-faced nature of man. Man's dark side—lazy and or corrupt. This is why the so-called "8-sided paragon of discipline" was proclaimed and executed to a fearsome degree. Jiang Jieshi either could not see corruption in his ranks, or pretended not to see them. He lost the center. So it follows that his sense of balance was lost. At Rui Jin, he lost to Mao Zedong several times. Mao Zedong was not a military man in any sense of the word. Chiang Kai-shek, a military man, would lose all because he had lost his center or his sense of balance.

If you devour Confucian classics, you will come upon a common narrative thread: all that is good and pure. Mao Zedong, fascinated with history books, would come to know both the good and the bad in man. He retained the virtue of balance. So it follows that Mao Zedong would come to lead and modernize China. At Yanan, the Red Army, well-established there, would come to surround Shanxi and fight Zhang Xueliang. Zhang Xueliang was the Northeast's commanding officer (a feudal warlord) and served as a deputy commander-in-chief during the Chinese Civil War.

Zhang Xueliang, in truth, was more hostile toward the Japanese forces than the Red Army. He had lost his homeland, Manchuria, to the Japanese army, and the same forces had killed his father. In his mind, it was of vital importance to defeat the Japanese before fighting the Red Army. Thus, Jiang Jieshi's policy of "Unification, then Resistance (against the Japanese)" did not sit well with him. In early 1936, Zhang entered into a secret agreement with the Red Army. They drew up a secret ceasefire between the two parties, and in exchange, decided to establish a unified front against Imperial Japan. This secret end of hostile activities between the warlord and the Red Army remained a secret from Chiang Kai-shek.

On December 7, 1936, Chiang Kai-shek sent troops to Xian, to encourage the people there to annihilate the Red Army and stamp out communism before resistance against the Japanese. But the commanders on location opposed this move. They believed first in unifying against Japan. They also wanted to develop an alliance with the Soviets to end the Chinese Civil War, and these are the terms that they stressed to Chiang Kai-shek.

Chiang Kai-shek, who headed the Chinese government at this time (at least, his government was legitimately regarded by foreign nations) was surprised and a bit dumbfounded by the unexpected resistance from his commanders. "This is strange, how dare they disobey my direct commands? This cannot be. Oh no! They must have been won over by the Commies." Realizing the gravity of the situation, Chiang Kai-shek decided to switch out the officer corps along with the warlord Zhang Xueliang. He wanted to eliminate those who didn't support his government in wanting to stamp out communism as much as they wanted Imperial Japan to leave their premises.

Zhang Xueliang proved to be swifter than his enemies. Once he found out he might be replaced, he used his brains to create a diversion. On December 12, he started a rebellion. At six in the morning, he infiltrated the city of Xian, took control of it, and arrested Jang's supporters. Chiang Kai-shek was actually vacationing in a nearby town known for its hot springs, and he fled from there but was shamefully arrested in pajamas at a hill around the hot spring.

Those who had taken part in the rebellion included regional militia such as men from the Northeast and the Northwest. They believed in fighting the Japanese first, and drew up eight clauses or provisions for Jiang Jieshi to approve and sign. Chiang Kai-shek, to the very end, refused. But he made some oral agreements instead.

"Ok, fine, let's fight Japan first." But to the end, he refused to sign any documents regarding the eight clauses proposed to him by the rebels.

The Chinese rebels let him go. Chiang Kai-shek upheld the oral agreements. Isn't this grand? I find both sides to be gentlemanly. This is the Chinese way. Just two days after the initial rebellion at Xian, 14,000 men led by Zhang Xueliang, 40,000 men from the Kuomintang, and 9,000 members of the Red Army merged to create the Second United Front. The leader of China, Chiang Kai-shek's fate was undetermined after his own commanders helped stage a rebellion. This was due to several of them calling for him to be severely punished. If Zhou Enlai or a chivalrous gentleman like Zhang Xueliang had not been there to save President Chiang Kai-shek, he might have been executed at Xian. The powerful warlord blocked his president's potential execution with his own body.

Zhang Xueliang was suffering from a crisis of conscience. He had pointed a gun at his president, whom he had an unspoken duty to protect. He had done something that he thought would be good for the people, but still, his heart was heavy with guilt and shame. Zhang Xueliang then makes a big, momentous decision. He decides to ask his president for his forgiveness. He makes plans to go to Nanjing to do so. This is a risky move. His life may be taken from him if he travels there. The former head of the rebel forces goes to the capital to ask for forgiveness? But without hesitation, he boards his private plane, and off he flies to President Chiang's Nanjing.

Zhang Xueliang was only a 36-years-old man, and previously, with President Chiang, he had had a close mentor-mentee relationship. He couldn't forgive himself for having turned on his president. No matter how much he tried to convince himself that his subordinate had acted for the good of the people, President Chiang Kai-Shek himself felt a bit peeved. But Zhang Xueliang had come all the way to ask for his forgiveness.

"My sworn brother, Zhang Xueliang, to betray me like that? Maybe I'll just…". What a disgrace. He's walking into a lion's den willingly. As a public figure, as the head of a country, he must have wrestled with unkind thoughts. Rebels were usually treated as those who knowingly committed treason and thus executed. But surely his subordinate would know of this. And he did.

President Chiang Kai-shek was embarrassed by the whole spectacle. On December 31, his former subordinate, Zhang Xueliang, was court-martialed. The circumstances behind the uprising at Xian were considered, so the death penalty was ruled out. Instead, Zhang received a 10-year sentence and a five-year suspension from exercising his civil rights. The very next day after Zhang Xueliang was sentenced, President Chiang Kai-shek handed down a presidential pardon.

The love and hatred between the two men, and the ensuing drama, whew! Zhang Xueliang is a fine gentleman, and Chang Kai-shek is another man of virtue. Later, when Chang Kai-shek escapes to Taiwan to evade Mao Zedong, he takes his subordinate with him. After the uprising at Xian,

Zhang Xueliang lives like a POW, and never ventures into politics ever again. In 2001, on one of the Hawaiian islands, Zhang breathes his last.

So why was the uprising at Xian of such importance? Due to this particular event in history, the Communist Party of China changes from that of usurper and always on the run and instead gains some legitimacy. This is the first time they are actively allowed to get involved in political maneuverings and military actions, and they effectively fan out to spread their motives after this. After Xian, the CPC does encounter some troubles, but the tide turns now toward the Communist Party of China. So who was the hidden figure behind the Xian uprising? Who masterminded it all? According to my knowledge, I believe it must have been Zhou Enlai. Zhou was a really important figure in history. His vision, along with his power of persuasion, wisdom, and cruelty, and face would make Chinese intellects love him way more than Mao.

If we speak of Chinese communism, two of the most important figures are Mao Zedong and Zhou Enlai. If Mao was an outstanding, boss-like figure, then Zhou was a great staff member. If Mao was a large mountain, then Zhou was a big river. If Mao was a huge mountain and stubbornly resilient, then Zhou was like water, moving through the valleys, permeating the land, filling it, and refining it. Mao Zedong made mistakes once in a while, but Zhou was perfectly mistake-free. Both were wily and cold-hearted fellows. Without Mao, we cannot discuss Chinese communism; without Zhou, we cannot discuss communist China.

Ever since his days at the Whampoa Military Academy, Zhou Enlai propped up Chiang Kai-shek who was its head, but secretly worshiped another political system. He was secretly undermining Chiang the whole time. In later years, he would systematically recruit outstanding students who would eventually join the Red Army. In 1946, when the Red Army had almost been annihilated, the one who brought it back to life, Lin Biao, was one of Zhou Enlai's former recruits. A member with the fourth class of Huangpu Military Academy, he would earn the nickname of the "Unbeatable General" in the years to come, as he was an excellent commander.

During the Chinese Civil War, the one person who really destroyed Chiang Kai-shek was Zhou Enlai. Including the Xian uprising, and until the end, Zhou Enlai, in a cat-and-mouse type of game, would keep on attacking Chiang Kai-shek. But ironically, Chiang liked the fellow. This is the irony of history. If there is a goddess of history, then who would she prefer? She might be subject to variable moods. The People's Republic of China is the result of the leadership of Mao Zedong and the wisdom of Zhou Enlai. This is my personal opinion again, but I would like to say that the Chinese Communist Party, upon its formation as a new party, faced five big hurdles on its way to wresting control of the country. These include 1) The Long March, 2) the Xian rebellion, 3) Mao Zedong's deception, 4) the Cultural Revolution, and 5) Deng Xioping's "Reform and Opening."

Let us continue. In July 1937, the Japanese Imperial Army caused the Lukow-Kiao incident[44] as an excuse to invade China. They were not just satisfied with Manchuria (March 1932), and sought an even bigger prize: a bigger piece of the pie that belonged to China.The Japanese Imperial General Headquarters planned to invade China and add to its land within two years.

---

44) The Lukow-Kiao incident refers to the area southwest of Beijing that was invaded by the Japanese Imperial Army. Also known as the "Marco Polo" bridge, in 1937, the Japanese Imperial Army fabricated that one of their soldiers was missing and demanded entry into a walled town of Wanping. Upon the Chinese's refusal, both sides started firing (Japan fired first). This incident would lead to the Sino-Japanese War.

Preparation to fight and initial deployment of troops was swift.

Before the end of 1937, they occupied the following cities: Beijing, Shanghai, and the capital of the Kuomintang (Nanjing). This is my own analysis, but they failed to take into account the sheer size of China against their own. For example, smaller countries' citizens, such as Korea, cannot understand the mindset of larger countries' citizens, such as China. China's national land mass is about 25 sizes bigger than Japan's. The Chinese have experience in managing empires such as the Tang and the Qing for over 5,000 years. They are a hardy breed and an ancient peoples. China is not a country that can be swallowed by Japan. Starting with the sheer size of China, a 5,000-year legacy bestows upon the country a metaphor like a large mountain, immovable and majestic.

Trying to occupy the entire country is a foolish act, for Manchuria is one thing, but the whole of China is quite another beast. Manchurian land was always contested. Physical strength, all by itself, has its limits. Time and distance (in addition to mass) render sheer physical strength incapacitated.

The reason why former dictators of the past, such as Napoleon and Hitler lost is due to this type of miscalculation. Additionally, the cultural force is another strength to be reckoned with, as it transcends time and space. Japan failed in its mission to take over China due to these reasons. History tells us now that it was a big mistake for Japan to make.

As a foreign invader advanced toward China, Mao Zedong, along with Chiang Kai-shek, agreed to unite to fight the Japanese. This became the Second United Front (Sept. 23, 1937). The Red Army, along with the Eight Route Army and the New Fourth Army, was attached to the National Revolutionary Army. But each side agrees to autonomously execute its plans against the Japanese. During the Japanese attack on Shanghai, many civilians died. The occupation of Shanghai took three more months than expected by the Japanese. Japan, angered by this delay, started murdering civilians left and right. "Sam Kwang Jak Jeon," refers to taking away, killing, then burning. In all of Japanese history, one of its worst stains is the Shanghai Massacre. Even after this event, the Nanjing Massacre followed.

Soldiers must think about the lessons these tragic events bestowed upon them. To put it bluntly, the Japanese Imperial Army behaved like a forcible, murderous group, like a gang or a mob wreaking havoc. But the mission of the military is one and the same, regardless of race or nation: to "protect the country and their countrymen." This noble mission begets noble actions, or at least, they should. So the military should always behave morally and ethically. So many are reluctant to admit this, or argue it's not possible. But see, the United States is already implementing this strategy of a military built on morals.

Plundering and the murder of civilians…any military man must think twice before resorting to such measures. History teaches us that when the military of any nation plunders and rapes, they will never be successful. This is why the Japanese Imperial Army failed and why China's Kuomintang fell. The history of the war in the West also attests to this. Throughout all of human history, a selfish, conniving, corrupt military has always failed and will continue to fail. There are no exceptions.

Until 1941, the Japanese Imperial Army kept on pushing the Second United Front to its brink, and many died. Most of the fighting was done by legions commanded by Chiang Kai-shek. Mao Zedong, on the other hand, used Japan as an excuse to say he was a fish out of water and instead, kept on "fishing" for the hearts of his countrymen so that they would end up supporting communism. He devoted all of his energy to this subversive plan. While keeping the Kuomintang-Communist Collaboration of the Second United Front, very often, Kuomintang and the CPC fought against each other. So while there was an official "pause" in the Chinese Civil War, the Kuomintang and CPC continued to fight, all because of ideological differences.

By 1940, the Communist Party of China had gathered enough strength to claim ownership of a large part of the country. So by then, the country was largely divided into three parts: Chongqing, under control of Kuomintang, Yanan, ruled by CPC, and Japanese-occupied territory. By 1941, the nature of the Sino-Japanese war had changed. This is due to Pearl Harbor. They had bombed the Pacific Fleet of the United States of America. This ended up becoming a foolish action on their part. It's obvious that Japan would lose when the United States joined World War II, but nevertheless, they committed this act with disastrous results.[45]

Ask anyone, and they will tell you that war against the United States is paramount to self-destruction. Only Japan did not know this. Well, what I really mean by this is that they would have gone down this path anyway. They are very educated. Korean intellectuals should read "The History of Showa," especially the end of that era in history.

Let us return to the war between China and Japan. Up until the Pearl

---

45) There is a conspiracy theory that the United States induced the Japanese to attack them at Pearl Harbor. This theory states that they intentionally left an old battleship in Hawaii. But this is wrong. The United States had, since 1920, agreed to a treaty for the limitation and reduction of warships. The Japanese fleet effectively destroyed Pearl Harbor, so I would venture to say that this conspiracy theory is wrong.

Harbor incident, the United States did not care to interfere between the two countries. In fact, some may have been grateful for the way the war with China tied up Japan. Even in their worst nightmares, the United States never dreamt that Japan would attack them first. But attack they did, and the United States responded in kind.

"Remember Pearl Harbor!"

The whole nation stood up. As literal bombs blew up on the state of Hawaii's shores, the course of history was changed forever in East Asia. The United States would come to carefully assess the situation in this region of the globe, and would continue to exert its influence there. Even though this was a strategic mistake and a miscalculation on their part. The bombing of Pearl Harbor would influence even the circumstances surrounding the Korean Peninsula in the years to come.

Chiang Kai-shek, well versed in international affairs, quickly declared war on the Axis powers of Japan, Germany and Italy. He also came to direct troops and help the United Kingdom in Myanmar. From this point onwards, during World War II, China would be recognized as one of the Allies, and the Sino-Japanese War would gain traction on China's terms. After the Pearl Harbor incident, the Sino-Japanese war would come to be seen as an act of aggression on Japan's part by the international community.

In truth, some can argue that World War II started not in September 1939 (when Germany invaded Poland), but two years prior, when Japanese forces invaded China in July 1937. Chiang Kai-shek's China had fought the Japanese alone until Pearl Harbor. About 800,000 Japanese soldiers were tied up (metaphorically speaking) for four years in China. His Western allies should have paid homage to him for doing this for them. But the cost of the Sino-Japanese (now seen as part of World War II) would be dear. About 20 million Chinese would lose their lives, and another 80 million would lose their homes and become refugees. About 80 percent of the national infrastructure, if I may be so bold, was destroyed. All the large cities were left in ruins.

Within China, domestic trouble was brewing as well. While Chiang was busy fighting the Japanese, the CPC strengthened their powers by swaying the farmers to their side and creating strong supporters. Touting social reforms was how the CPC came to captivate the hearts and minds of the Chinese. The strictly disciplined Red Army proved to be very effective compared to the chaotic army led by Chiang Kai-shek, and this helped them increase their supporters and their stronghold on the country.

Now listen to this anecdote; when the Red Army entered Shanghai, they actually slept on the streets to avoid inconveniencing their countrymen who lived there. On the other hand, the Kuomintang Army, whenever they entered a new city, they would immediately take over the best house in the neighborhood and plunder their wealth. And so it goes that Chiang Kai-shek won the war but lost his country and his people to the Communist Party of China.

And the Japanese lost again and again in the Pacific. During the Sino-Japanese war, which dragged on to its seventh year, Japan's complete defeat came to light. Japan, as if it knew already that it would lose the war against the United States, tried to recover in China by way of invading the channel connecting Myanmar-Vietnam and started the Battle of Imphal. Japan lost over 40,000 men in this fight. Many words were spoken before and after this battle, and all these words were critical as this maneuver was a failure from beginning to end. In April 1944, Japan entered Hainan Island, tumbling into defeat after an initial success. The balance was broken and could not be recovered.

After getting nuked twice, Japan finally surrendered on August 15, 1945. While Japan may have left the Asian continent, China succumbed to civil war again. In 1946, phase two of the Chinese Civil War started with the Kuomintang attacking the Red Army. At first, the Kuomintang did well at the start of 1947. In March of that same year, they reached the Soviet-controlled capital of Yanan. But the Kuomintang made a huge mistake. Corruption was rife within its ranks, and the economy was sinking, which caused them to be alienated by the public.

In 1945, the Red Army numbered at 1.2 million. They were outnumbered by the Kuomintang's 4.3 million. The Kuomintang may have had more military strength, at this time, thereby allowing Chiang Kai-shek to restore peace for the most part. Until this point, luck was on their side. The Kuomintang then set their sights on the northeastern part of the country, Manchuria. Only Lin Bao's regiment was left of the Red Army at this time.

In late spring of 1946, Chiang Kai-shek's Kuomintang Army began its offensive on the northeastern province of Harbin, where the last remnants of the Red Army were stationed. If present circumstances prevailed, then the Red Army would finally be annihilated, from Chiang Kai-shek's point of view. This is what they call a "coup de grace." At this time, the United States Secretary of State, George C. Marshall, stepped in. He negotiates with Chiang Kai-shek and orders a ceasefire. "Stop the attack. Instead, we will reach an agreement with you and give you $500 million to help rejuvenate the economy."[46] Chiang Kai-shek was a bit aghast. This was the moment when Communism in the country could be wiped out forever and its roots eradicated. This was a golden opportunity going to waste. He was upset and undeniably angry. But he could not disobey the U.S. Secretary of State.

So he accepted the deal. He couldn't but otherwise do so. But $500 million U.S. dollars! He wiped his tears and tried to calm down. This dramatic situation changes the course of history forever. Why? Through this deal with the United States, the communist Red Army would be resuscitated and unite China once again. Why did Marshall make such an absurd deal with China? This was not a mistake, but all was planned in advance. But there were holes in the plan.

The United States was always interested in Russia's involvement in the Asian continent. After the attack on Pearl Harbor, and afterward, the whole plan for Asia's so-called "management" was recalculated and reconsidered. From 1941 onwards, the United States would send its diplomats and military personnel there. They were not just sent to Chang Kai-shek, but to Mao Zedong as well. In particular, another U.S. diplomat, John S. Service, was sent to Yanan to discuss the future of China with Mao Zedong.

So who is Mao Zedong? It's hard to say. Out of the ashes of the bloody revolution vortex, he emerges as a sly old politician in the struggle for power. Out of all of China's storied history, one would be hard-pressed to find someone like him. How could Service, who was a second-class diplomat and a gentleman of good breeding, not be swayed by the wily Mao Zedong?

---

46) Richard Bernstein, *China 1945: Mao's Revolution and America's Fateful Choice*. Alfred A. Knopf, 2014.

"We highly esteem the United States of America's democratic ideals."
"I want to inherit a Lincoln-type of the democratic ideal."

Mao Zedong takes the initiative. Service falls into a type of dreamy stupor as Mao Zedong waxes lyrical about former U.S. President Lincoln. He used to think of Mao as a bandit in a cave, and now, he starts viewing him very differently.

Due to Service's official assessment of China, which he detailed in a series of reports, all of America started to view the country very differently, or at least Mao Zedong and his communist ideals. Service, in my view, lost his head. He promised Mao Zedong that the United States government would financially back not just the Kuomintang led by Chiang Kai-shek but also the Communist Party of China.[47] The United States came to trust Mao Zedong, and decided to "Give Manchuria over to Mao Zedong and stop Russian influence in that region, and the Chinese mainland would be turned over to Chiang Kai-shek, again, to stop Russia in their tracks." This became the United States' strategy toward China. In other words, "divide and rule."

Mao Zedong would become known in the Western world in another manner, through the publication of a book. *Red Star Over China*, written by Edgar Snow (1905-1972). In the genre of nonfiction (written by journalists), I would say that it ranks among one of the best.[48] It is so well written, in fact, that Mao Zedong reportedly said of it, "this book will replace my

---

47) According to *The Wall Street Journal*, John S. Service, until he died in 1999 at the age of 90, would continue to voice his support for communist China. "I hope that the CPC wins [and prevails]," he would confess shortly before his death.

48) Snow's *Red Star Over China*, John Silas "Jack" Reed's *Ten Days that Shook the World*, and George Orwell's *Homage to Catalonia* are regarded as the triple crown in long-story form non-fiction today.

biography." At only 30, Snow heads over to China and lives there for seven years while canvassing the northern Soviet-controlled area. During this time, he would meet repeatedly with Mao Zedong and other important members of the Chinese Communist Party. Snow would interview them about their lives until the present, and about their plans for China's trajectory. This would alert the world to what was happening in China, down to the minute details.

The legendary journey of Chinese communists became real life figures, and the poorly dressed main figures would become heroes. This was all due to Snow's brilliant writing. Mao Zedong, all of a sudden, became a hero of sorts. The United States started regarding him in a positive light as well. Even though technically he was a communist, he was being packaged as a nationalist. This mood would have enormous repercussions for the future of post-war Asia. On December 20, 1945, U.S. President Harry S. Truman sent General Marshall to China as a special envoy.[49] This was the first time Marshall met with Mao Zedong. Basically, in simple terms, the United States' chief strategist was meeting with the scheming Mao Zedong.

But what did Marshall have to say after this initial first meeting?

"I had a long discussion with Mao Zedong. He did not voice any complaints, and promised to partner with and work with the United States." This is Marshall's official report. If the venerable Marshall wrote such a report, then it points to how brilliantly eloquent Mao Zedong was. But again,

---

49) George Marshall (1880-1959) was a graduate of the Virginia Military Institute (1897). He was not a West Point graduate. During World War II, he served as the Army Chief of Staff and a military adviser to F. D. Roosevelt. He would serve in important posts during several Presidents' tenures, including Secretary of State and Secretary of Defense. In 1953, he won the Nobel Peace Prize.

there was a catch, because there was also artifice behind his eloquence. This is why the United States placated Chiang Kai-shek with $500 million U.S. dollars, and stopped the attack on the Red Army and saved Mao Zedong. In reality, the Red Army was so depleted of strength by this time that had the United States not stepped in and all had gone according to Chiang's original plans, Mao would have met his end.

On the other side of the front, Lieutenant General Joseph Stilwell, who had served on the China-Burma-India offensive, was assigned to help advise President Chiang Kai-shek in 1943. Unfortunately for Chiang, Stilwell and he had an uneasy relationship. At first, they clashed concerning matters regarding the military, and then as time passed, this rift became personal. Stilwell was a respected man in U.S. military circles. The fissure in the relationship between Chiang and Stilwell would have devastating consequences in delivering results. Unfortunately for Chiang, he always seemed to rub the American officials who were assigned to help him the wrong way, and vice versa.

But Mao Zedong was simply charming to all he met. If Chiang loved the Chinese classical texts, Mao loved and devoured history. They viewed life in vastly different ways. Chiang would stick to the script and was honest. Mao, on the other hand, would sway whomever he met to his side. Ultimately, Mao would even win over Henry A. Kissinger.[50] Mao Zedong would leave a copy of *Zizhi Tongjian* by his bedside. This book, written during the Northern Song Dynasty, spans 1,362 years of history from Emperor Weilie

---

50) Henry A. Kissinger (1923-present) was the U.S. Secretary of State and National Security Advisor under two presidents. In 1971, he visited Chiang Kai-shek in Beijing under a cloak of secrecy. A year later, he arranged for a historical summit between President Nixon and Mao Zedong. In 1973, Kissinger won the Nobel Peace Prize.

of Zhou (403 B.C.E.) to Emperor Shizong of Later Zhou (959 C.E.). About 1,300 years of historical events are chronicled in the book, which details the governance of what would become present day China, from the emperor and his ministers, while dispensing worldly wisdom and stressing the importance of interpersonal relationships in a lively fashion.

If just one person's life lends a lot of valuable experience to a reader, imagine a book spanning 1,300 years of invaluable knowledge gleaned from previous rulers of China and their subordinates or challengers and their ensuing fights and contemplations. Mao Zedong's delight in this book speaks to how carefully he devoured and paid attention to lessons from prior historical events.

In the end, Chiang Kai-shek lost. History is cruel, sometimes. You may call it retribution, even. His downfall was not due to his quirks, but it was something much larger, in the greater scope of things. Tens of thousands of Chinese suffered, and in the future, China's political landscape, along with that of the Korean Peninsula and the whole of Asia, would suffer from turmoil and confusion for a while. If one is completely honest, Chiang Kai-shek's strategies for uniting and fortifying China were never entirely backed by the Americans. Why? This is an unanswered question. This is a question I will leave to you, young reader.

In 1946, at Harbin, the newly fortified Red Army attacked the Kuomintang. Two years later, they controlled about 99 percent of Manchuria's Hebei Province. In October of the same year, Zinzhou fell under the Red Army's invasion, and the Kuomintang, which had been defending Changchun, lost their 60th Army and 700,000 men. In November 1948, Manchuria's farthest outpost, Shenyang, fell under the Red Army control.[51] On April 23, 1949, the Kuomintang's capital of Nanjing fell under CPC control. On May 27th, the Red Army invaded the large city of Shanghai. On October 1, 1949, Mao Zedong proclaimed the birth of the Democratic People's Republic of China at Tiananmen Square. And so it goes that the Chinese Civil War ends after eight long years, and the curtain falls on the struggle between the two heroes battling over their homeland.

How can the world change so much and so quickly? We cannot but shake our heads to history's stark and aloof chain of events.

D. China, formerly the Great and Powerful

a) The Heavens, Earth, and Man

Long, long ago, around 5,000 B.C.E. A group of people, in search of water, reaches a river. Red clay water flows forth steadily. This is the Yellow River Huanghe. Within its yellowish depths, fish swim, and giant clams filter sand.

These people of the Yellow River Huanghe would live mid-stream, and downstream, then live in caves, then build houses, and fashion pottery until they became the future ancestors of the Longshan (3,000-1,800 B.C.E.) and the Shantung-Longshan cultures. They rank among one of the first four major civilizations of humankind.

In 2,100 B.C.E., they would establish the Xia Dynasty, then by 1,600

---

51) The Laoshan-Shenyang Campaign was part of the Red Army's three-part attack on the Kuomintang. This is where the Kuomintang lost Manchuria to Mao Zedong's Red Army.

B.C.E., the Shang Dynasty. The Xia Dynasty was recorded in the pages of history but archeologists of today still struggle to find evidence to verify its existence.

But archeologists of the 20th century have found evidence of the Shang Dynasty. In the early 20th century, at Henan and Anyang, they would discover cultural artifacts dating back to centuries ago, leaving the world amazed by their findings regarding their complex social structure and their mighty civilization of yesteryear. A large number of bronze ware and oracle bone scripts that were found points to how advanced the Shang Dynasty civilization used to be. In addition to weapons, bronze work and exquisite pieces were made. With these bronze weapons, they would subdue the Qiang people and send them far away or expel them further upstream to the Yangtze River area.

Inscriptions on tortoise shells and or cattle bones (the upper shoulder part, to be precise), indicates their advanced writing system. The Shang peoples would actually use these bones, which they would burn using red-hot metal, and use the resulting cracks to read the future. Shamans would use them to tell fortunes. The Shang peoples would closely consult the cracks made by the red-hot metal and regard them as oracles to foretell the Heavens' will. They would ask, for example, questions regarding battles to whether the current year's harvest would be bountiful or not. As I stated before, they would use these animal bones or tortoise shell cracks for divination. These ancient peoples thereby believed in a divine being in the heavens.

By 1,000 B.C.E., the Shang Dynasty would fall, and the feudal country of Zhou would, for about 800 years, become the longest-running dynasty of ancient China until 221 B.C.E. In that year, the Qin people would unite all of

China and lose much of their power after that. The Zhou Dynasty is divided into Western Zhou and Eastern Zhou. From 1,000 B.C.E. to 403 B.C.E., it was called Western Zhou, and from 403 B.C.E. to 221 B.C.E., it was called Eastern Zhou.[52] For ancient China, the most important period is the Warring States period. From 770 B.C.E. to 403 B.C.E. is the Spring and Autumn Period, and the Warring States Period lasted from 403 B.C.E. to 221 B.C.E, when the Qin Dynasty united all of China.

Why do I speak of the ancient past to you today? During the 5th century B.C.E., an extraordinary historical event happens. The 5th century B.C.E. is when the Spring and Autumn Period ends, and the Warring States Period begins immediately. This is, to me, indicative of something like a puzzle. During this period in greater China, three wise men emerge: Confucius, Lao-tzu, and Mo-tzu. But the emergence of brilliant men is not just limited to China, but they are also found in other parts of the world. For example, India's Siddhartha (later Buddha), Greece's Socrates, Plato, and Israel's Jeremiah and Isaiah, are all great men who also emerged during this time period in history.[53]

So how did these luminaries of thought and reason emerge during this period? I will focus right now on Confucius and Lao-tzu.

Let me tell you about 500 years in history before the advent of Christ. From 771 B.C.E. to 221 B.C.E., also known as the Warring States Period,

---

52) In 771 B.C.E. Quanrong would invade the Zhou Dynasty, so they moved their capital to Luoyang and founded the Eastern Zhou Dynasty

53) German philosopher Karl Jaspers' book, *The Origin and Goal of History*, published in 1949, said that today's most well-known religions and schools of thought belong to this period in history, and calls it "die Achsenzeit."

saw a kind of dark ages that had previously been unknown in Chinese history. In particular, the darkest period lasted from 403 B.C.E. to 221 B.C.E. This period was one of the harshest and the deadliest, with everything seemingly thrown into chaos. Previously advancements were destroyed through warfare, and millions of people died, including feudal lords and those from the noble classes. In the fifth century B.C.E., man created iron. When weapons were fashioned out of this material, they became much more deadly than weapons of prior years (which were fashioned from out of bronze and stone) and resulted in heretofore-unseen bloodshed.

Agricultural tools made out of iron were much more efficient than bronze, so that they could reap more during harvests. When hunting with iron tools, hunting became easier, so more meat resulted in more nourishment for mankind, and man became smarter. As farms began producing so much food that they ended up with surpluses, the ordinary people's wealth grew, and along with the peasant class, they became much more upwardly mobile.

This would have consequences for China, however. As the peasant classes became more upwardly mobile, society started to wobble. The relationship between feudal lords and their peasants grew sour, and the strict social structure began to break down.

The relationship between the emperor and feudal lords also soured for a while. Before, class structures had been determined by bloodlines, with each passing to his son, but by the Eastern Zhou Dynasty, this was no longer the case. Another reason behind this was that lineages became murky. The neighboring states, of which there were about 70, would wage war mercilessly. By the end of the Warring States Period, only seven remained. They were as follows: the Han, Zhao, Yan, Wei, Chu, Qi, and Qin. With the absence of an emperor and the will of the heavens now being considered as nothing more than natural science, the veneration of a deity or gods diminished, and their faith plummeted into nothingness. Mankind now felt like they were in an advantageous position. Mankind went through a type of metamorphosis of self-discovery.

In other words, they had found their original will. The fates did not decide man's actions; rather, he chose them himself. When faced with problems, it was up to man to make his own decisions and fight his way through. This was a real revelation. So instead of putting faith in the heavens, it seemed that wise men and their teachings emerged during this time to replace deities or supernatural forces. Thus emerged "Tao" as a substitute for deities. "Tao" was one of the teachings of Confucius and Lao-tzu. Thus the focus shifted from that of the other world's deities, to the world of mankind, and from myth to philosophy.

b) The Hundred Schools of Thought

The Warring States Period was tainted by blood and cruelty. Many heroes fought against one another in droves, with the fortunes of each individual shifting and constantly in flux. But amidst this confusion, many scholars and philosophers waged a contention of hundred thoughts unprecedented for that time and age. In truth, a kind of enlightenment, the first of its kind in Asia, blossomed during this time. It was as if man was discovering his consciousness for the first time.

The contention of hundred thoughts is a period in history that is incomparable to any other incidents in the world. In essence, it is a testament to the brilliant thinkers of this long-ago age that Chinese philosophers and thinkers can stand tall among those who were to follow in other parts of the world. Without this campaign, I personally believe that China wouldn't have been able to achieve this. Without this ancient wisdom, I would not consider China one of the greats. That long ago, which lasted for about 300 years to be precise, the intellectual battles and controversies that took place are unable to be imitated by any nation of any race. These are my thoughts, but I believe they bestowed upon the world a great, monumental world heritage that will shine forever like a golden tower of knowledge.

Among these arguments between scholars, many different types of political ideas and opinions, along with sometimes sharp, biting criticisms of each others' works and ideas, blossomed. Some might call this a magnificent bloom of wisdom, like a beautiful rainbow in the sky. Not to mention that this is one of the first times that man would question his existence on earth, which would lead to a highly advanced system of ethics and philosophy so profound that they would pursue "Victory which requires no battle." This esoteric military science is something that we can benefit from even in this day and age, centuries later in the 21st century.

There is a phrase I am fond of in Chinese. From *Great Learning*, it reads as xiūshēn qíjiā zhìguó píngtiānxià. In English, the phrase means this: "The regulation of the family lies in the cultivation of the person, before governing the country, you must first regulate your family, bringing peace to the realm lies in the ability to govern the country." Doesn't this strike you as the ultimate phrase that sums up a male man's duty in this world? So, who came up with this phrase? It is found in one of the Four Books and Five Classics. So, what is the "Four Books and Five Classics?"

I myself was unfamiliar with these texts. But I had heard about xiūshēn qíjiā." In my opinion, this sums up a man's daily life. Isn't it grand? But it's nine characters long in Chinese. Who made up this phrase? Through this phrase, I became familiar with the Four Books *The Analects of Confucius, Great learning, Mencius, Doctrine of the Mean*, and some of the greatest minds of Chinese classical thought and philosophy, such as Confucius, his grandson Zisi, and Mencius. These classical texts of the Orient are a treasure trove of knowledge. Confucianism, Mohism, Daoism, and Legalism are discussed in those venerated pages about 3,000 years ago, and this systematic knowledge is explained thoroughly in these texts. The ancient Chinese are truly excellent thinkers. For these alone, I truly admire and venerate the ancient Chinese.

So what were we Koreans doing during that time in history? We were a new foundling state, established by the heavenly celestial being, Dangun. Whatever we were, there is a lack of records. However, from the *Samguk sagi*, which recounts the Three Kingdoms period of Korea, along with the *Samguk yu sa*, also known as the *Memorabilia of the Three Kingdoms*, we learn about Bak Hyeokgeose, the founder of the Silla Dynasty, which was established in 57 B.C.E. Did I fail to mention that Bak Hyeokgeose hatched from an egg?

According to legend, Emperor Kim Suro, the founder of Gaya Kingdom, hatched from one of the nine eggs wrapped in gold cloth. This was in 42 C.E. And also, Kim Alji, the progenitor of Royal Kim's family of the Silla Dynasty, was discovered in a gold box in 65 C.E. The Hundred Schools of Thought had already been parlayed in China about four to five hundred years even before the establishments of Korea's kingdoms and dynasties, which were shrouded in myth.

So who do I like the best out of the Hundred Schools of Thought?

Confucius. Why Confucius? Do you think Confucius is still the best sage even though our ancient forefathers ruined the nation by having unnecessary arguments based on his teachings? That is not correct. Confucius hated impractical arguments.

There is a saying in Chinese that I will quote for you today. It says, "The superior man is modest in his speech, but exceeds his actions." Confucius also said, "Gentleman desires to be hesitant in speech, but sharp in action." As such, he was exactly like this. His approach to life, even in that of political theory, was always practical and able to be executed quite easily. According to Confucius, a person should act with filial piety, loyalty, and faithfulness. In the political arena, politicians should "cultivate themselves to give rest to others." How easy is this to understand?

Confucian philosophy bled into metaphysics after the life of his grandson, and during the Song Dynasty, Neo-Confucianism became too sublimely groomed, so it became too ideological. In fact, Zhu Xi was too talented, and this became a problem. Confucius was a practical man, who understood reality all too well. He even spoke of the afterlife. "I do not know life, [so] how can you know about death?" He also refused to speak about ghosts, the grotesque, and violence.

Our Korean ancestors would ruin the country in the years to come because of impractical arguments and not because of Confucianism. They, unfortunately, relied on follow-up scholars who misinterpreted Confucius.

Confucius was a lover of words like, "virtue," "loyalty," "fidelity," and "righteousness," more so than words like "xing" or "li". He respected a person's emotions, and his ability to feel the joys and sorrows of life. Thus, he disliked stoicism. What he held in high regard was man's natural state as an existential being and life itself.

There are many phrases that are of use in *The Analects*, but one in particular comes to mind. It is one of my favorites. One of Confucius's students asks him a question:

"Is there one word which may serve as a rule of practice for all one's life?"

Confucius answered, "Is not reciprocity such a word? What you do not want to be done to yourself, do not do to others."

Don't make someone do something that you yourself wouldn't do? This may sound simple and obvious, but this is an excellent remark. If you follow this rule in all sorts of human relationships, then most problems can be resolved. For example, article one of leadership serves as a model example, a paragon of goodness. To serve as a good leader, one must volunteer to do what the average person doesn't. You have to do what other people don't want to do. You have to do it first. This is not easy. But only through this method can one foster leadership. This is common, but how remarkably astute does Confucius champion this rule long ago?

His ideas regarding philosophy are also simple, some might even say, unsophisticated. But they can be put quite easily into action. For politicians, the summation of his most valuable phrase is "make the people comfortable." This is Oriental Humanism. But Oriental Humanism, as I call it, has a spirit of reformation rather than stasis. This is because Confucianism respects the person's virtues that he is born with, and these virtues will "Manifest their bright virtue to all in the world"[54] as he seeks wisdom throughout his life. Confucius's Oriental Humanism, as I call it, or Confucius's realism can be expressed in one phrase.

Lao-Tzu says in one of his texts, "Return love for hate."[55] How like Lao-Tzu to say something like this. But when someone asked Confucius, "What do you say concerning the principle that injury should be recompensed with kindness?" Do you know what he said in response?

"With what then will you recompense kindness? Recompense injury with justice, and recompense kindness with kindness."

Confucius also sheds light on another profound idea.

"A gentleman, in the world, does not set his mind either for anything, or against anything; what is right he will follow." What does this mean in simple terms? Always act morally, or with the idea of what is morally sound, in accordance with the present circumstances. In this complicated world, there is no official blueprint for the correct action taken at the right time, as long as one remains morally sound. Why or how could Confucius say this? This comes as a surprise to me.

About ten years ago, a Harvard professor named Michael Sandel visited Korea. He wrote a book titled *Justice: What's the Right Thing to Do?* and it sold about 10 times more copies in Korea than it did in the States. Over two million copies were sold, and some universities in Seoul organized a public

---

54) *Great Learning*, Chapter 3
55) *Tao Te Ching*, Chapter 3 page 63.

lecture and arranged for him to speak. I myself wasn't able to attend, but I bought a CD. My mouth fell open. I was so surprised. It was a great lecture. It was magnificent. This was the first time I had listened to a talk by a world-class, top-notch, brilliant professor.

My generation studied during wartime. We learned without classrooms, in factories, and even by riverbeds, where impromptu lessons were held. My generation of men, and our education, here in Korea, may be spotty because we were a poor nation back then, and embroiled in war during our formative years. So how could we, and I myself included, have attended lectures by such a luminary? It made me think of many things. While explaining philosopher Jeremy Bentham's axiom, "it is the greatest happiness of the greatest number that is the measure of right and wrong," he gave an example.

A train is moving at a fast pace. Far off in the distance, the train driver sees five men working. He is shocked. The brakes are broken. If he keeps speeding, five men will die or be grievously injured. This is a crisis. He looks over at the next lane. There is one person working there. It is just one person. So if he keeps on speeding in his lane, five men may be lost forever, and if he switches to the other lane, only one person will be injured.

Here, the professor tosses a question to the audience.

"What would you do if you were the train conductor?"

Of course, most students choose to switch lanes, which may end up killing the sole worker.

"So is it just for that one man to die?"

A debate starts. Bentham is discussed, American philosopher John Rawls's theory of "equal fairness," is discussed[56] and ancient Greek philosopher, Aristotle's ideas, come to light. But "this is the right answer" never comes into play. This demonstrates the inability of any simple logical argument to correctly solve this very real crisis. There is no way to judge, no "right way," and there is no way to satisfy happiness, freedom, and good deeds, all at the same time.

Here we need to examine Confucius's words again. "What is right, he will follow." How wise is this!

There was a banner hanging in Sandel's classroom that aptly summarizes that lecture's title and purpose. "'RIGHT [OR] WRONG'— It is not always black and white."

Strictly speaking, doesn't this point to how it is impossible to judge what is right and wrong in today's modern society? This may be due to my limited understanding (due to the lack of serious study about the said subject), but I believe Confucius's middle way comes from this very reason. Not too much or not too little, without bending to one side and constantly adjusting to varying conditions, as present circumstances permit… this may be the "right" answer to addressing the problems of today.

---

56) Rawls's *A Theory of Justice*, published in 1971, discusses how to achieve justice by ensuring the greatest benefits to all, and justice as a means to put this into practice. He also speaks about "distributive justice," meaning that the disadvantaged should be supported, and not only the talented should reap the benefits of everything, because that would be unfair. So to return to all people the greatest amount of benefits, and the problems that arise while following this route, is a just and fair process.

When I was younger, I could've read more classics. But they were difficult. Instead, we soldiers needed more knowledge of military strategies and tactics, so this genre is what I focused on back then. I really don't understand Lao-Tzu, to be honest. From the very beginning, he gives me a headache. The first chapter of the *Tao Te Ching* starts off like this: "The Tao that can be named isn't actually the eternal Tao. The eternal Tao is the nameless origin of everything there is."[57] This is too metaphysical for me. Maybe it's because I am a former military man, but I don't really understand what he means by this.

In the *Analects of Confucius*, there is another quote that I would like you to remember. "Is it not pleasant to learn with constant perseverance and application? Is it not delightful to have friends coming from distant quarters? Is he not a man of complete virtue (a gentleman), who feels no discomposure though men may take no note of him?"[58] This is from the *Analects*, in the Chapter titled, "Xue er" Isn't this much easier to understand? Lao-Tzu, on the other hand, breaks your spirits from the very beginning. The way he starts by talking of Tao is too abstract. But everyone always praises Lao-Tzu's *Tao Te Ching*, so I did read it a couple of times. It's very esoteric. The talk of "Wu wei" is difficult and doesn't sit well with me because I am a man who values active participation.

But Zhuangzi, or Zhuang Zhou, as he's commonly known, and his *The Pure Classic of Nanhua* is a fun read. The text is also referred to as, purely, *The Zhuangzi*, and is titled after the ancient Chinese philosopher. I take delight in the fables and analogies he uses in his texts. He loves discussing

---

57) *Tao Te Ching*, Chapter 1
58) *Analects*, Chapter 1 Xue er.

things on a grand, larger-than-life scale.

Zhuang Zhou's wife passed away. As soon as she left this world, Zhuang Zhou started pounding on a tub and singing. His friend, Hui Shi, alarmed by his strange behavior, asked him why he was doing this.

Zhuang Zhou replied: "I looked back to her beginning and the time before she was born. Not only the time before she was born, but the time before she had a body. Not only the time before she had a body, but the time before she had a spirit. In the midst of the jumble of wonder and mystery a change took place and she had a spirit. Another change, and she had a body. Another change, and she was born. Now there's been another change, and she's dead. It's just like the progression of the four seasons, spring, summer, fall, and winter."[59]

In this world, there are strange men, and yes, they do exist. There are strange men, entitled men, those lacking, and madmen. This is what makes the world a fun and enjoyable place to live. The world is yours to experience and enjoy. Another man's life is not yours to judge. You are uniquely you.

King Wei of Chu Dynasty contacted Zhuang Zhou, in hopes of having him serve as a prime minister. But Zhuang Zhou dismissed the representative.

"Do you know of the ox that is used in ancestral rites? For several years, he is fed the best feed and then, in the not-so-distant future, clothed in silk and becomes a literal sacrifice at the altar. You may think that I am playing in a

---

[59] *The Complete Works of Chuang Tzu*, by Zhuangzi

dog hutch, but this is a pleasurable life for me. I am happy here; what use do I have for coveting power and putting my life on the line for it? This is my wish, to live like this."

Zhuang Zhou lived a life that is freer than a bird, soaring near the heavens. His seemingly idle nature, or "Wu wei zi ran" carries wisdom. He even transcended death. Zhuang Zhou's "Wu wei zi ran" may be a follow-up version of Lao-Tzu, but both are in the fact that man's insatiable desires may have caused this troubled world. Thus, Confucianism's artificial morality only adds to the confusion. "Zi ran" should be free to express itself and rely on no one. A person should not be forced to do anything and be free to live as he pleases. The way to save the world is to embrace the "idleness" of "Wu wei."

But Lao-Tzu says, "If nothing is done, then all will be well." Is this maxim true? The following lines are even more complicated so I will summarize them in a short line.

"Those who seek knowledge, collect something every day. Those who seek the Tao, let go of something every day. They let go and let go, until reaching no action. When nothing is done, nothing is left undone."

Generally speaking, a person's work is not "inaction" and "idleness," but rather, talent in action. So when he says, "When nothing is done, nothing is left undone." What does he mean? Does he mean that the Tao is working in the natural order? Moreover, Zhuang Zhou turns down a very important position as a government official. If such an offer had been made to me, I would have accepted it immediately. The higher the rank, the better. The more duties, the better. I want it on the grand scale of things. A high-ranking position of power gives me even more authority.

I am not actually coveting a position or title as a high-ranking government official. It's because I want to put in the hard work. If I have to work, then I have to have money, authority, power, and gather people together. If I am not a government official, then in this universe, if everyone is content with poverty and lives without worldly cares, then who will work?

Let's stop here. Did I, as a former military officer, go too far? To be honest, as I was discussing these philosophers and scholars, I was a bit anxious. I did not have the confidence to discuss the classics. But I did feel that I needed to really read and study them, otherwise I have no authority to discuss them.

My lads, you may have been bored by these passages on the Chinese classics. Let us now discuss *The Art of War* by Sun-Tzu. I think it is impossible to speak about China without a discussion of military science or war strategies. The Warring States Period teaches harsh lessons regarding history, and China and its people who struggled to survive and did must have something in their hearts that they buried deep—emotional baggage.

If today we don't understand China for whatever reason, it is because we lack this experience of having ancestors who lived through the Warring States Period. The reason why I am now going to discuss Chinese military strategies with you is to look at the heroes of difficult times and study those who took a leading role, and through this lens, view China from a different angle.

c) Sun-Tzu

The first line of Sun-Tzu's *The Art of War* starts like this: "The war is vital to the State. It is a matter of life and death, a road to safety or ruin. Hence it is a subject of inquiry that can on no account be."[60] This is included in the first chapter, titled, "Laying Plans," in the Lionel Giles translation of *Sun-Tzu on the Art of War: The Oldest Military Treatise in the World*, published first in 1910 (I am referring to the latest version of this book, published in 2000 under the Classic E-texts Series).

Sun-Tzu regards war as something that decides a nation's fate. This is not a record of wars fought and won. And it follows that the first chapter's second lines refer to what is known as "Oh Sa Chil Gae," or the five "constant factors" and "seven elements" that determine who rules the battlefield. I will list the five constant factors here: "The Moral Law, Heaven, Earth, The Commander, Method and Discipline."

The Seven Elements, which also determine who emerges as the victor on the battlefield, are as follows: the government sound, the cable commander, the natural phenomenon and topography sound, maintaining the organization and the regulation, the stronger military, the well-trained troops, and finally, are the constant and just rewards and punishments. Sun-Tzu examines the government before he examines engagement in warfare. Just because he is a Chinese military strategist does not mean that his work is limited to that of the battlefield.

In truth, in order to understand the China of today, it is of vital importance

---

60) http://suntzusaid.com/book/1, Lionel Giles version (1910)

that we understand this book. From Sun Yat-sen to Chiang Kai-shek and Mao Zedong, who built modern China, we must understand that they are all military strategists, from a certain vantage point. Sun Yat-sen wrote *Sun Zhongshan zhibing yulu*, and Chiang Kai-shek wrote *Jiang Zhong zhi bing yulu*, and Mao wrote On Contradiction, Problems of Strategy in China's Revolutionary War, and On Protracted War quoting Sun-tzu. These facts teach us that reading Sun-tzu is a key to understanding Mao.

Let me summarize a quote from Mao. "If the enemy advances, then retreat, if the enemy stops, then stop, and when the enemy is tired, strike, and if the enemy is running away, then follow him." This part originated from Sun Tzu: "Avoid a strong enemy, make the enemy angry so that he loses his cool, look like you're underprepared and in disarray so that he takes false comfort in his superiority, and make up false plans to mentally fatigue him." Why do you think that Mao Zedong would rely on a classic such as Sun-Tzu's book on military strategies, published over 2,500 years ago? This book intrigues many people. Even former U.S. President Donald J. Trump takes interest in it. So where and what is the deep meaning behind this book?

I don't look at *The Art of War*, from just one perspective. This may be myopic of me, but I don't think he is as brilliant as the philosophers Lao-Tzu or Confucius, but I do believe he is a true luminary of Taoism. They may argue with me here, but his grand vision of the universe, and his perspective on human nature is really similar to Lao-Tzu. You can even say that he believes in the "flow of nature, as she is," and you can find traces of this belief in his work.

Sun-Tzu also says in his book to "avoid attacking the enemy, and instead, wait for them to flounder by themselves." Basically, he espouses "winning without fighting," and his philosophy speaks volumes about this irony and his infinite wisdom regarding humanity as a whole. Sun-Tzu believes that this universe comprises opposing elements, like strength and gentleness, coldness and warmth, heaven and earth, and man and woman. These opposites actually act synergistically, like yin and yang in Oriental ideology. That is why the "opposing side and I are actually as one, act synergistically, so how are we supposed to fight? There is a path to winning without fighting," he says.

Basically, one must know the enemy and know oneself, and this is again similar to the Oriental philosophy of yin and yang. From this point, it seems like nothing, but "hence the saying: if you know the enemy and know yourself, you need not fear the result of a hundred battles."[61] Even those who are unfamiliar with *The Art of War* know this phrase. But out of this ordinary phrase, how many are familiar with its hidden depths?

About 2,500 years after Sun-Tzu, and in modern times, Mao Zedong would take Sun-Tzu's heart and write his famous three works, *On Contradiction, Problems of Strategy in China's Revolutionary War,* and *On Protracted War*. Mao Zedong would take Sun-Tzu as the basis of his theory. Though he made countless mistakes, it is because of these works that Mao Zedong is still regarded as one of the greats by the modern-day Chinese. In 1937, Mao Zedong's *On Contradiction* would call to attention to other CPC members an element central to his rule. He writes, "We must watch out for subjectivity and looking at only one side. Knowing the CPC but not knowing the Kuomintang, knowing the proletariat but not knowing the bourgeoisie, means that you're unaware of the aspects of contradiction, meaning that you

---

61) *Sun Tzu on The Art of War*, Chapter 3, SunTzuSaid.com

cannot find the clue and you will fail at the task at hand."

Mao Zedong approached Sun-Tzu's teachings via a method we call in Korean "Jeong Ban Hap." Loosely translated, it means "thesis-antithesis-synthesis." He used Sun-Tzu's works and approached it via a dialectical method, "When orders are issued to attack, the sitting soldier's collar is wet with tears, while the tears of those lying on the ground flow below his chin."[62] Sun-Tzu is familiar with the soldiers' mentality on the battlefield. Soldiers cry in secret. How frightened they must be. This speaks to their humanity. A general must know their pain, is what he means.

Sun-Tzu was a humanist. That is why he preached for finding a way to win without engaging in combat. There is always a way. That is why winning 100 battles out of 100 battles is not the best way. The river flows, regardless of night or day. One comes, and passes from this earth. A new life is born after the other passes— this universe is a big river that keeps flowing without rest. Winning once and losing once, how is this different from being born once and dying once? This river of life bears both winners and losers swiftly flowing toward the completion of history.

Warfare is the outcome of karma, the product of interaction between a leader's misjudgment and his blurry vision. So, a leader must prevent his soldiers from tearing up if they fall into an inevitable war and find a way to win without much bloodshed. Sun-Tzu is a great humanitarian, and a profound philosopher.

---

62) *The Art of War*, Chapter 9, "The Army on the March"

4 The nation we call Japan

A. The "real" Japan

What is the real Japan? Why do we Koreans use a slur (sometimes) when referencing this country? (Some) Koreans actually still dislike Japan. This may be the first response when I mention "Japan" to you. Why do you dislike this country? What makes your blood boil? You just don't like it without having a proper reason. If you could live your life according to your feelings, that wouldn't be grand. But is this possible? No, it isn't.

If you don't like the country of Japan, then you shouldn't hate it, but surpass it. If you dislike something intensely, it's your loss. It's bad for your health. If you want to surpass something in excellence, then you must know your competitor. Know thyself, but know your enemy (competitor) too. We call this, "Ji pi ji gi," a four-character idiom in both Korean and Chinese. If you want to "Ji pi ji gi," then you must not act first in accordance with what your feelings dictate. You must approach the problem rationally.

Let us now examine the actual conditions of the nation we call Japan. Population 130 million, or tenth in the world. A GDP of 4.98 trillion dollars, according to a 2020 estimate, which ranks it 3rd in the world, and R&D investments of around 130 billion U.S. dollars. 15 Nobel Prize laureates in the field of science, 12th in the world with regards to quality of life, and military expenditure of up to US 49.1 billion dollars, ranking ninth in the world.[63]

They started using the hiragana, their own written character, about 1,000 years ago. They are the producers of the world's oldest novel, the "Genji Monogatari," or "The Tale of Genji," which dates back to the 11th century, and their ancient capital Edo (the prior name of modern-day Tokyo), had more than a million people living there in 18th century.

Japan is a formidable country. That is why the world is frightened of Japan. But only one country in this world underestimates Japan. It's the Republic of Korea. (Some) Koreans don't consider Japan to be much of a threat, or a competitor at all. The Republic of Korea is a really scary country. This bravado says a lot about us.

So let's say that today's Japan really is like what I described. Then what was Japan like in the past? Japan learned everything from us Koreans. Our ancestors crossed the sea and became emperors, and became the ruling class there. They learned about Buddhism, the writing system, and architecture from us. However, if I keep talking about this period, I would be a narrow-minded person, so I will stop here for now.

What was it like in Japan during the 16th century? In 1592, the Imjin War (the Japanese invasions of Korea) broke out. Japan mobilized 220,000 soldiers to attack Joseon. Of those, about 160,000 were sent to Korea as an attacking force, and 60 to 70 thousand remained in Japan. And hundreds of

---

63) Stockholm International Peace Research Institute (SIPRI), 2020 report

ships were used for the invasion. What a national power they had![64]

The Japanese Navy's main ship was Atakebune, with the capacity to hold 90 men. It went quite fast due to its narrow, flat bottom. Though changing directions was tough, it was still fit for crossing a channel between Joseon and Japan. The ships were made out of Japanese cedar and were weaker when compared to Joseon's Panokseon, or "board-roofed ship." Panokseon's undersides were flatter and slower, but by the coasts, very easy to navigate and quicker to change directions compared to the Japanese warships. With all types of Joseon cannons on her deck, Panokseon held Atakebune in check in the distance, preventing the Japanese force from engaging in close combat, which was their strength. The Japanese couldn't fire back because Atakebune's lighter weight couldn't hold recoil of a cannon.

Even in modern day warfare, sending over 200,000 men aboard battleships is a massive operation. Japan has done twice of this massive operation in Imjin War (1592) and Jeongyoo War (1598). Managing, sustaining and employing 200,000 men can be done by only a powerful nation.

In September 1543, about 100 missionaries from Portugal made their way to Tanegashima Island, Japan. This island is about three hours away by ferry from Kagoshima. At the time, Tokitaka, a lord of the island, bought two arquebuses from them, as he was already aware of their value.[65]

---

64) During the Japanese invasion of 1592, they say that Japanese naval ships crowded the seas, but the exact number of vessels remains unknown. With these commissioned ships, their army crossed the sea several times, making several round trips.

65) Tokitaka took one of the rifles to someone. He wanted him to take it apart in a feat of reverse engineering. But he was unable to do so. The would-be gunsmith wanted his only daughter to marry a Portuguese, and upon the marriage, he learned how to be a real gunsmith from them, as he was able to acquire the technology. He thus

Guns were first introduced to Korea during the Joseon Dynasty in 1554. The border defense council of Joseon requested gun molds from King Myeongjong (1534-67) but the request was denied. Joseon people named this Arquebus "Jochong," which means "bird gun," because it could shoot a bird down. Why did Joseon want rifles? It even downed sparrows flying in the sky. They wanted the technology to go bird hunting. Joseon became obsessed with the idea of shotguns.

I am not here to talk about "bird guns". It's about the leaders of Joseon, who underestimated Arquebus. In the Imjin War (1592), this so-called "bird gun" harassed Joseon. Technically, in the early moments of the Imjin War, it was hard to call it a "war." Joseon couldn't fight back properly at the beginning. What would have happened if not for Admiral Yi Sun-sin or the Righteous Army? When I think of the Japanese invasion, my heart aches. How unfortunate for us that King Seonjo of Joseon was on the throne during this time. Besides appointing the king, what else had Joseon's politicians done?

How dare a man named Kim Seong-il falsely report about Japan's attempt at an invasion? Politicians of Joseon falsely reported about Japan's attempt to invade, for their party's fate, thereby risking the nation's fate. The elite's loyalty lay elsewhere. The elite, ruling class has to be loyal to the people, rather than the dynasty. Personally, I believe that even now, many elites are wrong about this.

---

successfully built a rifle. Afterward, merchants from Izumi, or current day Osaka, learned the technology from him and this knowledge spread to even the Kyoto region. In just six years, by 1549, a 15-year-old Oda Nobunaga bought 500 rifles and in June of 1575, united Japan by obliterating the mighty Takeda horseback riding corps.

Hideyoshi's vanguard, Konishi Yukinaga, landed in Busan in the afternoon of April 15, 1592. Starting from Busan, he occupied Hanyang, the capital of Joseon on the eighteenth day. Nothing interfered with him. Joseon had a lack of soldiers, weapons, as well as training. Which translated to "totally unprepared." Before we cast blame on the King, we should place the blame on middlemen such as state governors, mayors, and local commanders. If they are not alert, then it leads to the mismanagement of the entire nation.

So what was 18th century Japan like? There is a book, called the *Hae Yurok*.[66] It is a record about Japan written by Joseon envoy, Shin Yoo-han (1681-1752). Rather than being an account full of the usual anti-Japanese sentiment of Joseon's elite, this record is quite objective. Shin describes Japanese society as consisting of a "four caste system," with "samurai" as the ruling class. According to Shin, Japanese society back then is stable and orderly. For example, he is pleasantly surprised by the well-mannered crowd who congregates to greet the Joseon envoy. And the elite's oratorical skills as well as their talent for writing surprises him as well. Lastly, the cleanliness of Japanese cuisine at full display in bars and streets impresses him, as well as the easy smiles of the women and their clear and ringing voices.

The publishing business was quite the vogue; books were everywhere, and even the non-elites read voraciously. Actually, the development of the Tokugawa shogunate surprises us in many ways. As a diplomat who served at Joseon's embassy in Japan, according to his book,[67] Shin Sang-mok

---

66) Written by Shin Yoo-han, translated by Kim Chan-soon. *Haeyurok*, Bori, 2016.
67) Shin Sang-mok, *Japanese history not taught in schools*, Poori and Ipari (Roots & Leaves), 2017.

Chapter Two Gazing away from Korea_177

writes that Japan had already surpassed Joseon during the 16th century. He insists the Tokugawa Shogunate ushered in an age of conversion equal to that of the Western world's Renaissance and their Age of Discovery. The Tokugawa Shogunate undertook public works to make Edo as a center of power. They paved roads and canals, and reformed moats and castles. They set the bar high, so that it was regarded as a city worthy and comparable to the "Western standard" of the day.

The Shoguns controlled their regional princes through various methods, but the most representative method was the "sankin kotai," or "alternate residence duty." This method was introduced in 1635 by the Tokugawa shogunate, and the regional princes (feudal lords) had to live for several months every year at the Tokugawa capital and serve the shogun there. The word may have been "serve." Depending on the size of the region, 700 to 2,000 people moved to Edo with their lords.

The Japanese peoples' life flourished, and the regional economy improved dynamically. Improvements in the financial industry led to individuals increasing their wealth, which led to changes in the social structure. Wealthy merchants, for the first time, became as well-respected as the samurai.

As I have stated before, the publishing business flourished during this time as well. During the late 17th century, a man named Ihara Saikaku wrote an erotic novel titled *Koshoku ichidai otoko*, or *The Life of the Amorous Man*. It became an instant bestseller. The book follows a man named Yonosuke, and his turbulent sex life. And many other authors' popular books followed Ihara's sensational novel. Books sold well, a testament to the high literacy of the average Japanese, and his ability to enjoy cultural past times. Such was Japan, 300 years ago.

B. Spiritualism

Japan is a country to be reckoned with. The Japanese have many good traits. Let us acknowledge this as a fact. Japan's biggest selling point is its purity. This is their spiritualism. This is from my viewpoint. There may be people who disagree with me. If you disagree with me and dislike Japan, I would like you to keep this as a reference.

There is something called "Wabi" and "Sabi" in Japanese. This is found in the traditional Japanese tea ceremony, "Chado", and is a testament to Japan's emphasis on beauty refined to a seamless simplicity. They teach simplicity and quietude. It is said that we may attain a spiritual state of selflessness while meditating. To be sure, I do not have personal experience with this, so there is no way of knowing.[68]

There is another phrase I am fond of, and it is called "il-gi-il-hwae." It can loosely be translated as "once in a lifetime." It is also used in the "Chado," or the art of ceremonial tea making. "This may be my first and last chance to receive you as my guest, and I will do my utmost to make you comfortable while our paths converge." This is a truly beautiful mindset. This is a final pure stage of spiritualism, also called, "Hwa Kyeong Cheong Jeok," an outcome of harmony, respect, purity, and stability.

During the early 18th century, under a snowy night, a group of 47 samurai stealthily made their way to Migawa (now known as Aichi Prefecture). They beheaded the feudal warlord Kira Yoshinaka and took his head to Sengakuji

---

68) Oda Nobunaga and Toyotomi Hideyoshi are known as the Sen no Rikyu. They are also known as the founders of the original Wabi tea tradition, and in Japan, are called the "Fathers of the Tea Ceremony."

temple. This place was the samurai king's last resting place, where Asano Naganori's remains were held. A year prior, Asano had tried to kill Kira, who had insulted him. He had raised his sword against him but failed to kill him. But amidst the shogun, he had drawn his sword and ended up committing hara-kiri, or suicide by disembowelment.

The samurai avenged their master's death that night. But their act of loyalty became problematic later on. They had acted out of revenge, during the relatively peaceful Edo period. Beheading another feudal lord was viewed as an unforgivable act by many. The samurai who had taken action against him knew that they would not receive forgiveness. Thus, they placed the beheaded Kira's head on temple grounds and, acting on orders from the shogunate, committed hara-kiri en masse. This incident is known as the "Chushingura." This act became legendary, and was made into a Kabuki theater production and commemorated by other works of art, and is still famous today, several centuries later. Its popularity in Japan surpasses that of *Chun hyang jeon (Story of Miss Chun hyang)* or *Sim Cheong jeon (Story of Filial daughter Sim Cheong)* in Korea.

This speaks to how Japanese society still honors the samurai spirit. Their loyalty to their feudal lord was so great that they were prepared to die for him. This type of sacrifice and taking secrets to the grave are viewed as beautiful acts in Japan. On August 15, 1945, around 4 a.m., Anami Korechika, the Minister of the Army, quietly sat in the courtyard of his residence. His upper body was unclothed. He was about to commit suicide by disembowelment. Next to him was Lieutenant Colonel Takeshita, who was his brother-in-law. The Minister's wife was Takeshita's older sister.

In a shaking voice, Takeshita asked:

"Your excellency, your last words?"

"I ask that my wife takes good care of what happens after this."

"Then, your excellency, kaishaku[69] is now my…."

Waves of grief hit him.

"That is useless! Leave me!"

Anami drew his sword and sliced himself open near the stomach area. He did not die until the sun was high in the sky. His tremendous pain ended with a painful gasp. This is the result of rejecting kaishaku. Minister Anami had rejected "unconditional surrender." This was because the Allied Forces' call for an unconditional surrender did not guarantee the survival of the Japanese imperial system. The Japanese's political system relied on it, and within the Department of the Army headquarters, the elite officers also believed in preserving their imperial system. This Japanese imperial form of government was the pillar of the Japanese way of life.

So they planned a coup d'état with the Imperial Guard Division and Eastern Command (troops in charge of Tokyo) as a contingency plan to upend public opinion. The Prime Minister, the Foreign Minister, the Minister of the Navy, all supported ending the war and the Cabinet Council would be sure to follow their chain of command. But a day before August 14th, a day before the announcement of the Japanese surrender during World War II, there was an agreement that they would agree to a formal surrender and accept the terms of the Potsdam Declaration.

---

69) Kaishaku happens after hara-kiri. To lessen the pain of self-disembowelment, another person stands behind the person who commits hara-kiri and beheads him.

Anami, Minister of the Army, grew faint when he received this news. He already knew that Emperor Hirohito was against the war. However, the Emperor's firm will shocked him. The Emperor's will is a holy decision. Anami, as a soldier, at all costs must abide by the Emperor's wishes. This is the mindset of all true imperial soldiers. But this went against his own principles. Not to mention, there was the promise that he had already made to his subordinates.

Lieutenant Colonel Takeshita, an elite officer of the Military Affairs Bureau of the Department of the Army, came to Anami. He was also a member of a coup d'état.

"Your excellency, how should we proceed?"
"I will follow the command."

Then he added, "Over my dead body!"

At this, Takeshima's mind fell to pieces. He wasn't the only one feeling stunned. Minister Anami must have thought of suicide at this time. He could not disappoint his subordinates, and his will refused to bend to this chain of command to surrender completely. But at the same time, he could not disobey the Emperor's will. Up until this point, he had lived with two honorable codes in mind: leading his subordinates and complete veneration of his Emperor.

History was calling upon him to make a choice between the two. He chose to honor the Emperor for the great cause. But he had failed in the minor cause. Minister Anami was a man who couldn't fail his subordinates either. Then, what was his final choice? It was death. He chooses "Seppuku."

This is the way of the samurai. American anthropologist Ruth Benedict writes about the Japanese mindset, in *The Chrysanthemum and the Sword: Patterns of Japanese Culture*.[70] I believe this duplicity that is mentioned even in the title is the reason why. The Japanese hold a chrysanthemum in one hand and at their waists, they carry a Katana (sword). The image they project onto the world differs from their inner worlds.

This dichotomy is called "honnae" and "tatemae" in Japanese. "Honnae," refers to how a person feels within, and "tatemae" points to how a person behaves on the outside. This is why a Japanese person's words may differ from his real feelings.

The duplicity that I mention here is not limited to just Japan. Every society and every person has a drop of this. But it is worth noting that Japanese culture exhibits these traits en masse. This is why during the Second World War, the U.S. Army could not understand the behavior of the Japanese soldiers that they took into custody. Japanese soldiers were educated by the Imperial Army that being a POW was the worst dishonor. So, in the early days of the war, most Japanese soldiers committed suicide before capture. Once captured as POWs, however, they readily cooperated with the U.S. Army. At first, the American army was befuddled. They wondered if the Japanese prisoners of war were lying. But everything that they confessed to turned out to be accurate. They were telling the truth.

The word duplicitous may come to mind. However, we must remember that the Japanese people are pure at heart. That is why they have an eye for beauty and are born with taste. This spiritualism has its merits but its side

---

70) Ruth Benedict, *The Chrysanthemum and the Sword: Patterns of Japanese Culture.* Houghton Mifflin, 1946.

effects as well. No matter what, anything in excess is harmful. Even death is viewed as beautiful, and an aesthetic surrounds it.

During World War II, while fighting against the Japanese, the Americans had one main question. Wartime customs and codes of conduct, seemingly did not apply to the Japanese. They may die but they never surrendered. If they cannot withstand any more onslaughts, they commit what is called a Banzai charge. On their planes, these kamikaze pilots carried a bomb and charged at the opponent's aircraft carrier. Their very bodies turn into weapons. To the American army, these behaviors contradicted what they considered "normal" behavior during times of war.

C. Harmony

The Japanese hold "Wa" or the concept of a harmonic culture, deep within their hearts. Over a thousand years, this mindset has been flowing within the Japanese people. This tradition of "Wa" dates back to antiquity. Japan is a nation made up of islands. If a terrible event occurs, there is nowhere to run. That is why within the islands, there must be harmony within, and people need to get along with each other. Prince Shotoku established this "Wa" as a founding ideology of an empire.

"Wa" is an implicit requirement that individuals cooperate for the community's common purpose. For the greater good of the community, a person must never push his own personal agenda too much nor harm others to the point that they feel uncomfortable. That is why one must be careful in his personal thoughts and actions, always think about what is best for the community at large, and act as a member of the community. That is a society governed by a collective living standard.

Japan, like Korea, was traditionally agricultural. Hydroponics are prevalent in Japan. This type of agriculture required a large labor force, and each generation passed on their ownership of their lands to subsequent generations, resulting in an obsession with retaining their ancestral rights to land and settlement. Farmers, regardless of race and culture, always adapt themselves to Nature, and the cultivation of crops is always seasonal, so it became natural for them to embrace a collective, harmonic culture.

Traditionally, the Japanese village community sticks to following rules.
1) Do not murder, 2) Do not steal, 3) Do not raise a fire, 4) Do not sue. These regulations ensured not only the maintaining peace and harmony of the village but also the stability of the whole of Japanese society. And scary punishment ensures observance of these rules. If a person flagrantly disobeys these rules, they would be treated as an outcast, so-called "Murahachibu", collective and thorough punishment by the whole community. (A person who flagrantly disobeyed these four laws would become "murahachibu," or the village idiot, and would become ostracized by other members of his community).

Japan entered the bloody Sengoku Period in the late 15th century and for about 100 years. Following 250 years of prolonged peace, the Tokugawa Shogunate provided industrial development, calm and stability. The "Wa" culture, of not harming others, not being stubborn, and sacrificing one's own for the community's prosperity, once again bloomed.

During the 1980s, Japan had a GNP of $14,807 U.S. dollars, while the United States had a GNP of $17,843 U.S. dollars, ensuring its place as the second most powerful economy. Back then, their pride was skyrocketing. Japan raised its national flag on the Empire State Building in New York City, and bought the Pebble Beach golf club. Nothing seemed to stop Japan's ambition.

Ezra Vogel, a Harvard professor with research interests in East Asia, wrote a book titled *Japan as Number One: Lessons for America*. This raised worldwide attention to Japan. It appeared as though Japan would soon catch up to the U.S. Even Ishihara Shintaro, then-mayor of Tokyo, wrote a book titled *The Japan that can say No: Why Japan will be first among equals*. In the 1980s, Japan seemed to have no end in its slightly arrogant attitude. This is what happens when a country gains power.

In September 1986, the Japanese Minister of Education, Fujio Masayuki, wrote a piece in a Japanese magazine that said, "the dispossession of Joseon sovereignty was the result of a negotiated agreement between Joseon's Emperor Gojong and Japan's Prime Minister Ito Hirobumi." This essay, published in the Bungeishunju in its October issue, caused a stir. As soon as it was published, it became a political hot-button topic, forcing the Prime Minister, Nakasone Yasuhiro, to dismiss him. Prime Minister Nakasone was known to be pro-Korean, or friendly towards the Korean people. Surprisingly, the following month, the same magazine published another piece by Fujio, where he expressed his justification and unbending attitude towards what he had written before.[71]

Looking at Japan before and after World War II, when compared to Germany, some Japanese politicians seem not to understand the gravity of its

---

71) It surpasses my understanding that Fujio won the Bungeishunju's Reader's Prize for this piece.

crimes, and in my opinion, has justly received criticism for this. This is true. On the other hand, Germany has repented for its past, immaculately so. The Chancellor of Germany, Willy Brandt, even knelt in the rain at a cemetery in Poland to honor the war dead. Even now, when people are exposed and found to have Nazi connections, they are punished mercilessly and justly. The German people do not forgive them.

But the Japanese are a different breed. Postwar Prime Minister of Japan, Kishi Nobusuke, was a class A war criminal. The world may not forgive, but the Japanese people think differently. The entire tone towards former war crimes veers away from the general German sentiment. This atmosphere makes war criminals more brazen.

The German peoples see Nazis as murderers. The Nazis murdered the Jewish people, and far too many, at that.[72] The Japanese, on the other hand, see those who led them to war as patriots. They do not see the need for those who led the nation to war to apologize. That is why their apologies are weak, and insincere. They are just pretending. The reasons are complicated. In Japan's collectivist culture, there exists the other side, exclusion. A collectivist culture fundamentally implies a sense of rivalry or exclusion within. This is what it means to be part of a group. Within them, their family, the groups to which they belong, matter to a Japanese person. If you are not in our group, then you are the other, an outsider. Talking to an outsider is uncomfortable, because they are not family. Along the same lines, they cover most of the faults committed by family members, because they are our family.

---

72) About six million Jewish people died in Europe during the Holocaust. About nine million lived in Europe at the time, meaning that 2/3 of them were wiped out due to the Nazis. A million children, two million women, and three million men died.

Japan's collectivist culture has no choice but to be generous to its own. This is why a former war criminal even became a prime minister. The German individualist culture would never have seen a similar fate. According to a Governor-General of Korea official named Morita Yoshio,[73] the Japanese Governor-General of Korea listened closely to radio broadcasts right before the Potsdam Declaration was announced. The Japanese Governor-General of Korea was concerned for the safety of Japanese people residing on the Korean Peninsula who could be threatened by riots right after disarmament and release of political prisoners as the Soviet Union participated on August 9, 1945.

The Soviet Union, on August 9th, occupied Woongi, Hamgyeongbuk-do Province, then on the 12th, occupied Najin. Everyone was on edge for fear that the Soviet Union soldiers may reach the capital of Seoul at any moment. Even after Japan's unconditional surrender, the Soviet Union's army kept advancing through the peninsula, and on the 23rd of August, reached Gyeseong. Thankfully, the United States had already drawn the 38th parallel, so the Soviets withdrew to the north of the parallel.

The Japanese Governor-General of Korea was in a hurry to make peace with the leaders of Joseon, and cooperate with them. On August 15th, the No. 2 official in the Government-General of Korea, Endo Ryushaku, called Lyuh Woon-hyung to his side. It was at 6 a.m. in the morning, about six hours prior to the Japanese Emperor Hirohito's declaration of surrender. Endo sought from Lyuh Woon-hyung the cooperation of the Koreans. Lyuh accepted gladly. Thankfully, on Liberation Day, there were no disruptive accidents.

---

73) Yoshio Morita, *Chosen shusen no kiroku*. Gannando Shoten, 1964

Japan and we, as neighbors, cannot actually separate from each other completely. In terms of politics, economics, society, culture, and security. Unfortunately for both of us, we became a mutual enemy through the Korea-Japan treaty of 1910.

In the financial world as well as the world of sports, I have a lot of Japanese friends. Once, I asked one of my friends what bothered him the most about Koreans. His face hardened, and he seemed very disconcerted. I was sorry to have asked such a question and asked not for his personal opinion, but what the intellectuals really dislike about Korea. He gazed at me for what seemed like hours. Then he started talking very carefully.

The first issue that the Japanese take with Koreans, in general, is that of an apology. Every single time a new president comes into office, it seems as though they keep insisting on an apology. So my Japanese friend's point was that the Japanese feel as though they have already offered their heartfelt apologies. They're sick of this requirement. To reiterate this point, they are so "tired." The second refers to that of compensation and conscription.

When the new President Moon Jae-in was sworn into office, for example, he broke promises made by the prior administration. The Supreme Court of Korea requested compensation from Japan again. From my friend's viewpoint, it is hard to understand why Korea keeps changing her mind. This is a complicated legal matter, and I agree that the Supreme Court of Korea keeps changing its verdicts, too, so no wonder our honor seems at stake sometimes.

But if we are really to discuss this, then it's a really complicated issue.

Why? Because the issue lies with the stealing away of national sovereignty 100 years ago. Why invade and annex another nation? Whatever the reason was, Japan was at fault. But under international law, there are no laws regarding colonization. So where do we go to appeal? Who do we hold responsible? I am at a loss to say anything.

The more oppressing part is that if we forced compensation, the international court would side with Japan; at least, this is the way the lower courts of Korea see the issue. This is the reality and this is international politics. The world is still ruled by sheer might and power. That is why Korea must strengthen its national power.

When a foreigner compares the Japanese to Koreans, they say Koreans have a lot of "Jeong," affection. On the other hand, they say that the Japanese wear a mask, and their outsides don't match their insides. This is the truth. Of course, they feel this. Koreans are quick to confess to what they are feeling, moment to moment, but the Japanese never really confess their true feelings. No wonder why foreigners feel closer to us Koreans. They feel "Jeong" for us too.

So why is it that the Japanese do not speak of their innermost feelings? They can't. They are careful. It's because the other person may become offended. This is called "maywaku," in Japanese. It refers to causing trouble. If it goes further, this is about "Wa" culture. It has roots from over 1,000 years ago. That is why they are sometimes called reserved.

The young people of Japan may have changed, but the generations that I do know don't even express their own opinions during a business meeting. That is because it violates the "Wa." I have worked with the Japanese in the Middle East. As soon as the day's work was almost over, the managing staff would congregate for what is called uchiawase, or a business meeting. It was a daily ritual. Sometimes there wasn't anything really on the agenda for discussion, but they never ruined the mood. All the Japanese seemed to swallow their own opinions during these meetings.

The Japanese prisoners of war only cooperated with the Americans because they didn't know how to behave when captured. In the Japanese army, they haven't defined POW, so there was no SOP (Standard Operating Procedure) for that. Additionally, when they became prisoners of war, they gave up in despair. They believed that they would become outcasts of society where they could never go back. This was a mistake of the Showa soldier. The Meiji era soldiers were different. After the Russo-Japanese War, there was a case where a returned POW was given a medal.

Personally, I like the Japanese people. They are mannerly, honest, obey the public order, and dislike slovenliness. I especially admire the Japanese leaders' spirit of public service and sacrifice; I find it beautiful. Do you judge me for liking them? Yes, the ills of the past are shameful, but I choose to forget. But I still want to win over Japan sometimes.

Wait up, Japan! Here comes the Republic of Korea.

Chapter Three

What is the Problem?

1 Korea is disappearing

A. Demographic cliff[74]

All this time, I have been asking myself this question: "Who am I?" Then I turned to our surroundings and where I should be standing. Now it is time to turn to our society and see and think upon the problems that it bears. But our problems are not ordinary. They are grave. The world is changing at a fast pace. The survival of the fittest is the natural provision of nature. If you cannot keep pace with the changes, you die. What is the most pressing issue at stake here?

It has to do with the population. As I am not an expert in this area, I am treading carefully. But when I look at the severity of the situation at hand, I cannot even for a moment delay what I wish to say to the younger generations of today. According to the Oxford Institute of Population Ageing, if this trend continues, the Republic of Korea is the first nation that will disappear from this Earth. This horrifies me. I almost want to scream. How on Earth did we reach this point? It has to do with the young people not having children. This is the direct result of the abysmally low birth rate (just

---

74) According to American economist Harry Dent, Jr., his book *Demographic Cliff*, describes when the working age population (15 to 64 years of age) drops dramatically. The elderly population (65 years and older) grows at an alarming rate, and countries reach the phenomenon (a demographic cliff) that he named the book after.

0.92 in 2018). The world faults the young people of today for not getting married, but how is this their fault? It is the fault of their elders!

Their elders got rid of their jobs, raised the prices of homes, all without a strategy for effective measures to combat the ills associated with these deeds. How can they just scold the young adults of today? The problem of the rapidly decreasing birth rate, and the resulting demographic cliff, is a problem that decides the fate of the Republic of Korea. We cannot hastily take action. This is a really serious problem. To the ones who will inherit this nation, the younger generations of Koreans, this is the problem that I want you to focus on and worry about. However, the constraints that I mentioned before may hamper your ability to take action on a grand scale. That is why the demographic cliff is tied to work, housing, the educational system, childcare, social security, and more.

All these things require the full mobilization of national power and strength, and the older generations had to pave the way for you, which we failed somewhat to do. But because the fate of this nation depends on us answering these questions and solving them, we all need to figure out a playbook of sorts to deal with these issues.

B. Super-ageing society and youth unemployment

The National Assembly of the Republic of Korea recently published a study, called the "Prospective Population Survey." According to this study, in about 80 years, "By 2200, our population will have shrunk by more than half, and many cities on the outskirts of rural places will disappear." The population in the capital of Seoul will also dramatically decrease, and out of the nine subway lines, about four will have to be closed. Does this make sense to you? This is a tragedy upon tragedy. If we continue along this path, doesn't it mean that the Republic of Korea will disappear?

According to the National Assembly's investigation, during the past 10 years, about 650,000 young people between the ages of 15-25 have disappeared. Well, they haven't "disappeared," per se. Still, due to the aging population, the rise of the middle-aged, and the falling birthrate, the new generations will be unable to support a healthy, growing society. If the young population drops, then it creates societal problems across all spectrums. At first, the number of military forces and resources shrinks, the labor supply stumbles, then the national strength and the societal power engine sputter to an end.

But what I am rather suspicious about these days is the issue regarding youth employment, or shall I say, youth unemployment. If more than 600,000 youngsters are "missing," then shouldn't more jobs be available to those who have been born and who haven't died? But I keep hearing that the youth unemployment rate is the worst these days. What in the world is going on? Did the number of jobs shrink in keeping with a shrinking population?

The most "super-aged" society is Japan (2006), followed by Italy (2008), and Germany (2010). I looked at these countries to see if I could gather some insight into what it means to be an ageing and an aged society.[75] Japan and Italy are already grappling with problems. They are struggling especially with how to support the youth. In Italy, for example, the unemployment rate is 13.4 percent, but amongst the youth (15-to-25-year-olds), the

---

75) If the number of those older than 65 years of age exceeds 14 percent, then it is an aged society and if it exceeds 20 percent, then it is called a super-aged society.

unemployment rate jumps to 43.9 percent.[76] For Korea, we will enter a super-aged society by 2025 or 2026. But when we reached the 2000s, for about five years, the youth unemployment was already about three times that of the national average. Even before reaching a super-aged society, Korea already had to and is currently grappling with the problem of youth unemployment.

About 70 percent of Italy's youth are adult dependents. Every year, it is estimated that 40,000 go abroad searching for work. They are losing their precious labor force because their own youth turn their backs on their own country![77] Why turn your back on your motherland? Because you cannot live! Why? Because there are no jobs! If there are jobs and the living is nice, then why would they leave? That is why I think creating jobs is the first thing a nation should supply.

Japan's problem with their youth, and the severity of the problem, is something that Italy also understands all too well. Japan's youth population shrunk by about a third, but from the latter half of the 1990s, it was coupled with that of an aging population, resulting in a higher unemployment rate and the lowering of wages. Additionally, only temporary, seasonal, or day laborer jobs have grown. With the shrinking youth population, the expectation that there would be more opportunities available for the remaining youth became the stuff of legends; in other words, this will never come true. Due to the (high) youth unemployment, societal ills have come

---

76) Italy is home to the highest rate of NEET (Not in Education, Employment, or Training) people, with an estimated 19.9 percent as of 2016. This is the highest out of all EU nations. (Korea Labor Institute, "Europe's NEET: Characteristics, Cost, and Policy Mechanisms," May 2013).

77) KBS PD Journal "Myung kyun man rhee," ("Good Insight"), "The Country that Lost its Youth," April 10, 2015.

into play. For example, for the Satori generation, 600,000 to 700,000 people, do not have jobs, are not actively seeking jobs, and do not marry. Of course, they do not even date or make friends with the opposite sex. Sometimes they make friends online.

So how does this generation make its income? They take on part-time jobs and maybe make money for a month or two. With their low pay and the fact that it's only part-time, no wonder why they do not make a good living. In real life, Korean broadcaster KBS's program, "Myung kyun man rhee," which translates loosely to "Good Insight," showed the harsh conditions in which they live. Sometimes they live in a tiny room, sometimes even three to a room, and eat ramen or perhaps kimbap or rice balls for meals. The youth who agreed to be interviewed said that they had not thought of their future. They are more preoccupied with staying true to themselves and abiding by rules at the present moment. At least, this is what they said during the documentary.

Satori means "to realize" in Japanese. So the "Satori" generation is the generation that has reached some kind of realization. In my view, the only fact that separates them from the homeless on the streets is the fact that they have a place to live. The Japanese hate shame, most of all. In the ways of the samurai of old, once ashamed, then they would actually kill the other opponent or commit hara-kiri. This is (or was) the Japanese way and the virtue of virtues. But the Japanese's current Satori youth endure this shame in droves. I feel sorry for them. How on earth has a situation like this come to pass?

The issue of population is not irrelevant but one we must face head-on right now. Though Korea has not yet reached a "super-aged" population, we're still reeling from similar problems that Italy and Japan are currently grappling with. We may face even bigger hurdles in the future than these two aforementioned countries. Germany has already reached a "super-aged" society, but unlike Japan and Italy, they are trying to fix the problem of youth unemployment. This is the wise policy of the Germans.

Japan tried to create more jobs by using several trillion yen of social overhead capital. They built bridges and even made a new airport. Afterward, when assessing their new policies' impact, they were disheartened to discover that employment was affected only by 30 percent. They should have just given the extra yen to the unemployed youth and invested in them, and they are still repenting.

On the other hand, Germany has been investing in the youth for quite some time. For example, while we dole out unemployment compensation after someone loses his job, Germany gives this money out, regardless of whether they have lost their jobs or not. In the early 2000s, Germany's Volkswagen built a new factory in its home city of Wolfsburg. At first, the company wanted to build a new factory overseas. This was because the competitiveness of German cars was falling. But the company decided to scrap the first idea, and build a company in their own country. They were then able to employ 5,000 people and guaranteed their salaries of at least 5,000 German marks per annum.

As the youth were able to make a better income, the consumer market was given a new breath of life, and the city regained some of its vitality. To top it off, excellent German technology contributed to the company regaining some of its lost competitiveness. This feeling spread throughout the nation. In the past, a man was called wealthy when he had a lot of land and resources. But as the birth rate continues to fall throughout the world, human resources are more important now than assets, and out of these assets, the youth are really invaluable, so investing in them is important.[78]

Germany's efforts to invest in their youth are not just about numbers, but it's a testament to investing in the country's future and displays that the first order of business is to create jobs first. Japan and Italy are reeling from the dissatisfaction of their youth, and have lost their way. On the one hand, Germany chose a different route from them, so let this be a lesson to us as well as we move forward.

---

78) KBS "Myung kyun man rhee," ("Good Insight"), "The fifth of the series, The Republic of Korea is losing its youth!" in *The Rules of Investment*. Park Jong-hun, KBS business reporter, April 14, 2015.

2 To become a developed nation (A first world nation)

According to "Transparency International's 2020 Corruption Perceptions Index" (CPI), Korea ranked 33rd out of 180 countries. Denmark and New Zealand tied for first place, and Japan was ranked 19th. You have to rank within the top 20 to be a developed nation with less public corruption as perceived by the rest of the world at large. According to the United Nations' "World Happiness Report 2021," the Republic of Korea ranked 50th out of the 95 countries. The first was Finland, followed by the United States at 14th, Taiwan at 19th, Japan at 40th, and China at 52nd place. This is what Korea is today. While it may rank within the top 10 in terms of economy, the political arena is unable to catch up with that of the economy.

What is the virtue that defines and is the very essence of a human being? It is honesty. The government should be the same. Whenever we speak of politics, we always aggrandize it, but even in government, we should place honesty first.[79] A government that isn't honest, a government that lies, cannot follow the right course of action and be fruitful. Unfortunately for Korea, our government is decaying because of the lack of honesty and transparency. I am reluctant to repeat some of the most recent political scandals, such as the

---

79) During the Nuo Dynasty, Confucius said to a man who inquired about politics, "Politics means to right what is wrong. If the teacher demonstrates the correct way, then who would dare defy this course of action?" *The Analects of Confucius.*

one regarding Justice Minister nominee Cho Kuk. Another one is the Korea Land and Housing Corp.'s (LH's) land speculation scandal as of late.

If you look at the root of the problem of these political scandals, you will find just one conclusion. It means they stemmed from having the wrong thoughts. Having the wrong thought, employing a method that is incorrect, serving your interests first before worrying about what may happen to others; these all demonstrate the fallacy of abandoning the right way and the right thoughts. If you look at it from a different angle, an honest person would never have these types of thoughts and thus, would never engage in actions like this. That is why in order to grow a prosperous and benign nation and become a developed nation, you have to start with honest citizens, and this will be the road to a righteous government.

In order to reach a righteous government, you need a leader—a trailblazer. The reason why Korea became one of the economic success stories of East Asia in a relatively short period of time (after the Korean War) is that the government initiated it. This is because a pioneer like former Korean President Park Chung-hee led the country through economic reforms and transformed it into an economic powerhouse. When I mention former President Park, some people still dislike him. A few go so far as to say that he should go down in history as a terrible military dictator. My thinking is a bit different. He liberated our ancestors from crippling famine, and under his leadership, most Koreans enjoyed a normal, if not comfortable life. Though of course, when discussing his economic reforms, you cannot but remember that some members of the opposition party or some university students may have suffered from repression back then.

Alvin Toffler (1928-2016) once said: "A democracy is only possible after the growth of the economy. To call this type of individual a dictator is a linguistic fallacy. Former President Park Chung-hee's [economic] model is one that the world wants to emulate, no matter what anyone else says." This may be a paradox, but according to Toffler, former President Park Chung-hee is one who pulled the Korean people towards democracy. This is why Deng Xiaoping respected him, and even figures like Lee Kuan Yew wanted to imitate him.

I would like to mention fourth-generation American philanthropist and doctor John Linton (1959-present) at this point. His great-grandparents came to Joseon during Emperor Gojong's rule, and were missionaries. His father served in the Korean War with the U.N. forces. He was born in Jeonju, North Jeolla Province. He once said something like this: "When I was young, I believed that [former President] Park Chung-hee was bad. When I grew up and became wiser, I realized that he was a great man, a man to admire and respect. Some people take issue with his human rights policies [during his presidency], but you have to guarantee a livelihood before you can discuss things like human rights."

Starting with middle class Koreans, it is safe to say that each household owns at least one car. Since then, Korea, for the first time, became more economically advanced than China. It ranks within the top 10 economies in the world. This is a miracle amongst miracles. This is why Korea has naturally become a country of democracy as well. Nature says that it's virtually impossible for dirt spoons (those born to parents with modest backgrounds) to catch up with gold spoons (those born to wealthy parents). Why?

Let's think about the analogy of a 100-meter dash. Everyone at the starting line wants to win. They are the dirt spoons. But the gold spoons start from 50 meters ahead of the dirt spoons. The finish line is the same, but how can the dirt spoons ever catch up with the gold spoons?

The 19th century's Industrial Revolution saw the United Kingdom, France, and Germany, become first world, or developed nations. They are still developed nations today. More than 200 years later, the Industrial Revolution has largely defined the world economic order. Developing countries cannot catch up. This is due to the gold spoon analogy. But, there is one nation that has shattered the analogy. It is the Republic of Korea. The country that is on the cusp of becoming a developed nation! Who brought Korea to this point? It is former President Park Chung-hee. He is the one who shattered the gold spoon vs. dirt spoon analogy and gave Koreans a miracle. This is also why Korea is a democracy today.

I will mention a story about the ambassador to Myanmar, General Kim Jeong-hwan (a Korea Military Academy graduate, Class of 1963), who served as the representative of Korea for that aforementioned country from 1993 to 1996. He spoke of someone from the United Nations Development Program (UNDP), Mr. Larzo, who said something to General Kim ahead of his retirement.

"I am sorry. I am repenting over something. I must mention this to you so that my heart doesn't feel overburdened. During my younger years, while working at the UNDP headquarters, I assessed the economic strength of the developing nations in Asia. I said that the Republic of Korea simply could not become a developed nation. In my report, I said it was a nation without hope. And our subcommittee picked the Philippines as the beacon of hope for economic development in Asia. But what is this! Korea has already surpassed developing nations and progress in the Philippines has stalled. After watching the Korean economy go from strength to strength, [I wish to apologize] to the Korean people."

Personally, I don't think that the initial assessment by the UNDP representative was wrong. As economic pundits, they must have objectively made their assessments. This is because in most cases, a dirt spoon cannot win over a gold spoon, and the rationale here is the same. If the UNDP analysts were wrong, it's because they did not take into account the transformative power of "leadership." What they had missed was the great leadership of former Korean President Park Chung-hee. Leadership is not part of an economic strata but it is influenced by the humanities and philosophy. If financial experts missed this point, it may be an obvious yet moot point. President Park is a luminary, a great man, whose leadership propelled Korea into the economic East Asian tiger that it is today, much to the astonishment of officials at the UN Development Programme (and dare I say, the rest of the world?).

There are numerous requirements that must fit the bill when evaluating whether a country is a developed one or not, but one that is of pressing issue is "protecting the country." A stagnant economy can be revitalized. If national security is at stake, then the citizens and economy disappear. The second is the morality of the people. They must be honest, hardworking, and follow a code of conduct; if these three conditions are met, then the nation will be prosperous. The third is the economy. If you are hardworking, then the economy will follow in your stead. Look at Germany, for example.

But, there is something that is even more important. It is that of politics. If something goes wrong politically, then it spoils everything. It is a matter of great importance, and out of all these conditions, leadership is the be all and end all. A country metaphorically, and perhaps even literally, goes "bankrupt" if it picks the wrong leader.

3 Our bare faces

Are the politicians the only ones to blame for the current predicament of our country? No. The citizens of Korea must repent too. After impeaching former president Park Geun-hye, Koreans picked unqualified people to lead. The right to vote is a part of representative politics, and the very lifeline of democracy, and yet, just look at us throwing votes around without much thought. The problem also lies with the representatives who grouped together and made all sorts of laws that landed the Republic of Korea in a hot mess.

What is the law? It is the moral standard. It is the golden rule book that the nation must abide by. The law, and the laws governing the people and the nation are of utmost importance, and the people who make these laws have great power in their hands. And yet, we foolishly picked the wrong representatives; is it so wrong to say that we put irresponsible politicians in office? Koreans should repent. Let's talk about this, honestly.

Firstly, basic manners are disregarded. I would like to call this a disregard for the golden rule book that I mentioned before. If you do not abide by the most basic manners, then you appear undignified. It causes social disorder. It also is a cause for finger pointing. Abiding by these basic, universal manners is not hard. You must have manners. Manners refer to doing unto your neighbor as you would to yourself. If you have manners, then all relationships improve, and become comfortable. There is no need to fight. Society becomes the brighter for it.

The most important and the first of what I mean by basic manners can be boiled down to one point: compromise. Compromise is exactly what I mean. Take a step back and reassess. It's a small sacrifice. Sacrificing a large fortune and stepping away from large competitions are not what I mean. Compromise is a small step in the right direction. You'll get plenty after you give them tiny portion, like the Korean saying. This is because my small concession and goodwill will win over the other person. "My acquaintance feels interested in me" is a very important part of doing business. Relationships between people become beautiful and the society itself becomes brighter; this is a shortcut that paves the way toward an ideal society.

As I said before, this is the starting point towards developing a beautiful society. Because people feel interested in each other, they will naturally help and cooperate with each other. This is the essence of harmony. The creation of an advanced society starts from the act of yielding. It's not inaccessible because it's far away. If politicians want to usher in a newer and better nation, they should start small with concessions towards each other instead of droning on and on about policies and whatnot. But unfortunately, Koreans don't know how to yield. Even when it's evident to others that they should yield and compromise, they keep charging ahead at full speed. We don't even apologize when we bump into each other in crowded areas. Doesn't this make you feel bad too?

Mothers! Listen to me. Return to your senses. Children learn manners from their mothers' knees. The average person may push his way towards the front as they enter an elevator, talk loudly, and say all sorts of things while talking on the phone. Just imagine. You feel bad as soon as you leave home and go to work. When someone holds the steering wheel, a person changes (for the worse).

I myself have a lot of foreigners as friends because of the nature of my work. However, all of my foreign friends say to me that they are too scared to drive in Seoul. Foreigners abide by the rules of the road, and concessions during driving are common. They comply with this virtue. This means that the city's functioning is even more efficient and car accidents are scarce. It's called defensive driving. Think about this. Developed nations, and people from developed nations, tend to abide by the rules of the road more than people from other nations. This is one of the reasons why they are developed nations and became developed nations in the first place.

When Korea finally began to make some money, it was around the latter half of the 1980s. Korean tourism abroad really took off during this time. As the number of Korean tourists swelled, tour agencies started booking group travel. Their destinations of choice? But of course, developed, mainly Western, countries. But much to my embarrassment, in many countries, they would have a "No Korean Tourists" sign on their hotel restaurant windows. This was because Korean tourists flocked to tourist destinations and displayed an atrocious lack of manners. They talked too loudly, ate slovenly, and made a mess in the bathrooms. How they conducted themselves was detrimental to business. My face is reddening from what I have not said to you because there were even worse things that I have failed to mention. Let's stop here for a moment.

So why did Koreans display a lack of manners that did not reflect our ancient culture and heritage steeped in values? Firstly, the parents did not teach their children well, and secondly, people do not value their own lives. If a person has manners, he will not behave this way because they don't want to earn the scorn of their peers. Because they do not know their self-worth, they do not honor other people's self-worth as well. That is why they do not know how to concede. Doing something that may be the cause for public ridicule chips away at a person's honor and makes a mockery of it. It causes people to disdain you.

My friend, please remember who you are. You are right next to me, and you are just as valued and important as I am because life is a gift.

The second is slander. This is another cause for embarrassment, but in Korea, there are lots of lawsuits and complaints lodged by the public every year, which is 60 times that of Japan.[80] They do not trust each other, which means that they lie to each other much too often. This is embarrassing. Conceding to the other party and recognizing that they are just as important... These values are not present. No wonder why they disregard the importance of the other party and file lawsuits against each other.

During the Joseon Dynasty, most people did not tolerate each other, and ridding the other party through public exile was about average. Too many gifted people were handed the death sentence. There were four rounds of purges of scholars,[81] and during the Gichuk purge in 1589, 1,000 scholars

---

80) In 2015, Korea's rate of lawsuits against another party was about 80 per 10,000 people, making it 60 times that of Japan. In Japan, there are 1.3 lawsuits per 10,000 people. (Korea Patent Attorneys Association, kpaa@kappa.or.kr).

81) The Muo Purge of Scholars (1498, four years after King Yeonsan came to power),

were murdered or forced into exile. Slander has become a part of politics ever since then. If you keep criticizing others and hurt them with words, your mouth becomes dirty, then your relationships sour, and society becomes lawless.

My dear youth of today, how can't you make a society that espouses warm-heartedness? At least, let us say hello with our kind eyes! And let us return to very Korean values such as, "You first, older brother, you first, younger brother." You, as well as I, live only once and have inherited one splendid lifetime to spend as we wish. Your life is just as valuable as mine. Don't you want to make the world a great place to live too?

Thirdly, it is the "public" spirit. Especially, there is not enough respect for one's superiors. In his book, *National Reformation*, a writer named Lee Kwang-soo laments this way. "There is no spirit of doing charitable works. There is no 'public' mindset. In thought, speech, and action, there is no sense of national homogeneity as one people, and there is only a sense of greed as they pursue personal goals for a profit. They do not take care of national affairs." Lee believes that the fall of the Joseon Dynasty was tied to moral corruption and that the Korean people needed to reform their morally bankrupt selves in his book *Gaebyuk*. This makes me embarrassed, but this was our reality back then.

In 1894, the Austrian tourist Ernst von Hesse-Wartegg[82] wrote, "Joseon's

---

Gabja Purge of Scholars (1504, ten years after King Yeonsan started his reign), Gimyo Purge of Scholars (1519, fourteen years after King Yeonsan started his reign), and Eulsa Purge of Scholars (1545, King Myeongjong's ascension year) are called the "Four Rounds of Purges."

82) Hesse-Wartegg wrote a German version of his book in 1894, then published a version in Italian, and towards the end of the book, he mentions the Korean Peninsula, Japan,

full of thieves. A corrupt official has wrecked Joseon and left it penniless and weak." This is really a cause for embarrassment too. Before the fall of Joseon, Japan sent many spies to report on its real conditions to their motherland. Their investigations proved largely to be the work of professionals. The Korean peninsula's natural landscape, national character, slavery system, military, and officers' average standing, and the proliferation of the Korean alphabet, Hangeul, was all reported without frills and was chillingly accurate. Honma Kyusuke, in *Exploration of the Joseon Dynasty*, writes a severe and cold report.[83]

"Joseon's officials steal their countrymen's assets to the point that it is worse than thieves." If a public official forgets his place and starts seeing his personal interest as above the public good, then the nation will come to an end. How horrible that 500 years later, the Joseon Dynasty was gobbled up by Japan. Let's stop talking about these embarrassing events.

---

and China by including them in a map. The disputed island of Dokdo is marked as "Liancourt," and as such, it lays a clear claim to Dokdo's sovereignty to Korea and is one of the documents in favor of Korea. (*Joseon, Summer of 1894*, Ernest von Hesse-Wartegg, translated by Chung Hyun-gyu, Cum Libro, 2012.)

83) Honma Kyusuke, translated by Choi Hye-joo, *Exploration of the Joseon Dynasty*, Gimyoung, 2008.

4 National reformation

Chun-won, also known as Lee Kwang-soo, laments in his book *National Reformation* that Joseon is "filled with falsehoods, takes pleasure in fantasies and desk argument, is lazy, lacks fidelity and loyalty, doesn't have enough courage, is selfish, lacks a sense of service to society, and lacks unity." He stresses that the first order of business is to "rid the country of negligence and prevent it from backsliding. By negligence, I mean, let us not lie, let us not deceive, in words and deeds be true, carry out works with due diligence, not talk a desk argument, and always put into practice the right thing once we think of it."

Chun-won, even in the early 20th century, thought of Korea's legacy far off into the distant future, and for this, I am humbled. But I believe in today's youngsters. Even though they may not take the complicated path outlined in Chun-won's "National Reformation," I think this generation will bring glory to this nation.

The important work starts in the home. If the mother teaches her children to be honest in the home, then the world is our oyster. In this, mothers have more access and are more responsible, in my opinion, than fathers. Oh! To the daughters of this nation, please remember that the reformation of this country starts in your hands. My beloved granddaughters, please take the lead. Honesty must be taught to children; this is a mother's loving care for future generations to follow.

To the young generations! Roll up your sleeves and get to work. It is time. It is time for you to take the lead. While during the late Joseon period the Korean monarchy fell from power due to incompetence and stagnation of its politics, leading to Japan wresting power from Korea, this is not what modern-day Koreans are. We are different! Korea will recall the spirit of the Goguryo period, and bring it back to life. The 21st century's younger generation will inherit the greatness and the dreams of former presidents Rhee Syngman and Park Chung-hee and bring back glory to the Republic of Korea.

Look! The Hallyu, or "Korean Wave." The young Korean generation has and is already doing what the developed country of Japan and so many Chinese are unable to do: shaking the very foundations of the world in cultural prestige and art in all forms. This is not the only way Koreans impress the world today. In the sector of science and technology, the world is gazing with wonder at our prowess. Korea's shining star of science and technology lies in its weapons system. Currently, the weapons that Korea develops are comparable to the ones produced by the United States, Russia, etc. Especially the K2 Black Panther, the K-9 self-propelled gun, and submarines are the ones that defense officials around the world gaze at with wonder and greedily crave.

The K2 Black Panther built upon the technology behind older generations of American tanks and adapted it into an advanced type of tank that is suitable for Korea's mountainous terrain and ensuing tactical operations. It was designed to find, target, and destroy the enemy while moving, and stands shoulder-to-shoulder with world-class main battle tanks such as ones in the United States, Germany, and Russia. Along similar lines, Korean submarines' original technology is from Germany. Germany, which handed down the technology to Koreans, is still amazed because the latter developed an even more powerful submarine than its teacher. The nuclear submarines of Koreans are world-class ones. A nuclear submarine outfitted with one of our atomic energy technologies is a powerful deterrent to potential enemy threats.

The Korean navy has about 20 years of experience with submarine technologies. But even the United States navy, which boasts a 100-year history with submarines, is frightened of Korea's submarines. During the joint exercises, our diesel submarines outmaneuvered and evaded capture for many years, while sinking about ten battleships including U.S. nuclear submarines and aircraft carriers. The Korean navy is a formidable one.

Special attention is being paid to another area in particular regarding Korean-produced weaponry: fighter jets. They are developed solely from Korean technology. This supersonic aircraft and trainer, KAI T-50, has even been exported to other countries. The KAI KF-21 Boramae is another type of fighter aircraft that is astonishing in other countries. This is all true, but most nations never share weapons technology with other countries, no matter how close. So it follows that advanced technology is up to us to develop on our own. Four types of developments impact fighter technology. These are radar, engine, defense, and stealth. The KAI KF-21 Boramae is comparable to the world's number one fighter jet, the F-35. But this technology was developed on our own. Small wonder why the Republic of Korea surprises the world. They are frightened by Korea.

In the field of guided missile systems, Korea has also garnered praise. For intercepting missiles, there is the Patriot. Of course, the United States produces first-class weaponry, and many allies own this short-range guided missile. But the type of short-range guided missile that Korea developed and produced on its own (with a little help from Russia) is superior to the American Patriot. The KM-SAM (Cheon-gung) is a type of missile defense system. Remember how good we are with bows and arrows? Our missile defense system is yet another area in which Koreans should take pride.

There is another one I'd like to mention. They are surface-to-surface missiles, called the KT-SSM (Hyun-moo). There are four generations of it already. It has the potential to be just as powerful as nuclear weapons. Thanks to negotiations with the United States, the distance limit of 500 km was forgone some time ago. When the fifth-generation comes out, what will it mean for Korea's nearest neighbors? It may have the potential to reach Japan, China, and even countries on the European continent. The Korean military is also formidable.

In "The Later Han" and "Eastern Ok Jeo," our ancestors are described as having large physiques and being very brave. They were skilled in infantry combat. The Korean Army, Navy, and Air Force inherited this tradition of excellence from those long ago. How could we not boast a little! The period prior to that of the Three Kingdoms' showed Korean ancestors' fighting spirit.

"The country of gentlemen [Joseon] lies to the North, and their attire is modest. Men wear a sword, and hunt animals as a main staple for food. When they travel, on both sides, two large tigers act as servants. They honor each other and yield when necessary, and do not fight. They are elegant and simple, and as such, they have the air of gentlemen."[84] Such is written of our Korean ancestors by Chinese scholars of Xian Qin Dynasty in the *Classic of Mountains and Seas,* or the *Shan Hai Jing.*

Meanwhile, a novel written by a long-ago Chinese scholar-official named Dongfang Shuo, called the *Shin Yi-Kyung,* praises that these "Men of the East do not offend each other, do not slander each other, and help and rescue those in need, sometimes risking their own lives to do so. At first glance, how foolish, but in ensuing glances, how beautiful and kind."[85]

In *The Book of Later Han*, the "Buyeo people are stern. They do not plunder and pillage another country, they are of a tall and large physique, their nature is stubborn and brave, and they love to sing so much that one cannot hear their songs cease."[86] In the "Eastern Ok Jeo", another person writes, "the Buyeo are simple and honest and are good at fighting with lances and talented in infantry combat."[87] So it follows that our Korean ancestors earned the praise of those from other countries, and were strong and brave, intrepid and heroic.

Our ancestors were indeed of large physique and full of valor, and additionally, were talented swordsmen and fought and won valiantly in battle, so does it not suffice to say that men from other countries may have also met them with a bit of fear? And yet, they loved to sing, so much that

---

84) *Classic of the Mountains and Seas*, Shan Hai Jing

85) *Shin Yi-Kyung* written by Dongfang Shuo, translated by Kim Ji-sun. Communication books, 2011.

86) *The Book of Later Han*

87) *The Book of Later Han*, Vol. 85; "Eastern Ok Jeo" in *The Chronicles of Eastern Ethnics*, Vol. 75.

their songs never ceased; they must have known how to enjoy life. They must have loved peace.

Our young Koreans! Puff out your chests! We are sturdy, brave, and gentlemanly and have inherited these traits from our ancient Korean ancestors. Lee Kwang-soo also had this to say about the Korean people:

"When looking at Joseon's history, there was no feudalism. Of course, during the period of the Three Kingdoms, there were countless small countries, but all of them were independent, and even if a greater, more powerful country destroyed them, they were not vassal states. The Tang Dynasty's China and Shilla were separate and established foreign relations between themselves, and the Tang Dynasty did not rule over Shilla. During the Joseon Dynasty, the latter-day Korea was not a vassal state of the Ming and Qing Dynasties. It was never formally governed by China. And if you look at the Koreans from that time period, there was a strong sense of independence."

Former Harvard University professor Mark Peterson (who now teaches at Brigham Young University) said, "First, Korea's 5,000-year history is full of aggression and chaos. It also, to use a metaphor, is a small fish in a large pond (in Korean, we say the shrimp burst because of a fight between two whales). In other words, it is full of sacrifice and weakness, and its history is that of an innocent bystander that gets hurt in a fight. Thirdly, the Joseon Dynasty was too long and was full of corruption and incompetence, and because of its [stubborn] upholding of Confucian ideas, eventually, ruined the country."

Peterson's view of current Korean history is also full of mistakes. In his opinion, if you take the long view, Korean history is not full of chaos and dismay but has enjoyed long periods of peace. Even when transitioning from one dynasty to another, it was relatively peaceful, and periods of stability were longer than periods of warfare. Additionally, Korean history is not marked by constant attacks and tainted by periods of invasion. It is not a history of a people with a history of suffering, as Peterson laments. These are misconceptions, in his view. Korea has been attacked only twice in modern history, during the 1231 invasion by the Mongolians and the Japanese invasion of 1592. To say it was attacked hundreds of times is because the verb "attack" is being misused.

So the invasions commonly spoken of may include more minor incursions on coastal villages, for example, by Japanese raiders who may have plundered, or the northern Jurchens who may have stolen some livestock from the Koreans. These types of deviant behaviors cannot be called attacks. But Koreans can be proud of something here; they never struck first. In truth, "[Ancestors] of modern-day Koreans have never attacked another country," which makes us hold them in high regard. In short, he valued our history as "History of Korea is neither that of ordeals nor of sheep much more. In which period of each dynasty was longer than that of any other, legitimacy has been well protected through prolonged peaceful history."

According to the University of Zurich, the average I.Q. of Koreans is among the highest in the world. Koreans' average I.Q. ranks among that of those from the following countries: Japan, Taiwan, Singapore, Germany, the Netherlands, Austria, and Italy.[88] Koreans' tradition of excellence has a

---

88) Professor Thomas Volken's paper, "I.Q. and its effect on national income and growth," examines the correlation between I.Q. and economic growth. He concludes that there is no causal link between I.Q. and economic growth (*Daily UNN*, May 22, 2004).

storied history, from the past to the present.

My dears, do you not wish to unshackle yourself and stand up tall for once? You can do it! The time is now! I am certain. Your generation will turn the Republic of Korea into a developed country!

Let us go!
Onwards towards the world!

Chapter Four

Rise, Young Ladies and Gentlemen

1 The turning point

Corona! The ancient Romans used to crown their victors or those with authority with a type of crown called a corolla. Do they not sound similar? In the early 21st century, the world was crowned with the wreath of death. About a year later, so many have passed away from this virus, or more than 4.7 million (as of September 20, 2021). Schools have closed and adults are isolating themselves at home without going to work. In a single day, thousands of businesses have shuttered their doors, and thousands more have lost their jobs. The world has become topsy-turvy. The flow of history has come to a standstill. What bad luck! No wonder why the world is changing (for the worse). Is this the turning point?

So, how is it changing? Even when the sky falls, they say there is always room to escape, or so says a Korean dictum. Even when the world falls to pieces, some survive, and others don't. Do they not mention that even if you enter a lion's den, if you keep your wits about you, you can manage to survive?

My young ladies and gentlemen, come to your senses. A time of crisis is a time of opportunity. It's an opportunity to leap forward, or so they say, a time when the Republic of Korea can finally become a developed nation, a nation to finally stand shoulder-to-shoulder with the rest of the first-class countries.

How is the world changing again? Who will rise and who will fall? Even during this pandemic, there are those who have seized the opportunity and gained wealth and perhaps power. So which are the businesses that are losing ground during this time of crisis? Let us take a look.

I have found a good guide. It's called *State of the Future*.[89] I have read the Korean version. I encourage you to read it at least once. This book states three important facts in particular.

The first is telecommuting.[90] Because people no longer commute to work, large office spaces have become obsolete. On the other hand, the Internet and related infrastructure for single homes have gained interest. This change and the surrounding commercial districts may have also hit the real estate market hard. Restaurants and coffee shops have been impacted the hardest by this change. But the need for oil may has shrunk, resulting in a less polluted environment, from a different standpoint.

The second is the change in university educational systems. Its very foundations are shaking. Why? It's due to the virtual classroom. Many worried. What if the world goes backwards instead of forwards? But the Internet has saved them. They put out the small fire first by continuing classes online.

---

89) *State of the Future* by Jerome C. Glenn, Elizabeth Florescu, and The Millennium Project, the Millennium Project, 2017 (Korean version, trans. by Park Young-sook, *Segye Mirae Bogoseo 2030-2050*, Kyobo books, 2020).

90) In Silicon Valley, working from home has become the new normal. Twitter founder Jack P. Dorsey said working from home for his employees would be a new fixture for the company. He ensured that employees would receive $1,000 U.S. dollars to buy the necessary equipment so they could telecommute. Facebook's Mark E. Zuckerberg has said that in the next five to ten years, about 50 percent of his company's workers may work from home.

At first, it may have been uncomfortable. An online class may feel like an imposter. Staring at a computer or a laptop screen is so different from a real person talking in a classroom. It seemed that knowledge could not be passed on through this mode of learning. However, humans adapt quickly. Homo sapiens, as we all are, have evolved very quickly within the past 300 million years due to our ability to adapt quickly. Because of no in-classroom lectures, the world quickly adapted to providing learning online.

In Japan, renowned universities that accepted Korean students have kept this e-learning going for about two semesters or about a year. In Korea last year (2020), about 85 percent of four-year universities made adjustments so that online classes became the norm for the first semester. The savvy student is already saying that enrollment fees, or tuition discounts, should be available. He is fast. University and students alike, how quickly they adapt.

Young people! Stay awake.

As some businesses boom and others perish, life is simply a fact. Thanks to the pandemic, offline meetings have shrunk. Since meetings held online, such as Zoom, have become the norm, there is less need for business travel. Even the need for business trips has dwindled. There is no need to take a 10-hour flight. Vacationing near the home is a new trend. Department stores and supermarkets have also taken a hit. For example, Woohan Brothers' food delivery has really taken off, and online shopping is thriving. Korea may be the only place where you can order pizza in the middle of a cornfield.

Even sports spectators have moved to watch the games on TV. Televisions these days provide crystal-clear images. The game is easier to watch and hear at home compared to the sports stadium. Close-up images broadcast on the screen enable us to see better than the referees. TV has brought the excitement of the game right to our doorsteps. For example, track and field events such as the high jump or the pole vault are fun to watch from the comfort of our living rooms. In slow motion! A narrow win (or miss), and the thrill of watching sports matches, have been brought to our TV screens.

The petroleum industry is shrinking; this is a mere fact. Morgan Stanley predicts that gasoline will not exceed $50 U.S. dollars per barrel. Which industries will take off is now so easy to predict. Everyone is gazing at Silicon Valley and biotechnologies. This is too easy. Of course, everyone wants longevity; is this not the most basic of human desires? Stem cell research, new medicine development, and biotech are meant to thrive.

In the world of today, you need to earn money in order to live and eat well. Earning a good living is important. But what is even more important is how you spend your money.

During the 14th century in Europe, disease and pestilence wiped out about a 1/3 of the total population. It was clearly a pandemic, and yet they could not pinpoint what it was or how to treat it, leaving millions to die. Europe panicked. Even those in the clergy were not immune, leaving people wondering as to why God's representatives on Earth were not protected. Sometimes those doing God's work died in droves, or even more so than the laity. Why? Churches are places where people congregate and come together. No wonder why the religious died in droves.

One of the reasons why I penned this book is because I wanted the younger generations to see the golden opportunity at this particular moment in time because it is one in a thousand, or so they say in Korea and China. Settle your minds and please assess where to go from this point onwards.

First, you must believe that if you can, then you can. Open your hearts. The world is now turning to the Fourth Industrial Revolution. We are just one step away from becoming a developed nation. Let us go forth! We know. That we can.

2 The Republic of Korea and the 4th Industrial Revolution

The 4th Industrial Revolution was mentioned first by Klaus Schwab, at the 2016 World Economic Forum in Davos. Schwab said, "the world's societal, industrial, and cultural renaissance will be ushered in by new scientific advancements."[91]

Germany has its "Industry 4.0" (2010), Europe has its "Horizon Europe" (2014), the United States has its "Advanced Manufacturing Partnership 2.0" (2011), Japan has its "Reconstruction Strategy 5.0" (2015), China has its "Made in China" (2025), and so on and so forth. In these ways, these nations are heralding the beginning of the 4th Industrial Revolution. While South Korea is behind these more advanced nations, I believe that it is still aware of and can keep up with the overall change in the times. We put forth our best efforts into growing national strategy and policy, and deliberated on similar topics in 2017, hence the establishment of the "4th Industrial Revolution Committee" that same year.

---

91) However, according to Great Britain's *The Independent*, "Artificial Technology (AI), robots, etc., are not new technologies, and the 4th Industrial Revolution is simply a continuation of the 3rd one." The American writer Jeremy Rifkin says, "The 3rd Industrial Revolution is in progress," and is one of the many who oppose the idea of the 4th Industrial Revolution.

So, what are the essential core technologies of the 4th Industrial Revolution? After investigating this phenomenon via 22 books published domestically, I can confidently say that they mentioned AI and IoT (the Internet of Things) the most, 16 times. Other items that were mentioned include self-driving cars (mentioned 15 times), robots and 3D printing (mentioned 14 times), and Artificial Reality (AR) (mentioned 13 times), in addition to big data, blockchains, cloud computing, and 5G telecommunications.[92]

But the situation at hand is not easy. While Korea has been called one of the leading countries when talking about Information and Communications Technology (ICT), it is still behind the times when compared to other countries such as the United States, Europe, Japan, and China. I am saying that we have not adequately prepared for the 4th Industrial Revolution. According to Roland Berger, a German consulting firm, Korea's manufacturing industry output is about 30 percent higher than other G7 nations. That is why it will be dealt a severe blow if Korea adapts to the new paradigm of the 4th Industrial Revolution.[93]

In late August 2021, the Korea Institute of Science and Technology (KIST) issued a report titled, the *Scientific and Technological Innovation Competency Analysis Report*. In this report, they said that from 2010 to 2019, Korea ranked third out of 44 countries, right behind the United States then Japan, in terms of patents issued in nine areas: AI, big data, cloud computing, IoT, intelligent robots, self-driving cars, 3D printing, biomarkers,

---

92) Moon Byung-sung, *Understanding the Core Technologies of the Industrial Revolution*, 2020.

93) Roland Berger, translated by Kim Chung-hee, *The 4th Industrial Revolution is Already Here*, Dasan Books, 2017.

and digital health. So how many patents are we talking about here? 188,160 as of this writing. But when measuring how impactful these patents were within the country or a company's technological innovations, measured by citations per paper (CPP), it ranked 20th. (only 2.8 citations) That is why while Korea has a high number of patents issued, high-quality patents were not issued, displaying that Korean patents in these areas generally failed to meet the highest quality standards.[94]

Korea has to overcome this hurdle. That is why we must find a way to leap over this hurdle. Corporations and the government need to develop cooperation relationships on Information and Communications Technology (ICT) through concentration and flexible application, and options to maintain the momentum. This is why retaining young generational talent is so important.

I would like to introduce a type of creative and innovative technology that is representative of the 4th Industrial Revolution developed right here in Korea. It is Harex Infotech Inc.'s "UB Pay," a type of contactless payment system that cuts out middlemen and puts users into direct contact with businesses that were the first of its kind in the world. It won a prize at a conference held at Harvard University in 2013. This innovative technology developed by a small-to-midsize Korean business was introduced to the world at the 2015 World Economic Forum. A year prior, the founder, president, and chief vision officer, Park Kyung-yang, had been invited to the 2014 World Economic Forum to share his vision with the world. For you youngsters, this technology is actually a Godsend for you, because it helps businesses run by younger generations and is not just user-friendly, but user-

---

94) Yonhap News Agency, August 29, 2021.

centric. This synergistic effect is so powerful.

First, as a user-centric platform that cuts out middlemen, it reduces fees for young startups and is risk-averse. But its benefits don't just end there. As you use the UB Pay system, the more it gives back to you in the long run. Through the platform that you share with others, the younger generations' ideas and products can be easily created and help grow your customer base. I would like to reiterate here that it's a type of payment system on your mobile phone so that you can "conduct safe and secure transactions," according to its official website. UB Pay also reduces the digital gap between the user and artificial intelligence, and continues to support young startups and thereby becoming a lifeline.

Secondly, for the young entrepreneur, all banks, cards, and stores are connected, and it doesn't stop just there. In all, financial investments, remittances, loans, business transactions, loyalty points, order deliveries, travel, stays, parking, self-development, hospitals, pharmacies, gyms, and cultural attractions are just some of the types of businesses that UB Pay users can use. This lifestyle platform connects various services with the customer in mind, and its customer interaction approach has unlimited potential in constructing or establishing a global presence.

Thirdly, the shared platform means that businesses do not need to develop their own software or related systems, thereby saving them money. In other words, the shared platform cuts out related costs, time, and effort, and businesses can focus on things like branding instead. Of course, this app is provided free of charge.

In May 2021, the local Korean government hosted a spring academic symposium roughly translated as, "Young Entrepreneurs (My Job) and Our Shared Tomorrow." A Youth Startup Platform Committee was inaugurated here. It announced that this committee would corporate and link each supporting startup group. Then for the next step, it would build a "sustainable" Korean "youth entrepreneur ecosystem" through a shared platform consisting of the voluntary corporation. The goal is to grow this so-called ecosystem to the level of those in Israel or the United States' Silicon Valley and surpass them by at least 100,000.[95]

A shared platform helps young business entrepreneurs, small businesses, self-employed persons, small to mid-size and even the major conglomerates. It's a win-win situation for all, and everyone benefits from its coexistence and mutual strengthening. As a user-centric platform system, it will continue to break the past paradigm and usher in a new tomorrow. It is indicative of the 4th Industrial Revolution at work.

Within the Covid-19 pandemic and its ensuing problems, lies opportunity. It can be Korea's chance to grow with the 4th Industrial Revolution. Even if the prospect turns into risk, let us go anyway. You can do it. You are fully capable.

---

[95] According to the Ministry of SMEs and Startups, research on the actual condition of young entrepreneurial startups that employed regular workers was about 84,000. This exceeds those employed by the four major conglomerates in Korea by 136,000. In 2019, these new startups created 117,000 new jobs, which was about 5.6 more times the jobs than those of the four major conglomerates. Total sales in 2019 were about 193.3 trillion won, ranked second behind Samsung Group. The contribution of venture businesses' sales to the GDP was about 80 trillion won.

3 Artificial Intelligence (AI) and Man

In 2016, there was a match of Go between Google's Alpha Go and Korean Lee Se-dol. It was a game between Korea's best Go player and a Google-developed Artificial Intelligence. Unfortunately for Lee, he lost 1:4. In Western-style Chess, AI won over humans, but everyone believed that in the game of Go, humans would outwit AI. It was definitely an upset. When master Go player Lee Se-dol lost, people were shocked.[96]

Artificial Intelligence (AI) is displaying signs that it is highly advanced and its mental activity can actually replace humans, even the best of the best. Among humans, there is a growing fear it may even replace those professions that require a lot of brainpower and talent, such as law and medicine. However, I predict that AI's ability to replace humans may be limited in scope. Instead, I feel as though they will help increase the number of jobs available for humans, thereby being a boon and an asset rather than a loss.

Recently, the Massachusetts Institute of Technology (MIT) finished a three-year study (which started in 2017 and concluded in 2020), on the ability

---

96) The fact that Alpha Go won over Lee Se-dol is actually a matter of course. This is because Google's Alpha Go used Big Data and learned hundreds of thousands of ways to play the game, and chose only methods on how to win. One person's brain is no match for dealing with millions of brains.

of AI to impact human labor. This study spanned the areas of automatic driving, the medical industry, and the insurance industry. This field study demonstrated that instead of snatching away jobs from would-be jobseekers, AI actually helped increase the number of jobs available.[97]

American economist Jeremy Rifkin, the author of *The End of Work: The Decline of the Global Labor Force and the Dawn of the Post Market Era*, said in an interview with *The JoongAng Daily* in 2017:

"In 40 years, for the first and last time in history, there will be an era that I would like to call the Great Employment. Within the span of two generations, smart infrastructure will be established all over the world. In terms of Korea, for example, all buildings will have to become "smart" buildings. All buildings will have their own self-data center and will increase their reliance on renewable energy, and its important functions will be connected to IoT. Robots cannot control this type of infrastructure. Furthermore, fossil fuels and nuclear energy's ability to be converted into power, as well as running "smart" farms, 5G networks, etc. requires human labor. In about 40 years, because of this need, there will be hundreds, thousands, millions, and billions of humans needed for this type of labor."[98]

Hyper-connectivity and super-intelligence are two of the characteristics of the 4th Industrial Revolution. What makes it possible is artificial intelligence. AI really is excellent in terms of making possible unmanned aerial drones, self-driving cars, drone delivery services, and unmanned factories. Thereby,

---

[97] Japan's SoftBank, led by Masayoshi Son, developed a humanoid robot in 2015 named Pepper. However, its limited function and error-prone ways rendered it ineffective and it was removed from hotels, department stores, and the like and was replaced by humans instead.

[98] Jeremy Rifkin, interview with *The JoongAng Daily*, Sept. 17, 2017.

I am a firm believer that AI will never displace, replace, or usurp humans. This is an unfounded worry. For example, abacus calculations or mental math were replaced by calculators that are much more precise and faster, but have they replaced human labor yet?[99] No, they haven't. Humans invented the calculator and its use has led to improvements in the workplace.

The same is true of Artificial Intelligence. AI just speeds up the process that humans would normally have taken, thereby delivering results faster with more precision. Artificial intelligence merely helps humans, and acts in a supportive role. Instead of replacing human labor, artificial intelligence merely carries out the task assigned to them. This is why artificial intelligence actually helps make humans happier by taking on assignments that are simple yet difficult. They give humans more time to do other things. They will never replace nor rule over mankind.

The limits of artificial intelligence have already been tested by the Covid-19 pandemic. In June 2021, MIT's *Technology Review* reported that, "Out of the more than 600 algorithms that have been developed for artificial intelligence, only about two have been precise enough to move from theory to practice." This caused shockwaves throughout the community at large. The reason behind this was "false data." Artificial intelligence that is equipped with false data will inevitably fail because it reaches a wrong conclusion. This means that they will be unable to display their strengths to the best of their ability. It might risk a patient's life by misdiagnosis and cause severe medical and ethical problems by becoming prejudiced.

---

99) The Korea Institute of Science and Technology (KAIST)'s current President, Lee Kwang-hyung, said in a lecture titled "Understanding AI and the Future" that "AI cannot ever replace human labor." He said that robots are able to, because of the IoT, communicate…[but] it can never use [its strength in numbers] and organizational capabilities [in the same way humans can]."

The dangers posed by the commercialization of Artificial Intelligence are some of the hurdles that this technology faces in the future. The trillions of Korean won spent on developing a supercomputer named AI Watson, may have gone to waste due to its limited capacity as a diagnostic tool, for example.

4 Aim High

The motto of the U.S. Air Force is "Aim High...Fly-Fight-Win." I would like to focus on the first part of the motto. Their stage is the sky, yet they aim even higher, pursuing a more vaulted goal. The world's best Air Force can be summed up with one phrase: "Aim High." Can we not adopt this too? Our feet may be planted firmly on the ground, but we gaze toward the heavens. This is how we improve. Do not stay in the present. Go forth, climb that wall, and aim higher and higher.

How can Koreans scale the wall and keep on striving toward excellence? It is through action. Set your goals high. Strive to look further. Your thoughts will grow in depth and breadth. The very topic of discussion will change. The silliest topic of conversation is judging other people. Who does well, who doesn't do well, slander, rumors…all these topics are useless. So what should be the topic of conversation? Goals, dreams, wishes, and hopes. One of my American friends used to quote Eleanor Roosevelt saying, "Great people talk about ideas, average people talk about things, and small people talk about other people."

When discussing ideas, you cannot but talk about a metaphoric "wall." Let us rid ourselves of ideologies, inequalities, irregularities, and lies. No, we must go even further than this, and lose our past selves. That way, we can give birth to a newer, better self. This is what ancient Eastern scholars used to say, roughly translated, "everything must become new, every single day." Every day, you should make yourself anew and greet each day with this purpose in mind.[100] This will make you aware of new problems. Otherwise you cannot scale the wall in front of you.

So who is the new I? One who has self-respect, one who yields, one who behaves modestly, and one who has surpassed yesterday's self. So how does one make oneself anew? By discussing one's wishes and hopes, always setting the bar higher, and by reading books. Starting from today let us become voracious readers. Books are the world's greatest teachers. Should we not be thankful that we have risen to greet yet another morning, that we are breathing, and have friends to meet, and that we have tomorrow to look forward to as well?

I would like to tell you a story about a strange road on the island of Jeju. Are you familiar with the Dokkabi (Goblin) Road, also known as the Jeju Mysterious Road? Two years ago, right before the Covid-19 pandemic, I went to Jeju Island. It was my first visit in quite a while.

Located towards the mid-point of Halla Mountain lies Dokkabi Road. There is a sign here to mark this place. It is a tourist attraction because of God's mysterious sleight of hand. At first glance, it looks as if the road is going uphill. But when you reach the middle of the road, and put your car gears into neutral, instead of going in reverse, it goes uphill. Is this not strange? Even when you gather all your mental faculties and gaze at the road, it is definitely going uphill because the road looks like it slopes upwards!

---

100) During the Shang Dynasty, King Tang of Shang supposedly repeated this mantra to himself while washing his face at the sink.

I stopped my car and examined my surroundings. My eyes told me one thing, and yet the car definitely went uphill. I asked my guests who were in the car with me to step outside for a moment to examine this phenomenon. They all confirmed to me that it certainly looked like an uphill road. What nonsense was this? I had an epiphany around this time that filled me with doubt. Is all that I believe true? All my five senses tell me that this road is going uphill. And yet, it is an optical illusion. So how much can I rely on my five senses? What I see and feel with clarity seems to have become opaque and misled me? To what extent should I believe? Taking this one step further, what if I believe in something that is untrue? I decided not to be bull-headed. When my senses lead me astray, how can I keep insisting that I am right?

How far can you trust your sense and rationale? There is a book I would like to introduce to you titled, *Think Again*. Written by a University of Pennsylvania professor, one line comes to mind in particular. He writes, "The smarter you are, the more mistakes you are bound to make." Adam Grant, the writer of the book, insists on this fallacy.[101] *Think Again* is a book I highly recommend to everyone, because if you are a modest person with some level of curiosity it will give you the courage to make yourself anew, over and over again.

Let's just be humbler. Arrogance is always our enemy. "If you want to stand above your fellow man, then you must be below them, and if you want to be ahead of him, then you have to stand behind him."[102] So says Lao-Tzu.

---

101) Adam Grant, *Think Again*, translated by Lee Kyung-shik. *Korea Economic Daily*, p. 46.
102) Lao-Tzu, *Tao Te Ching*. Translated by Park Eun-hee. Goryeowon

5 1988 Seoul Olympics

When we hosted the Seoul Olympic Games in 1988, we were at the pinnacle of a developing country. Now, we must scale the wall ahead of us. We are at the cusp of becoming a developed nation. What happens if we fail to take this course of action? We will rot. Even at the pinnacle, we must set our goals higher and higher. This is the logic of this world that we must learn.

One of the many mottos we adopted during this particular game was "beyond the wall." We wanted a united front that would cast aside racism and ideologies. The official motto, "Harmony and Progress," reflects this change in the times. This may have signaled communism's rise and fall, or shall I say, the zeitgeist of the latter part of the 20th century?

I hesitate to write this even now, but in my opinion, the 1988 Summer Olympic Games may have even contributed to the fall of the Soviet Union's ideological beliefs, namely, Communism. And so we rose, the Republic of Korea, to the cusp of a developed nation. Is this an exaggeration? I digress.

After hosting the games, I traveled to Budapest for the IAAF Youth Championships. A year prior, the Soviet Union started showing some cracks in its facade. I hailed a cab. The entire time, rather than keeping his eyes on the road, the cab driver kept glancing at me and asking me question after question. What were the demographics of Korea like? What were our principal exports? How did we finance the Summer Olympic Games? How did we pull off that magnificent spectacle as a developing nation? He was bursting with questions. I was sitting, a cold sweat starting to form. He was holding onto the driver's wheel, but kept glancing backward at me as he spoke.

I couldn't continue. The car stopped.
"I changed my mind. Please drop me off at the nearest hotel," I said.
We parted ways an hour later, after conversing more about Korea in the hotel lobby.

They were sincere. He hadn't been asking questions out of just pure curiosity. To them, Asia was a land that they hadn't heard of or seen before, and yet, for a tiny East Asian country like Korea to have hosted the Olympics was astounding to them. And might I say, not just astounding, but surprising as well by how well Korea did overall in terms of serving as a host country. This is something that I found out later. The shock of the 1988 Olympics extended far beyond the Hungarian cab driver. From my perspective, it seemed as though the whole world was shocked.

My prominent Japanese colleague and counterpart told me afterward, "Sensei, we have now lost to Korea." Right after the Republic of Korea hosted the Olympics, Japan experienced a kind of shock, due to our new economic prowess. There was even some speculation that Korea may overtake Japan, according to some pundits from that neighboring country.

Hungary was a giant in and of the past. Up until the early 20th century, they were a European superpower. It was a symbol of the noble Habsburg Dynasty and the prestigious country that they inherited and built. Budapest was still a beautiful city. The Danube River that flows through the capital, and the Szechenyi Chain Bridge that bridges the divide between Buda and Pest, the palace nearby…are all prominent places that move even a first-time visitor to pure admiration. An old couple promenading by the river's banks may have seemed dwarfed in comparison to the prestige of their ancient and storied history. Yet there was still an elegant simplicity to their movements that I couldn't shake off.

Until the early 20th century, this particular country was a part of the Austria-Hungarian Empire that followed Russia in land mass. It was a part of the Eastern European bloc and ranked amongst the top four in terms of industry. It was not the smaller, weaker country that I was familiar with. He may have been a taxi driver, but he was full of pride. A person from a country that has been a superpower, and one with a storied past, are different. They see the world with different eyes. They have higher standards. I am sorry to say that I don't think most Koreans are like this at all. This is because we have never been a superpower.

So, Korea pulled off the Olympics…but what about Hungary? To the taxi driver, Hungary's current predicament and the rising star of the Republic of Korea were indicative on a smaller scale that the entire world was watching us with astonishment. To me, it seemed like the world had fainted before my very eyes. I think to this day, that the Eastern European bloc was the one who was shocked the most. Until the early 20th century, they were a part of developed nations and were immensely proud of that fact. Socialism ruined them.

For a country that they were unfamiliar with, that they immediately placed in the realm of a developing country, they were astounded that we had hosted the Summer Olympiad with great success. Where was Korea located? What did Korea look like? Do they have a storied past (like us Eastern Europeans)? They were in awe, curious, perhaps even wanted to travel there…so a Korean was in my cab? What does he look like, and what is his occupation? From where did he learn about culture? His curiosity knew no end. I could and did not understand their perplexing perspective until years later.

So, what is so admirable about the Olympics?

Listen well. In the world of today, technical merit counts the most. Politics and the economy are of importance as well. But the ability to change the world lies in the humanities. A wrist with an expensive gold watch on it is less valuable than a wrist attached to a hand that plays the piano well. We may vow to avoid being punched, and yet, our hearts do not yield to this show of brute force. For hearts to yield, the arts must be appraised appropriately.

The 1988 Seoul Olympics. We sure showed the world a grand time. What was so great about this particular Summer Games? It started with the official motto: "Harmony and Progress." Something that would allow us to go beyond the wall and leave discrimination and ideologies behind. Something to unite us all. Is this not grand? And every event was planned to reflect this spirit of the Games. We certainly won over people with our artistic merit.

I will now introduce to you some festivals and events that took place then. I am warning you that some of this may sound a little boring. But how our predecessors did before us and how they managed to succeed is something I believe we must all learn. We set the bar high for all events and imbued them with our unique culture. These included sports festivals, the opening and closing ceremonies, symposiums, orchestral festivals, dance festivals, and other performances, etc.

We earned a lot of praise for the 1988 Seoul Olympics Opening Ceremony. It took place on September 7th, at around 10 a.m. About 2,000 people took part in the "Festival of the Gangsanje" River and formed a formation as if 500 floats floated into the Jamsil Sports Stadium. Imagine about 160 Wind Surfers (symbolizing the 160 participating countries) holding the various flags of the world's nations and taking the lead, and a grand fleet of 500 boats following them. No other country could have pulled it off. Even if it wanted, they have no river attached to the stadium. Seoul is a "special one."

The Seoul 1988 Olympics was a spectacle involving 160 countries (the most enormous scale thus far) from around the world. The prior one, held in Moscow, had had only 80 participating countries due to boycotts, and right before that, the L.A. Olympics only had 140 participants due to boycotts against communism. An ideological confrontation between East and West that divided country from country could not be found at the 1988 Seoul Olympics. Democratic ideals versus communist beliefs could not be found here. The entire world watched with startled eyes.

But the real spectacle took place in the opening ceremony, at the main stadium. Big drums about three meters high moved from the Hangang River into the auditorium, and dancers of over 5,000 composed of high school and university students took the stage. Under the symbols of "Sunrise," "The Predawn Path," and "In the Beginning, Light," the choreography and its execution earned praise from all around the world. This dramatic spectacle took place in Seoul, and those at the stadium, those watching from television screens from the world over, right into the bedroom, so to speak, were stunned. Members of the Soviet Union were stunned. Some insist that the fall of Communism was due to the Seoul Olympic Games. The legend of Eastern European's blame 'What has Russia done for us?' might be true.

From 1988 to 2016's Summer Olympic Games, I have seen a total of eight Opening Ceremonies in person (as the IAAF representative from Korea). So I think I can say with some degree of certainty what was done right and what they should have improved upon. I think that the 1988 Seoul Olympic Games were the best of the best out of them all, from what I've seen. Even developed nations did not work so hard to pull off the magnificent spectacle that we did long ago, and developing nations were unable to raise the bar higher.

Moreover, the symposiums, music festivals, festivals of traditional Korean music, dramas and dancing festivals, and other cultural feats earned praise and interest from pundits from all over the world. It was an all-inclusive event that pulled together 150 professionals from within the country and 111 professionals from around the world. Various topics, including the changing family and its future dynamics, communication breaks, new inclusion, etc., were discussed worldwide due to these particular games. I think it suffices to say that such a Summer Games may never be seen again, unfortunately.

On a more personal note, I have benefited from the 1988 Summer Olympiad. As the IAAF representative from Korea, I was one of its longest-serving members (I am still an IAAF Personal Member). I also helped host the 2011 Daegu World Championships. This was all thanks to the 1988

Seoul Summer Olympics. The high standard of Korean culture and my oh my, did we not show them all that we were a force to be reckoned with? It was not just due to my innate talents, but also due to the talents of the Korean people as a whole.

We must learn an important lesson from this. If we dream of becoming a developed nation, then we must have the technology to back this. And the 4th Industrial Revolution is important, but so are the humanities and related cultural philosophies.

Let us learn, my brethren. Let us go beyond the wall to become a developed nation. No, let us not just go beyond the wall, but crush it.

Chapter Five

Our Choice

1 Ceaseless Endeavors

Up until this point, we have discussed many things. The problem that lies within us, the problems faced by our neighboring countries, and proceeding with history's turning point in the previous chapter. So what task lies ahead of us, and where do we go from here?

The first is building our competence. Growing our own power so we can stand on our own two feet. In the end, innate abilities are the answer to everything. This world's rules of engagement are endless competition, endless decision-making, and adjusting to the ever-changing clime. Within these unspoken laws of nature, if you are without ability, you will be weeded out. How do you grow your talents and abilities? Through ceaseless endeavors,[103] of course! You must work ceaselessly, hone your talents, and exercise your strength. You must do your best. David beat Goliath, didn't he? This is due to competence. It's not due to brute strength. The United States of America made Germany bow to them, and even stopped Russia in its tracks. This is all due to competence.

Oh, my young ladies and gentlemen! Build your natural competence and work on your skill sets. If you have these qualities, you need not be

---

103) "The laws of nature are never-ending and flow endlessly, adjusting to the current as necessary. A gentleman looks towards the Heavens and reaches enlightenment. He never rests. He works on his own to build his skill sets." Zhong Yong.

frightened by anything in this life.

Let me discuss with you the situation of Switzerland. By 2019, its total population was about 8.5 million people. Its land mass is less than half of Korea (41,300 km squared). It's a small nation. But Germany, France, and its neighboring countries never look down on this country. Its military may consist of only 200,000 men, but even Hitler was afraid of Switzerland. The entire country armed themselves and received military training. About 3 million guns are home owned, ranking them 4th in the world in terms of personal gun ownership. Meanwhile, their GDP per capita is about $80,000 U.S. dollars.

Israel is in even more dire straits than Switzerland, situationally-speaking. They have 9 million citizens (as of 2019 estimates), and their national land mass is about 22,000 km^2. This small country is surrounded by hostile Arab nations, with over 200 million population. And yet, Israel is doing well.[104] Everyone is frightened of Israel. This is all due to competence.

How is the Republic of Korea's national security? How should we deal with North Korea's nuclear weapons? Why are we pushing our own national security towards the United States' army? Do you not know that in these times, it's all about collective security? NATO, the Mutual Defense Treaty between the United States and Korea, shows us that it is effective to have allies. Making U.S. troops stay on the Korean Peninsula as long as possible is competence. Making an ally nation uncomfortable means benefitting the enemy.

---

104) Israel has an Army, Navy, and Air Force, but their main force lies in their reserve forces. Through regular, scheduled training, they are well prepared to deal with a state of emergency. They regularly practice mobilization training and while small in size, they play war games to guard against preemptive attacks.

We don't have to hurry for self-sufficiency of national defense. To be honest, we are not yet ready. Especially the transfer of wartime operational control matter is all about time.[105] National Security requires a lot of time and money. It's a big business. If you rush it, you may end up wasting money, time, and effort. Between you and me, keeping a firm guarantor is a wise scheme.

With regards to the North Korean nuclear issue, however, there is an answer. We can arm ourselves with nuclear weapons too. But if we take this route, we face scrutiny from the international community. If we actually take the time to quit the Non Proliferation Treaty (NPT), then we will be cutting ties with the United States and other western nations and suffer from worsening economic trade relations. Japan may decide to arm themselves with nuclear weapons too, and so on and so forth. At this point, we cannot use this strategy. We must use the second-best strategy.

This means using the advanced weaponry we currently have to our full advantage. We can use the recently developed weapons such as the F-15, KF-21, F-35, Hyunn moo-4, Chun gung-III, and the like instead of nuclear weapons. Of course, these are not as powerful as nuclear warheads, but they do serve the purpose of deterrence to a lesser degree. Do not take the Republic of Korea's Army, Navy, and Air Force lightly. The Network

---

105) The Korean army needs about 137 trillion won (about 3.2 to 3.5 percent of the total GDP) to replace U.S. troop's presence on our side of the peninsula. It is advantageous for Korea to have U.S. troops stationed here until we are ready to meet the requirements for self-defense. Additionally, the Republic of Korea must meet the high standards set by the United States in areas of intelligence, surveillance, precision strike, and protection capabilities. Our wartime strategy and war planning capabilities must be strengthened.

Centric Warfare (NCW) that uses IT technology will be a critical nuclear deterrence measure.

While under the nuclear umbrella of the United States, there is something that Korea must do. Our neighboring country of Japan, up until 2002, took only one week to obtain nuclear warheads,[106] but nowadays, they may only need three days.[107] The technology is obtainable, and they have established excellent ties with the United States to make this route a possible reality. At the very least, Japan's Prime Ministers, from the 1980s, have kept on working ceaselessly towards this goal of fostering friendly relations between their country and the United States. Korea is obtaining formidable technology about the same level as Japan's as well. Smart politics would allow for the technology of short-term nuclear development.

Nuclear weapons can be a scary topic to discuss, but we do not need to fear that of North Korea. If you start with the conclusion first, then nuclear weapons are something that North Korea cannot use. They are used to stir fear and threaten. Upon using them, it's game over for North Korea. They will die. Yet they cannot give them up. Once giving up its nuclear capabilities, they will also perish. So, either way, North Korea, with regards to nuclear armament or disarmament, is between a rock and a hard place. This is called "Ja Ga Dang Chak," or self-contradiction, in Korean.

Nuclear possess is the second-worst strategy (the most worst one is a dictatorship) North Korea ever take. 1970's 'March of Suffering' was also

---

106) Prime Minister Abe (now dead) said during a lecture at Waseda University on May 13, 2002, that "Japan arming itself with nuclear weapons is constitutional. If we decide to take this route, then we can be ready within a single week." In 1975, this process would have taken three months; now it would take only a week (December 28, 2005, declassified papers from the United Kingdom).

107) *The Donga-Ilbo*, Sept. 10, 2019.

due to its wrong-taken nuclear strategy. Its leader's choice of nuclear strategy caused 2 million people's tragic death by starvation.

Gentlemen! Do you not feel sorry for North Korean compatriots? If you meet the wrong leader or adopt the wrong strategy, then they may cause you and the rest of your countrymen to suffer from distress and even starve to death. The United States may be a country of learned men, but still, they dropped a nuclear bomb, twice, on Japan. It can't be possible that The United States may have been unaware that North Koreans may starve to death. In this cold world of international politics, any nation or nation-state can be cruel; this is the reality that we must face.

2 Strengthening the ROK-US Alliance

A. Before and After Independence

On August 15, 1945, Japan waved the white flag of surrender. Their nation had turned into mud, average citizens were in complete distress, and the territory had been completely devastated. This is what happens when the people meet the wrong leader. This was their fault. But for us, we got the jackpot of "liberation".

So, who liberated the Koreans? They were the Americans. We haven't won it. In the Pacific region alone, about 160,000 brave young men from the United States died and another 250,000 men sustained injuries. But we almost forgot that without this liberation by the Americans, the Koreans of today would not exist. In February 1945, during the Yalta Conference, our peninsula was almost put into a trusteeship for about 20 to 30 years. But due to the protests of Jiang Jieshi, this became, thankfully, impossible.[108] Jiang Jieshi, as he is known, immensely helped our fledgling government and independence movement. He was a man of excellent character. He was kind

---

[108] The Cairo Declaration stipulated the independence of the Korean Peninsula, and it was said that the independence of the Korean people was due to Kim Gu, and Jiang Jieshi was moved to support this provision. But in recent years, scholars have said that Franklin D. Roosevelt, the then-President of the United States, had "supported the independence of the Korean Peninsula, and Jiang Jieshi was merely passively agreeing with him."

to us, and after WWII, his magnanimity refused Japanese compensation for war toward China.

Some people said that the U.S. drew the 38th parallel to divide our nation. This is not true. For many years, the Soviet Union had already been eyeing the Korean Peninsula. They saw a golden opportunity at hand. The U.S. Ambassador to the Soviet Union, William A. Harriman, told the newly inaugurated President Harry S. Truman, that the Soviet Union had ambitions in the Korean Peninsula as well as Manchuria, but this initially fell on deaf ears, as the United States was preoccupied with the issue of a Japanese presence in the Philippines.

On August 9th, Russian forces, in flagrant disregard of the Soviet-Japan Neutrality Pact, made their way quickly toward Manchuria and entered what would eventually become North Korea, conquering these lands at a ferocious pace. The United States was stationed in Okinawa at the time. It was too far for the available forces to reach Korea. If the 38th parallel had not been drawn, then the current Republic of Korea would not exist.

After liberation, the land south of the 38th parallel would become awash in chaos. This is because we had not engineered the liberation ourselves. We did not even have the ability to manage the day-to-day operations of the country. The orders, however, were upheld thankfully, and ironically, due to some of the civil servants who had served under the Japanese occupation of Korea.[109] When we discuss North Korea or left-wing supporters, they may attack the Republic of Korea for using former Japanese sympathizers. In

---

109) After the surrender of Japan, the changing of the guards caused civil servants and police officers to go into hiding. That is why security and administrative tasks were made difficult for the fledgling nation of the Republic of Korea. The Special Committee on Anti-National Activities thus was unable to punish war criminals.

reality, however, North Korea's then-leader, Kim Il-sung, used even more former Japanese sympathizers than this Republic.[110]

Japanese sympathizers? What a joke. My parents' generation, in the blink of an eye, lost their country. In 1935, I left my mother's womb, only to find Korea under Japanese rule. I learned the Japanese language, and until I was of age, I thought of Japan as my country. Can a person select their parents or their country? Life and death, parents and country of citizenship, are all servants of Fate. Or shall I say, God? I think a person who fights his fellow citizens, especially those of the same ethnicity, is terrible. They are the Japanese sympathizers we're talking about.

Joseon, as we were called then, had lost its way and was floating in chaos. We didn't have a leader, or the power to decide our own fate. The organizations were weak, and our goals uncertain. Among this chaos, only Kim Il-sung of the North and pro-communist forces seemed strong. And amidst this ideological struggle, the army forces rose in revolt. Left-wing forces, in particular, seemed ready to swoop in and take over everything. For example, these include the October 1946 riots in Daegu, the 3rd of April 1948 incident on Jeju Island, and the October 1948 rebellion of the 14th Regiment in Yeosu. All these incidents were the product of communist forces. Within this time frame, good and innocent people died by the hundreds. In any era, leftist forces are really problem-makers and rabble-

---

110) When the Japanese occupation of Korea ended, and some intellectuals fled to the South, North Korean leader Kim Il-sung promised not to ask about past deeds committed during Japanese imperial rule. Kim's younger brother, Kim Young-ju, had at one point been a part of the Japanese military police. Furthermore, other leaders of the new North Korean government were made up of former Japanese sympathizers. Jang Heon-geun, for example, was appointed as the head of the Judiciary Department of the People's Committee, and Han Nak-gyu, who had served in Manchuria as a prosecutor, was newly appointed as the Prosecutor General.

rousers. Did the right-wing stage any revolts in North Korea? Of course not.

During this time, a leader like Rhee Syngman emerged, and established a government, and contributed to ending some of the social and political upheavals.[111] The United Nations recognized only the Republic of Korea's government at this time. Kim Gu, Cho So-ang, Lyuh Woon-hyung, and other illustrious leaders also existed. But compared to Rhee, their view of the world was myopic at best. Rhee Syngman was a graduate of Princeton University, where he earned a Ph.D. About 80 years ago, he published a book titled *Japan Inside Out*, which garnered high praise from the Americans. In this book, Rhee discusses the eventuality of an attack by the Japanese on the U.S. soil. As the events at Pearl Harbor unfolded, this book became a bestseller.

After liberation by the Americans, Koreans' poverty is still a difficult one to explain or process. With an income of only $60 U.S. dollars per person per annum, skipping meals back then was a norm. It's difficult to imagine starvation. Gentlemen who grew up in a land of (relative) plenty in a democratic society will never understand. You don't want to hear this, do you?

If the politics of a country go wrong, then the problem of hunger will arise just about anywhere in the world. Twenty-or-so years ago, Kim Jung-il's countrymen, or about 2.2 million people, starved to death. If Koreans had not received help from the Americans, we might have been privy to a similar fate. During this time, the United States helped us without reservation. The United States set up Government and Relief in Occupied Areas (GARIOA) and the Economic Cooperation Administration (ECA), and Korea received

---

111) In North Korea, then-leader Kim Il-sung proclaimed sovereignty over all of the people north of the 38th parallel, so the citizens of the entire peninsula could not come together to vote freely to establish one government for all. Inevitably, free elections were only possible in what would become the Republic of Korea.

about $600 million U.S. dollars from these organizations.

Right after liberation from Japanese colonial rule, Korea had to deal with a great deal of instability. The United States had moved the line of defense, so to speak, to Japan, rather than Korea. This was something we did not know. The United States abandoned the Korean peninsula for a while. The United States' line of defense in the Far East was limited to the Aleutian Islands, Japan, and the Philippines. In January 1950, the "Acheson Line," was created, which excluded the Korean Peninsula from U.S. protection. Most Koreans at this time did not know the significance of this line. We were left out of the U.S. line of defense along with Taiwan. The North, eyeing this crisis, seized the opportunity to stage a predawn attack on the South. So the Korean War started on June 25th, 1950.[112]

B. The Korean War and the United States

In the early morning of June 25th, a fight breaks out by the 38th parallel. In less than three days, Seoul falls into enemy hands. This is almost too absurd for words. At this point, the United States military presence on the Korean Peninsula was just around 500 advisors. They had scaled back their operations greatly a year prior to what would eventually be called the Korean War.

I would like to repeat a saying that encapsulates the speed at which the enemy forces advanced towards the South: "In the morning, they dined at Kaesong, at noon, they dined at Pyeongyang, and by dinner, they were dining

---

112) When some communist papers were declassified during the late 20th century, Kim Il-sung and Park Hon-yong's actions in instigating a civil war were revealed. Russia's President, Boris Yeltsin, handed over papers to the Korean President at the time, Kim Young-sam. These papers were titled, loosely translated, "Stalin's attack strategy and authorization of North Korea's invasion on the South."

at Sinuiju." This was the catchphrase of the times. What a shame. These are the words directly from the then-Minister of National Defense's mouth.

At the outbreak of the war, the First, Second, and Eighth Divisions in charge of defending Kaeseong, Uijeongbu, and Gangneung, respectively, all fell without a fight like dominoes. The enemy had broken through on an otherwise peaceful Sunday morning. They were only operating at about half capacity. Most of the soldiers were away on leave.[113] But the Chuncheon area was different. The man in charge, General Kim Jong-oh, who was leading the 6th Division, held their ground and managed to block the enemy forces. General Kim's decision to suspend leave and be alert from June 24th made this possible.

How strange. Why did the front divisions make the soldiers go home on leave? This is not all. On the 24th of June, on an otherwise fairly normal Saturday evening, the Army Headquarters Officers' Club held a ball, and the festivities continued until the early morning hours of the Lord's Day. All the important officials and military officers were at this party, including the Army Chief of Staff and the principal staff. They were too drunk to notice when the first alerts were issued. Only the Sixth Division was on high alert, suspending soldiers' leave. The North Korean People's Army's 2nd Division and 12th Division fought with the 6th Division. General Kim Jong-oh's tactics was so sound that the enemy couldn't get into the trench of his division. The 6th Division's stronghold threw a wrench into the North Korean People's Army's original plans.

---

113) The Information Bureau alerted the National Defense Minister Shin Sung-mo, that North Korea had invaded the South. Still, the Soviet collaborator failed to notify the heads of intelligence and issue alerts. This gave the North, led by the Soviets, to capture the South's capital in a matter of days without much effort.

The North Korean Army had already penetrated the capital of Seoul and Gangneung, but the 6th Division's surprising show of force meant that the line of attack momentarily stopped there. This was why the enemy didn't carry out the river crossing southward and attack immediately, and why they hesitated for three days. The 6th Division's contribution is enormous here. These three days became critical for the Republic of Korea. All the military and politically crucial decisions such as the U.S.'s immediate decision of participation in war and the U.N.'s declaration of labeling the North Korean People's Army as "enemy combatants" were made just in three crucial days.

The Korean War also involved student soldiers. Two hundred executive members of each school's National Defense Students' Corps in Seoul voluntarily gathered and enlisted in Suwon, just like the volunteers during the Imjin War (the Korean-Japanese war) back in 1592. These brave young student soldiers enlisted whilst still wearing their school uniforms, participating in the Battle of Nakdong, advancing North, without ranks or service number. In total, student soldiers' enlistment would number around 27,700 young men.

The President of the United States of America, Harry S. Truman, made the decision to help Korea. For us, this move would be a "Chun Woo Shin Jo," or, roughly translated, an act that showed us "the Grace of God."[114] On the 27th of June 1950, the U.S. Air Force was deployed, along with a maritime blockade of North Korea. Meanwhile, thanks to the prompt action of the Korean ambassador to the U.S., John Chang, the UN Security

---

114) The United States believed that if the Korean Peninsula as a whole became communist, then a "Domino Effect" would occur, leading countries like Turkey and Greece to embrace this political ideology as well. This is why the United States made the decision to aid Korea during the Korean War, to stop the advancement of the Soviet Union's ideology from spreading across the western front.

Council labeled the North Koreans as invaders and took the necessary measures. On July 7th, 1950, the Commanding General of the U.S. Forces in Japan, Douglas MacArthur, became head of the newly created U.N. forces deployed to fight in Korea.

On July 8th, the U.N. flag fluttered on the battlefield for the first time, representing the 16 countries that pledged to fight for the Republic of Korea. The first of the U.S. Army that fought in this war was Task Force Smith. This unit consisted of an infantry battalion reinforced by one artillery battery. The only anti-tank weapons that the unit had were some pieces of 105 mm howitzers and 2.3" Recoilless Rifles.

On July 4th, Task Force Smith met with the Fourth Division of the North Korean Army at Osan, Gyeonggi Province. This was the first military engagement between both sides. Task Force Smith tried to stop the advance of the enemy by using 105mm howitzers, yet this tactic was ineffective. This was because they used high explosives rather than armor-piercing ammunition. The 2.3 inch bazookas were also ineffective. Additionally, the North Korean 4th division had 20 tanks.[115] This was a fight that was unequally matched, in terms of weaponry and the number of men. Out of the 550 men fighting, about a third died, another third were taken as prisoners of war, and the rest broke through and ran away. The commander, Lieutenant Colonel Smith, barely escaped with his life.[116]

---

115) General MacArthur writes in his memoirs, "Task Force Smith was a type of 'Operation Death,' given that they had to engage in combat at Osan that they would be sure to lose in order to secure the Busan perimeter." But General Matthew B. Ridgway, who would come to lead the United Nations forces later in Korea, criticizes this move in his own memoirs. He writes instead of the excessive arrogance of the Smith Task Force, which put one battalion in front of ten divisions of the North Korean People's Army.

116) While Task Force Smith lost the Battle of Osan, when the U.N. forces joined the war 10 days later, the morale of the North Korean Army greatly decreased. Kim Il-sung,

The U.S. troops were pushed back at Jugmilyeong Pass but also at the Battle of Daejeon. The head of the 24th battalion, Major General William F. Dean, Sr, was taken captive by the enemy. So how did the world's supposed best, the U.S. Army, do so poorly initially at the beginning of the Korean War?

This may be attributed to policy failures. After World War II, the U.S. military was still reeling from the Japanese involvement in the war. The 12 million-strong forces had shrunk to just two million. The U.S. Department of Defense was also negligent in preparing the forces to fight, and there was a prevailing atmosphere at the home of wanting comfort instead of more warfare.

What worsened this atmosphere and produced pleasure-seeking youth was that Americans were tired of war. They were so tired of fighting after World War II. In the eyes of the Americans, the Japanese soldiers were odd. When the U.S. finally entered WWII, as a result of the bombing of Pearl Harbor, at the very beginning, the United States forces were baffled. Why? Because the United States' opponent was using tactics that defied common sense.

The idea of an honorable death, or "Gyokusai," is not present in American tactics. If combat capability reaches a breaking point, then U.S. soldiers surrender. That is the American army's way. Yes, there are exceptions to this unspoken rule. If there is a direct order to fight to the last, then the U.S. army will. But the Japanese army is always "Gyokusai". It seemed not to place value on human lives, leaving the Americans confused. Additionally, "kamikaze pilots" were conducting suicide missions, in their eyes. But for the Japanese military, they were committing an honorable act, a heroic act of true sacrifice for their Chrysanthemum throne.

---

on July 8th, would come to request in a letter more Soviet assistance.

To put it bluntly, the Americans arm themselves with weapons, but the Japanese use their bodies as weapons. To helm a fighter jet and become part of the weapon? This was absurd in the Americans' eyes. An American pilot would drop a bomb rather than sacrifice his own life as a part of the bomb. This disparity between the two cultures disheartened Americans and made them tired of war. The Japanese did this for five unbelievable years.

On June 25th, 1950, the Korean War broke out. The American soldiers fighting for Korea were the ones stationed in Japan. They were about 18-years-old, had never seen combat. The officers didn't tend to train their soldiers as well. It was fun to be stationed in Japan. In essence, they played and spent more time in cabanas drinking and partying rather than doing drills.

So the order was issued to deploy to Korea. The soldiers arrived on the Korean Peninsula without knowing where it was. If you examine the correspondence during this time, the soldiers that had previously been stationed in Japan were deploying to Korea under the guise of going on a picnic, so to speak. They were unaware of who they would come to fight and unaware of how to use weapons. They were just deploying because orders had been issued. Why? In the eyes of the greenies in the U.S. Army, the North Korean Peoples' Army would probably run away just by the very sight of them. The North had seasoned troops and tanks, whereas our side did not even have anti-tank weapons! Small wonder why the U.S. Army failed miserably at first. The problem was arrogance.

By August, the Americans had been pushed back to the Nakdong River. Pohang, Yeongcheon, Daegu, and Changyeong were connected in a trapezoidal line of humble defense. The Battle of Nakdong River was fierce.[117] The U.S. forces fought hard to push back the advancing line of North Korean soldiers and secure the bridgehead. This is where General Walton H. Walker, the commander of the Eighth U.S. Army, Commanded his troops to "Stand or Die."

On September 15th, 1950, General MacArthur landed at Inchon and demolished the North Korean forces in a single stroke. In truth, he did not just defeat them, but he practically made them collapse. The North Korean troops had already reached the point of exhaustion at the many battles at the Nakdong River. With their retreat route cut off, exhausted North Korean troops fled to the mountains.

The Korean forces and the U.N. forces charged ahead to recover lost territory. By September 28th, they had taken back Seoul; by October 1st they had reached the 38th parallel and pushed further north. It seemed like reunification was within our sights at this time. But after October 25th, something unexpected occurred. The Chinese People's Volunteer Army entered the war. Over 300,000 men hid in North Korea's mountains. The U.N. forces and the Korean army, kept advancing further north, unaware of the dangers ahead. In early November, the Chinese forces that had been in hiding came out of the mountains, surrounding the unsuspecting U.N. and Korean forces. We bid a hasty retreat, without a fight. To give up without a fight when reunification was within our grasp! I still believe that if it weren't for the intervention of the Chinese forces, then the Korean Peninsula would not be divided today.

---

117) John J. Muccio, the U.S. Ambassador to Korea, advised the then-Korean President, Rhee Syngman, to move the official government to Jeju Island when the enemy forces infiltrated as far south as Daegu. At this time, Rhee is said to have replied, "The communists will come for my wife and shoot her, then kill me with a single bullet. We do not plan on moving the government off the Korean Peninsula. We are not going to run away."

Chapter Five Our Choice 263

During this time, the worst of the fighting was the Battle of Changjin Reservoir. It was between the North Korean army and the First U.S. Marine Division and the part of U.S. 10th Army Corps. When was this? November 1950. The fight took place 2,000 meters above sea level in a mountainous area. Changjin Reservoir is located in North Hamgyeong Province where the temperatures can drop to a low of 30 degrees below Celsius. But in that very year, temperatures were around minus 40 degrees Celsius. The trapped troops in this mountainous area included the First U.S. Marine Division, two regiments of the Seventh U.S. Infantry Division, one battalion of the U.K's Royal Marines, and so forth, totaling about 30,000 men. They were surrounded by 120,000 troops of three Chinese Corps.

Major General Oliver P. Smith led the U.S. Marine Division at this time. On November 27th, for a period of two weeks, they bid the most difficult retreat in the U.S. military history but were successful overall in evacuating their men. General Smith was also able to return with his life intact. He used the airfield in Hagaruri, North Hamgyeong Province, to evacuate men via plane. They relocated the division headquarters from this area, but this plane evacuated the wounded and killed first. Until the very last, General Smith broke the siege and escaped to the port city of Heungnam with his men.

North, south, east, west. Everywhere they turned, they seemed to be surrounded by the Chinese Army. Every road seemed blocked. The only chance for survival was a local road toward the south. So the Division commander broke through enemy lines and made an escape route that led down south again.

"Are we retreating?"

Someone asked.

"Retreat, hell! We're not retreating. We're just advancing in a different direction."

These are the words, straight from his mouth.

Before penetrating the siege, this is what the General said: "I'm going to fight my way out, I'm going to take all my equipment and all my wounded and as many dead as I can. If we can't get out this way, this Division will never fight as a unit again." He actually collected as many wounded and killed as possible and evacuated them first via available planes. Not leaving fallen soldiers behind was a tradition of the U.S. Marine Corps. And he broke through the siege and came south.[118] While the retreat was widely regarded as a success, the losses sustained were severe. About 17,000 casualties and 7,400 more were taken out of action due to frostbite and the like. The casualties of the Chinese numbered over 50,000.

During the three-year war, the total strength of the U.S. forces deployed to Korea was nine divisions, amounting to as many as 1.8 million personnel. Out of these, there was a special unit that I would like to mention in particular. This was the U.S. 2nd Infantry Division. This Division was established in Paris, France, during World War I on September 21, 1917. During its 100-year strong history, it was stationed in Korea for over 70 years. This division became not just American but a kind of native Korean division. Ever since it was dispatched to Korea in August 1950, it has been stationed here.

The one that fought the hardest and the most was also this division. Its

---
118) The success of the U.S. Marine Corps in withdrawal can be attributed to Pace's special task force, who sacrificed themselves and became prisoners of war, so that the U.S. Marines could be saved.

nicknames include Warrior Division and Indian Head whose motto is "Second to None!" The first time they were dispatched to Bakjin Ferry in Changnyeong County, downstream of Nakdong River. This was around the time of the Inchon Landing by General MacArthur, most of the men were picked up for Operation Chromite, so there was a shortage of men. Bakjin Ferry was assigned to the 23rd Regiment, 2nd Division, and their front was 5 km wide, which was five times the standard front. On August 9th, the 4th Division of the North Korean Army fully attacked them. It was NK's final attack from Changyeong to Busan trying to isolate the U.N. Forces in the Daegu area.

The 23rd Regiment fought desperately with the one enemy division. Every company commander in the Regiment was killed; one company got filled up with new company commanders three times. Two-thirds of the whole Regiment were sacrificed. The North Korean Army's attack faltered and its 4th Division also became exhausted. The Nakdong River bridgehead was almost penetrated. If the 23rd Regiment had not fought well, what would have happened to the U.N. forces and the Republic of Korean Army?

Every November 30th, during the evening, there is a battalion that sets fire to its flag. It's the 2nd Division's Engineer Battalion. This tradition, called the "Burning of the Colors," started on November 30, 1950, in North Pyeongan Province, where the U.S. troops stationed there were about to meet the Chinese People's Volunteer Army and the North Korean Army in battle. The Battalion commander, Lieutenant Colonel Alarich Zacherle, felt the crisis of being wiped out. Rather than get their flag captured, he decided to burn the battalion flag instead. This was done so the enemy forces could not wield the flag upon capturing them. The annual "Burning of the Colors," commemorates, to this day, this very notion.

The reason for this crisis was that they were ordered to take the rear by the Division commander at the moment of complete siege by the Chinese army. The U.S. Engineer troops are traditionally fighters. During this retreat, the 2nd ID's Engineer battalion took the hardest fight. Though they got out of the Chinese siege with extreme difficulty, only 266 out of 977 men came back alive. Lt. Col. Zacherle himself was captured and freed after two and a half years in an enemy's prison camp.

The Korean War's dead and wounded, as well as the total number of participants and the like, can be seen through this graph below:

Participant nations	Total forces committed	KIA	WIA	MIA	POW
South Korea	1,269,349	137,899	450,742	24,495	8,343
The United States of America	1,789,000	36,940	92,134	3,737	4,439
The United Kingdom	56,000	1,078	2,674	179	997
The Netherlands	5,322	120	645	?	3
Canada	25,687	312	1,212	1	32
France	3,421	262	1,008	7	12
Australia	8,407	339	1,216	3	26
New Zealand	3,794	23	79	1	
The Philippines	7,420	112	229	16	41
Turkey	14,936	741	2,068	163	244
Thailand	6,326	129	1,139	5	?
South Africa	826	34	?	?	9
Greece	4,992	188	459	?	?
Belgium	3,498	104	336	?	1
Luxembourg	83	2	15	?	?
Ethiopia	6,037	122	536	?	?
Colombia	5,100	163	448	?	28

Data: Institute for Military History, MND, "The Korean War through Statistics," 2014.

During the three-year-long Korean War, the United States sent 1,789,000 men to fight for us. They suffered heavy casualties, as they sent the most number of soldiers. The U.S. Army's death totaled 36,940, wounded at 92,134, 400 Airforce fighter jets downed, and 2,000 airmen dead. Out of the combined U.N. Forces, they sustained the heaviest losses.

If we think about it, we are a nation with a deep relationship with the United States. More than hundred years prior, when Japan tried first to annex the Korean Peninsula, the United States pretended not to notice. This is what we like to call the "Taft-Katsura Agreement."[119] If the United States had just shaken its head back then, then the Korean Peninsula would never have had to endure years of Japanese imperialism.

Isn't this a bitter pill to swallow? But this is what international politics is. If you want never to be caught in a trap of international politics, then you must first grow your national power. But as fate would have it, Korea would gain an advantage from the U.S. for liberty. Even after liberation from the Japanese, they provided us with food and economic aid. After the Korean War, they continued to maintain a presence of forces and protect us. Thanks to these ties, we have risen as a country and are now even in a position to help other countries. Gentlemen, this is the first time that Koreans have lived a reasonably "good" life. Yes, I know. Some skeptics will say that

---

119) The agreement had three main points. First, the United States said that Japan should not invade The Philippines. Instead, the United States would rule over that country should the need arise. Second, to secure peace in Asia, Japan, the United States, and the United Kingdom's three governments would need to work towards the same goals, and the result would benefit all three parties. Third, the United States would agree that Japan's annexation of the Korean peninsula would be a natural result of the aftermath of the Russo-Japanese War of 1904-1905, and Japan's imperial rule over Korea would secure East Asia's peace.

the Americans only helped us because they would also benefit from this alliance. That is why I am still thankful.

I usually travel to the United States of America once a year for business purposes. I always go to the Korean War Veterans Memorial in Washington, D.C.'s West Potomac Park, to pay my respects to the fallen U.S. soldiers. This is my small gratitude toward the United States. Starting this year, every person who served in a branch of the U.S. military during the Korean War will have his name engraved on this war memorial. The interesting part? The first KATUSA members' names, or the Korean Augmentation to the United States Army's names, will also be engraved as well. Americans never forget their brethren that they fought alongside during the war. This is an American tradition, and the American Way.

At the West Potomac Park, in front of the fountain, there is a plaque engraved with the following words:

> "Our nation honors her sons and daughters
> who answered the call to defend a country
> they never knew and a people they never met.
> FREEDOM IS NOT FREE!"

C. After the Korean War

The Korean War left devastation in its wake; our entire country was in ruins. Our fate seemed sealed; we were in desperation. We did not have enough to wear or eat. This is embarrassing to admit, but it would not be a far stretch if we called ourselves beggars at this time. So who helped us during our time of need? The Americans. The United Nations Korean Reconstruction Agency (UNKRA) also helped enormously. The Americans borrowed the name from the U.N. because this tiny peninsula would come to symbolize the ideological war between the communists and the free world, and they needed a reason and justification for helping Korea.

Between 1955 to 1960, the assistance organization called the Foreign Operation Administration (FOA) was renamed the International Cooperation Administration (ICA) and provided about $15 billion U.S. dollars in aid. About two-fifths was to be used for bolstering the economy, while the rest was to be used for military assistance. At this time, the military aid budget constituted about 77 percent of our total national defense expenditure.[120]

This emphasis on military aid would transform the Korean army into a real army. The first and second headquarters of the army, along with the military base command and a military district command, etc., were founded back then. About ten reserve divisions were also founded at this time. It was 1954. In truth, the Korean army would be called a real army, with combatant capability, after it participated in the Vietnam War.

In June 1950, when the Korean War first broke out, the Republic of Korean army's capabilities did not extend further than a "National Defense Constabulary" of sorts. Instead of being a suitable organization with combat capabilities, it was more like a police force. Small wonder why we lost the capital of Seoul, just a mere three days after being invaded.

The dispatch of our troops to Vietnam was when the United States really

---

120) Kwon Oh-joong, *Post-establishment of the Republic of Korea, the United States' Economic Aid* (1948-1960), The Center for Free Enterprise, Oct. 4, 2018.

started looking at us as partners. During and after the deployment of Korean troops to Vietnam to aid the U.S. in their war efforts there, the military aid budget would increase and the quality and the content of the assistance from the Americans would come to change.

After the armistice, the U.S. Army's massive withdrawal[121] would see the U.S. send over tactical nuclear weapons deployment[122] to bolster Korea's defense system in the years to come. And through its military advisors, the Korean army's organization, weapons system, and force structure would come to be efficient and combat ready during wartime operations.

When the Korean forces were dispatched to Vietnam during the Vietnam War, Korea would benefit from its global positioning, not only from the modernization of its military. Moreover, the deployment of private corporations to Vietnam turned out to be formidable. Additionally, the expansion of middle-east advancement opportunities caused as an effect of deployment to Vietnam allowed Korean workers to perform economic activity all around the world. We should acknowledge that attaining trust from allies and becoming a partner in the international relationship enormously affects the nation's interests.

The R.O.K.-U.S. alliance would be further strengthened via the Combined Forces Command (CFC), established on November 7, 1978. You would be hard pressed to find such an alliance in the world. It has its roots in the

---

121) The United States Army deployed up to 325,000 men, but by 1954, it had shrunk to 223,000, and by 1955, it was just 85,500 troops.

122) The United States, in preparation for potential conflict between China and Korea, would establish the "Pentomic Division," along with sending the missiles "Honest John," and "Nike Hercules" to the Republic of Korea.

United Nations Command (UNC), which evolved into what is currently the most important R.O.K.-U.S. military alliance to date. The UNC was pivotal for the survival of Korea during the Korean War (1950-1953).

Under the command of a four-star American commander and a Korean deputy commander of the same rank, it is a unique combined forces mission consisting of members from the two nations, who have pledged to keep the peace on the Korean Peninsula from aggression from outside parties during times of war. It consists of "600,000 active-duty military personnel [as well as about] 3.5 million Korean reservists [should the latter be needed during times of war]," according to its official website. The two countries alternate the "chief of staff" and the "deputy" as needed.

In 1975, when South Vietnam became communist, the leader of North Korea, Kim Il-sung, who wanted to invade the South again, visited China and Eastern Europe in hopes of bolstering North Korean support for another invasion.[123] However, U.S. President Gerald R. Ford embraced the "New Pacific Doctrine," which entailed keeping the United States a superpower to secure and stabilize the East, including the Korean Peninsula. James R. Schlesinger, the U.S. Secretary of Defense at the time, warned that if North Korea invaded the Republic of Korea, the U.S. would not hesitate to use nuclear weapons on the belligerent country.

For the U.S. troop withdrawal, Korea required military aid for the five-year modernization plan of the Korean military. The U.S. provided $1.5 billion U.S.

---

123) William Colby, the former director of the CIA, tried to find support for North Korea invading the South again this time, but the Chinese convinced him otherwise. *The Dong-A Ilbo*, March 2, 1984; "Kim Il-sung's visit to Beijing during the Indo-Chinese embrace of communism," *Dong-A Research*, 39th edition, Book 1, 2020, pp. 221-244.

dollars. In 1971, direct military aid to Korea grew by about 15 percent from the previous year, and 95 percent of economic aid from abroad was from the U.S. during a decade.[124] Between the years of 1976 to 1980, U.S. military aid toward Korea was a key factor that grew Korea's economy and stability. President Park Chung-hee's strategy of boosting the heavy and chemicals industry, or export-oriented trade succeeded thanks to the R.O.K-U.S. alliance. And after the 1990s, the Republic of Korea won an ideological confrontation against North Korea based on the R.O.K-U.S. alliance.

Currently, the Republic of Korea has about twice the population of North Korea, and its nominal gross domestic product (GDP) is about 55 times that of North Korea.[125] Our practical prowess is outpacing North Korea by 100 to 1000 times according to criteria such as car manufacturing, shipbuilding, steel materials output, and number of holding ships.

---

124) Norman D. Levin and Richard L. Sneider, op., cit., pp. 48-51.

125) By 2020 standards, Korea's nominal GDP was 19,331,524 billion won, while North Korea's nominal GDP was 346,603 billion won. Ministry of Unification, Republic of Korea (https://nkinfo.unikorea.go/kr/nkp).

3 Mending our relations with East Asia

A. Chinese conduct

As for China, what happened to its ancient and storied past when it stressed humanity, filial piety, and brotherly love as virtues? The problem is the Chinese government, which has implemented the "Northeast Project" to appropriate other cultures and states, such as ancient Korea, and consider them former vassals of ancient China. This is just too Sinocentric. So why has China embarked upon this strange strategy? To make matters short, it is because it is afraid. What are they afraid of? They are afraid of division.

China's national land is too large. By 1,000 B.C., the Zhou Dynasty had united the feudal country under one imperial house. But while the Chinese are the same Han people, their identities are a little bit different. Regional dialects, for example, varied so widely that even just 50 years ago, they had difficulty understanding one another. Each region had its strong characteristics, so when the central government showed very few symptoms of vulnerability, China was divided into several regions. China experienced the Warring States Period, and the Xinhai Revolution of 1911 saw warlords rise and take their own land. Even nowadays, Xinjiang Province, Tibet, and some other regions remain unstable.

Some regions such as Gando and Primorsky Krai have deep connections to Koreans to this very day. Jilin Province, near the Yalu and Tuman River, is home to many Korean-Chinese, the only ethnic group who has a mother nation. China definitely cares about this. The Northeast Project is, in my personal opinion, a type of revisionist history. Furthermore, it tries to absorb one of our historical periods and make it a part of its own. According to China, "the Goguryeo people were a minority group of China. Goguryeo was founded within Chinese territory and should be considered part of one of the Four Commanderies of Han. After the fall of Goguryeo, the Goguryeo people were absorbed into the Han Chinese. Thus, Goguryeo was a part of China."

If we are to believe this version of events and that Goguryeo was part of the Han peoples' dominion, we have to examine the facts. According to the territorial as well as the personal principles, Goguryeo was never a part of China. These two criteria aren't even needed, for during the Three Kingdoms period of Korea, as well as *The Chronicles of the Three States* document the Korean kings' reign over the Korean peninsula. So I wonder why the Chinese are trying to, so many centuries later, not in those days when they were much more powerful, absorb a part of Korea as a part of China. Why is it partaking in revisionist history? It is due to trying to cut off the so-called "origins" of Goguryeo and modern-day Korea.

Out of the 55 minority groups in China, the ethnic Koreans rank 13th, numbering around 1.3 million. It is worth noting that they still speak the language (Korean), and still identify as ethnic Koreans all these years later. The areas in which many of them reside are actually a part of ancient Korea. Gando, for example, was a part of Goguryeo. As the Republic of Korea grows, the Chinese fear that we may declare those lands where the ethnic Koreans reside almost as a part of our own. But to actively engage in revisionist history? What a cheesy scheme.

Furthermore, about ten years ago, there was something even stranger. Chinese Communist Party incited young Chinese to slander Korea and threat Korean living in China. They fostered national extremists so-called "Young People of Anger," and made them take the lead.

"Do you know that Korea is, from ancient times, a tributary of China?"

"The Chineseness is the center of the world, and the Chinese people are a great people."

During the 1990s, this is the phrase that Korean compatriots heard from the so-called "Young People of Anger," or the "Furious Youth." They also engaged in "Guan Shui fa," active brainwashing. "Guan Shui fa" is the education of brainwashing hatred toward imperialism, capitalism, Japan, and U.S.

There is, unfortunately, more. The communist Chinese have created and continue to support something called the "Small Pink." They consist of the younger generation born during the 1990s. From birth, they are indoctrinated to love and support their nation. The Small Pink is different from the Furious Youth, who received this training from their primary or middle school years. Even from birth, the Small Pink seems to be indoctrinated. A fierce feeling of patriotism stirs from their very bones. They are also well educated. About 73 percent of them have bachelor's degrees, and about 37 percent hold degrees beyond master's[126] degrees. The Chinese Communist Party has created the 21st version of 'smart' Red Guards.

---

126) Kim In-hee, *The Chinese Patriotic Red Guards, the Furious Youth* (Blue History, 2021), p. 21.

Is it not good to develop a patriotic youth organization? On the one hand, that is fine. I am not criticizing the principle of helping the young be proud of their country. But the real problem lies in what these young people believe. In my opinion, the Chinese are indoctrinating their young with a revisionist view of history and planting seeds of hatred against other countries. This is seen, for example, through their dislike of foreign countries and their extreme and sometimes even violent ways.

The reason why I am bringing this up is that I worry about Korea. Koreans are mainly the targets by the Chinese. So why do they attack us? Even up until the 1990s, our small divided country of the Republic of Korea enjoyed better livelihoods, for the most part, than our much larger, neighboring country of China. The leftists tend to lean towards jealousy. When they see something good happening for someone else, they get jealous. This is absurd. At least, this is their thinking.

Not only are the Chinese communists jealous, they are also frightened. What if the Republic of Korea gains so much power that it sets its sights on former Goguryeo's lands? So, China's thinking was to tame them beforehand. China is trying to absorb Goguryeo into its own history. They are controlling the Furious Youth and the Small Pink so that South Korea never even dreams of taking back their lost ancient territories. They are trying to safeguard their future. One of the furious youth has even written thus:

"The tiny half-divided country of Korea is lying to the world and stealing away [our] culture. Korean culture is a hodgepodge of cultures brought in from other countries, yet their core culture is embedded in the Chinese ways of old (Confucianism), and only afterward did they incorporate elements of the culture of the United States as well as Japan." (Author's note: I cannot bear to translate the rest because it is so racist.)

Korea has deftly dealt with China for over 1,000 years, and yet, we have kept our identity. There are those who dislike our ancient ancestors and speak badly of them for bowing to China back then, but I think criticism leveled at them is unwarranted. I believe our Korean ancestors were wise. They kept their identity, which was such an excellent achievement. If they had not kept their worship toward China, what would have happened? There will be no end to arguing over this issue.

That for 5,000 years, our Korean ancestors kept the peace on this peninsula is nothing short of a miracle, due to the combined reasons of our wise ancestors and Chinese tolerance. But today's China does not display the same type of tolerance towards us. Why are the 21st century Chinese so different? Are they really that unconfident? Can they not see the people in front of their very eyes? They are arrogant. Yes, it is true that China made some money. They are rich now. Are they not the second largest economy in the world? By 2030, won't they have caught up to the United States of America? And yet, even if these projected forecasts turn out to be true, how can they treat their neighbors in this manner?

This is not fitting behavior for a great nation that is also very large, a great power, in other words. If they follow this route, I fear that they may fall into the Thucydides Trap.[127] If this type of disaster occurs, then the entire world

---

127) This trap refers to the tendency to go to war "when an emerging power threatens to displace an existing power" on the global or regional scale. In today's terms, it refers to an armed conflict between an established power and a newly emerging power when the emerging one threatens the economic world order via a new hegemony.

will suffer greatly. It will usher in tragedy for all.

"Tao Guang Yang Hui?" This Chinese phrase, roughly translated, means "hide brightness and nourish obscurity." Do not show yourself and grow your power and ability while in hiding. This is not a good phrase. It is wicked, in my opinion. Why hide and hone your skills? What kind of action are you going to take in the future? The very fact that you are hiding means that there may be a conspiracy at hand. It is not something that a gentleman would do. It is immature. If you are fair, then why hide some things?

These days, China is also doing something that puzzles me. They are claiming Spratly islands in the South China Sea belong to them. The Philippines and Vietnam have protested against Chinese sovereignty over these islands. But China has recognized only the 12-nautical mile limit of territorial waters permissible under international law. The rest, they say, or about 90 percent, belong to China. But with regard to Vietnam, the Chinese cannot always have their way. That is because Vietnam is home to a strong people. The Chinese have been pushing for historical sovereignty over 2,000 years ago over these disputed territories. And yet, these islands are missing from the historical record of the Chinese; they claim the land is theirs anyway because their imperial emperors ruled over this region long ago. No wonder it's a stretch to say that these islands in the South China Sea belong to China alone.

About five to six years ago, they started making man-made islands. On a rocky island, they have established a docking facility as well as an air base, and even made military bases there. What is civilization? It is leaving barbarism as far behind as possible. Why is barbarism destructive? Because barbarism means the law of the jungle, that's why people reject barbarism and prefer civilization.

China is a country that has vastly increased its wealth. Within the past 30 years, their economic growth has grown over 9 percent yearly; this is nothing short of a miracle. They are also home to about one-fifth of the world's population, a great country. Not only this, but starting from the early 1990s to 2015, their rate of spending on defense rose even more than their pace of rapid economic growth.

After President Xi Jinping's inauguration, the growth rate of the economy may have dipped to seven percent, but their spending on national defense has risen to above 10 percent every year. If a huge country like China has marked a 10 percent growth in its economy, and if it also increased its spending on defense year-on-year by 10 percent, then a complex problem arises. This causes tension in the realm of international politics.

Hasn't China changed already? China is flexing its muscles! And yet, the United States wouldn't stand this alone. Race for hegemony is inevitable. In a place like this, a small country like Korea must be careful. I think former President Park Geun-hye and the current administration conducted our affairs improperly. At first, they must have tried to use China as a powerful leverage to appease North Korea. Foolish fools! China cares more about North Korea than about the Republic of Korea. No matter what, they will protect North Korea. If something goes wrong with North Korea, then China falls into a quagmire. That is why they say, "Sun Mang Chi Han," or "lips keep the teeth from chattering." China, during North Korea's long-range missile launch of 2016, its fourth attempt, pretended not to notice. Rather than ensure our national security, China would rather ensure North Korea's survival. Former President Park Geun-hye missed simple math.

To play the double game is not a strategy you can pull out whenever you want. It only works if you have enough power so the others would study your face. If a small country like Korea tries to befriend two countries at the same time, then we will most certainly deserve the censure and be called a vulgar country. This is why I say our Korean ancestors were wise. This is why President Park lost her favor with the U.S.

Regarding the North Korean nuclear proliferation issue, I hesitate to say that there is really no solution. This is my personal opinion. The United States, and even China, have no solutions either. Four-party talks, Five-party talks are all in vain. There is one person who may have the answer: the young leader of North Korea himself, Kim Jung- un. But he does not wish to give up nuclear weapons even if he dies! If he gives up nuclear weapons, he thinks he may die. Who can reason with a man who believes he will most certainly die? You can cajole, you can threaten, but these tactics will not work. The best possible method, in my opinion, is to obtain nuclear weapons ourselves. But in reality, we cannot use them. That is why we must consider a second-best solution: conventional weapons. Of course, nuclear weapons are the best type of weapons. You cannot get more powerful weapons than nuclear weapons. So you are just going to give up? Of course not.

If well organized, even the conventional method could be a lethal weapon. So we should prepare the best suitable option with all possible methods all by ourselves. The Republic of Korea's Army, Navy, and Air Force are all fighters, only without nuclear weapons. The next step is to realign with our greatest ally, the United States of America. They have a nuclear umbrella and are also able to share nuclear weapons with NATO member nations.[128]

---

128) Belgium, Germany, Italy, the Netherlands, and Turkey usually share nuclear weapons. During times of peace, nukes are usually stored in a nuclear-free zone, and are

But is this a sure-proof strategy? No. The problem lies within us, and our credibility. We have become annoying to the U.S. government.

Once we regain our credibility in the U.S., there would be a better option. This is via what I would like to call nuclear fuel recycling, or nuclear fuel reprocessing. The amount of after-use nuclear fuel stacked in a single nuclear power plant in Gyeongju is already enormous. It's the same amount as 3,000 rounds of nuclear bombs.[129] The average life expectancy of nuclear fuel is 20 years in Korea. Twenty-three nuclear reactors are working now, and nuclear waste is almost full in the depot. If reprocessed, it could be used as fuel, a pure domestic energy resource. But the U.S. doesn't allow this nuclear fuel reprocessing at all.

Japan, on the other hand, has plutonium, 47 tons of it, in fact, which has the power of about 6,000 atomic bombs. It also has the ability to recycle nuclear waste products. The Japanese administration worked ceaselessly for about 10 years to bring this to fruition (getting the permission of the United States to reprocess the nuclear byproducts).[130] If Japan needs atomic weapons, it

---

overseen by the U.S. Air Force. Without the direct authorization of the U.S. President, the nuclear weapons cannot be used. The secret password, PAL, must be entered for the nuclear weapons to be launched.

129) The Republic of Korea currently has about 16,000 kg worth of Pu-239s. One nuclear bomb usually needs 5 kg worth of Pu-239s in its making, which means that we can make about 3,200 atomic bombs with the quantity of Spent Nuclear Fuel currently in our possession. The "Father" of Korea's nuclear power plants, Dr. Lee Byung-ryeong, said, "Korea is capable of making a nuclear weapon within seven months. It just needs to harness the manpower and use its technical and manufacturing capacity in an efficient way." This projection is shortened even more by American standards. According to Mr. Westinghouse, a former executive, Korea will "only need about four months to create two to three nuclear bombs" (*The Joong-Ang Ilbo*, Sept. 21, 2017).

130) The United States-Japan Nuclear Agreement has been renewed automatically after 30 years. Japan is the only one of the few atomic bomb-free nations that have been granted the permission to reprocess and recycle its nuclear waste products and

can make one within three to four days. This is all because the United States turned the other cheek and closed its eyes.

In early 2010, when China started to grow rapidly, the entire world became uneasy. The United States and its view of the world order, in which it was its center, became threatened. This is because many scholars predicted Chinese hegemony. Amidst this Zbigniew Brezezinski wrote, *Strategic Vision*. He writes:

"If the United States loses its hegemonic power, then Korea will stand at a painful crossroads. The first will be for Korea to acknowledge China's hegemony in East Asia, and create national security by relying on China. Secondly, it must put aside past hostility with Japan and strengthen its ties with this nation. The Republic of Korea must choose one of these options…the last choice is for Korea to ensure its national security by itself."

No matter what Korea chooses, it will be a difficult choice. This is the embarrassing crossroads that this nation will find itself at, in the future. But at least right now, the situation is a bit different. Many have put aside the idea that China will achieve regional dominance and hegemony in recent years. There are signs of China's decline everywhere.

I would say that the choice is obvious. In Korean, we say this is "Myung Yak Kwan Hwa." So, which will it be? China or the United States of America? You must choose just one. I choose the United States. This is a strategic choice. I love the profound history of the Chinese and its philosophy of old. But I disagree with Chinese hegemony. The China of today is not to my liking from a Korean survival perspective. From a moral perspective and

---

generate plutonium (*The Joong-Ang Ilbo*, July. 15, 2018).

via its actions, it is not acting like the adult it is.

Having lived some 80 plus years, I have come to realize that life is a series of choices! The success or failure of something is also relegated to choices. This is how important decisions are. But there is no need to worry; it's not that hard. You will not make mistakes if you always stay positive and select the "open" option, and or the brighter option. And you must think of which choice will be patriotic, then you will obtain the right answer.

So, should we head for the oceans or the continents? There is no need to worry over this choice either. The ocean is open while the land is blocked. The open place is the lucky place; this is what we call "gil ji" in Korean. The ocean is open. No matter which route you take on the sea, it is still a route. The continents have mountains and rivers. Of course, I select the ocean. This strategic choice I will explain to you right now in the following paragraphs.

Look at historical examples. Pax Romana, Pax Britannica, and Pax Americana: all are the result of maritime forces. Since the oceans are open, you are free to come and go as you please. We Koreans are without resources, so we must make a livelihood via trade. If we do not approach the oceans, then we cannot put food on the table and have a roof over our heads. For the past 500 years, we have been stuck near the mainland. This is so embarrassing. Did we not live in servitude? If we spend too much time thinking about which course of action to take, we run into problems. If we try to have it both ways, then we will get into trouble. If we yield to neighbors, calculate trade benefits, and try to save face, we will harm our national security.

According to George Friedman's book, *The Next Decade*, the world will not change much within the next ten years, but he makes some valid points that are worth noting.[131] Friedman says: "Within the next 10 years, China will face a crisis because of its reliance on export dependence and the paradox of poverty. On the other hand, Japan will rise as East Asia's greatest power. At this point, the United States will help the collapsing China and make a companion of the united Korea to hold Japan in check." This man, I believe, is on the right track.

Gentlemen! Stay awake!

Friedman is excellent, but I do not know if he delivers a miracle. But the think tank Stratfor that he founded in 1996 continues to operate and produces about 80 percent accurate material. This is why Friedman has been called the "Shadow CIA" and the "21st century's Nostradamus." There may be some errors, but we cannot but see that there will be a geopolitical shift in East Asia in the years to come. This is a scary thought.

But I am also excited. If luck stays with us, then what if we claim the rightful glory of ancient Goguryeo?

B. Strategic Vision

a) Strategic Paradox

In 2010, at the ASEAN forum, there was a discussion regarding the South China Sea and its sovereignty. The countries involved decided to invite the United States to serve as the arbiter, except for the Chinese foreign minister,

---

131) George Friedman, *The Next Decade*. Translated in Korean in Korean by Kim Hong-rae. Sam and Parkers, 2011. In 2009, Friedman wrote another book, *The Next 100 Years*, translated into Korean by Son Min-joong, Gimm-Young Publishers, Inc., 2010.

Yang Jiechi. He said, "China and your country have stark differences, and you must acknowledge this fact. That is why China is a big country, while you are a small country."[132] This is somewhat out of the ordinary. But this excessively imperious manner by China only struck the other Asian nations dumb.

In Korean, we have a saying, "the liver protrudes from the stomach." This is something we say when someone talks or behaves like a braggart. Why did China say such a thing? When a person becomes arrogant then he is unable to see clearly.

I would like to tell you about a real life example from a while ago. In 1959, during the annual Korean National Sports Festival, there was a rugby match between the Korea Military Academy (KMA) and Seoul National University (SNU). I hesitate to say this, but SNU at the time did not have a team worthy of competing back then.

The National Sports Festival gave a slot to each city or province, so SNU got a chance to play as a representative of Gyeonggi Province. That's what happened. I will tell you how it ended first: the match ended in a tie. This makes no sense at all, because the KMA boasted a powerful league, and was used to winning all their rugby matches. For about three years, they were unbeatable. On the other hand, SNU's team was closer to a neighborhood league in terms of ability. Korea's best team, KMA, tied with SNU. How did this happen?

The KMA was too strong back then. They used to obliterate every

---

132) Edward N. Luttwak, *Last Emperor: Xi Jinping*. Translated by Wokusan Shinji. Moon Yeo Chun Choo, pp. 31-32.

opponent. They were "second to none" domestically. They were an unbeatable team nation-wide. They became too prideful. Their livers protruded from their stomachs. No wonder why they suffered a defeat (even though they tied, I would still call this a loss). If you become too arrogant, then you cannot see clearly. Since you cannot see clearly, you mess up, make mistakes, and make even bigger messes that benefit your opponent. This type of error can be attributable to people, organizations, and even countries. I believe China has fallen into a strategic paradox due to its current arrogance.[133]

There is a problem with China's strategy right now. There is another saying translated from the Chinese that I would like to mention right now. In Korean, this is called "Jeon Bang Whi Kang Kyung Noh Seon." In English, it means "taking a hard line in all directions." Some news pundits take it even further and call it a "wolf diplomacy," and deplore its use.

When we deployed THAAD, we witnessed what China did to us. They shut down Lotte Department stores in mainland China, forbade travel to Korea, and started a nation-wide movement to boycott Korea. "My way or the highway," seems to be China's current strategy, from my point of view. From the 1990s to the early 2000s, there were no problems for Chinese diplomacy. In 1995, they joined the WTO, and in 2001, the IMF. It was demonstrative that they, too, were a part of a greater whole and willingly became global players in an increasingly interconnected world.[134] The world

---

133) "As you grow stronger, you lose your strategic advantage." This is what I mean by a strategic paradox. If there is no opponent to match your skills, then you become too arrogant. If you become too prideful, then your judgment clouds. If your judgments are clouds, then you start making mistakes. If you make mistakes, your friends will leave you. If you lose your friends, you become weaker.

134) China, at this point, seemed, through their actions, to promise and respect the

welcomed them into the fold. Until China reached its 10th anniversary with the WTO, it had shown a growth spurt (in its economy) that reached double digits. At this, the United States and Japan invested heavily in China because they believed that China would become global player.

In September 2008, Lehman Brothers collapsed.[135] While the rest of the world was spinning the wheels in the mud, China put in about 4 trillion yuan, or about $600 billion U.S. dollars, so they could revive and stimulate its economy. For about ten years, it continued to turn a profit. In foreign currency, by 2004, it had $500 billion U.S. dollars, but by 2008, it had $1.5 trillion U.S. dollars and became the first ranked country in terms of their foreign exchange reserve. It was obvious that the tides did not turn in their favor. The United States and other Western nations could not see a way out of their economic quagmire. There were no signs that they could recover. Even for the United States, there were some dire projections. If this is so, then based on modern China's economic growth rate, it may surpass the United States' GDP by 2030—it may become a hegemonic power by this time.

This was enough for China to think that Pax Americana is about to end. Starting from this point, China's policy started changing. It started following a more aggressive policy. This policy, called "One belt, one road," may have stemmed from this as well. From August to September of 2013, President Xi Xinping of China visited Central Asia and Southeast Asia and pushed this agenda. The scale and scope of the plan were magnificent. But the end

---

international Law of the Sea Convention, private property rights, intellectual property rights, and copyrights, and follow the international practice of these rights.

135) The global financial services firm, Lehman Brothers, filed for bankruptcy around this time, at close to $600 billion, causing a world-wide recession.

goal and its methods are still wrong. To aim for global dominance, and crush others who are weaker via money and or power are not to my liking.

Economic and military power are two important facets of a nation, but they are not the end all and be all. The United Kingdom and Italy's GDPs are not very different. The United Kingdom's is $2.8 trillion U.S. dollars while Italy's is $2.1 trillion U.S. dollars. But their dominance and role in the world differ greatly. I estimate that the United Kingdom's impact and role in the world are at least 10 times that of Italy. National power stems from economic power and international power, but also from its assumed "great" national presence in the world. Its contributions to culture and its moral actions must also be taken into account.

In 2009, China searched high and low in its museums and libraries for ancient documents and maps. Then they tried to use these documents as evidence of their international presence and claimed sovereignty over the South China Sea. Vietnam, Malaysia, Indonesia, and other coastal nations have thus been embroiled in a dispute all this time—and for them, there is only one choice. They must form an alliance or partnership with other nations. Not only this, but neighboring countries are frightened as well by China's actions. At the behest of the United States, Japan as well as Australia and India have joined "the Quad."[136] Even personal relationships take a hit when you ask for a huge favor or keep insisting on a one-sided argument. Even in international politics, your strategy is sound only if you remain flexible. An unreasonable strategy is hard to call "strategy."

---

136) The Quad may reject Korea's wishes to join the organization. At ASEAN, Cambodia's always taking China's side and as a result, meetings have not reached fruitful outcomes thus far.

Let us take a look at the Philippines, for example. The "Father of the Nation," so to speak, along with the upper classes there, are all overseas Chinese. Even economically speaking, China is its biggest trading partner. Even when left alone, it is a friend to China. While it seems like the United States may have a big influence there, there is a subtle anti-American sentiment stirring as well due to past U.S. colonialism experience. As soon as the conflict of the South China Sea arose, however, it sought the help of the United States, which it had rejected before.

But as to what China thinks of this is all too clear. It is inflexible and unbending. Has its liver protruded from its stomach? Or their Sino-centric ideology made them stuck? I am very sorry about this. If China were back on the right track as a member of international society, the world must become full of light, for the sake of the fame of "China," and its bright cultural heritage.

In April 2019, one of France's warships entered the Taiwan Strait. This is out of the ordinary. China was angry, but it did not retaliate. The United States has long stressed the "freedom of navigation."[137] There is no place on Earth where it has not been. This may always disgruntle China, but it cannot do anything. We need to think about France and their military action, with seemingly no interests or concerns in this area of the world, who did a brave thing to keep China in check via the aforementioned rule.

The British Royal Navy, in recent years, has deployed aircraft carrier

---

137) "Freedom of Navigation (FON)," states in one of its clauses that the United States Navy, in accordance with international laws of the sea, may enter foreign waters and pass through it if there is a dispute over sovereignty. Thus, the nation contesting the sovereignty of the sea is held in check by a public show of force via the United States Navy passing through its waters, and this has proved to be an effective method so far.

Strike Group, consisting of nine warships, mainly HMS Elizabeth. The United Kingdom has ties with Hong Kong and Singapore, so this presence is not a stretch, and yet, the German Navy has also announced its deployment to the South China Sea. The deployments' mission comprising the United States, the United Kingdom, Australia, and Japan's respective navies, are also present in that area to monitor North Korea's smuggling activities in the region. That was the official reason given, but it is definite that they are watching Chinese unreasonable activity around the South China Sea.

In recent years, Sweden and China have had strained relations as well, even though they are not neighbors. In February 2020, Hong Kong's Swedish bookstore manager was sentenced to 10 years of penal servitude. According to media reports from Hong Kong, he was charged with "releasing illegal information that [should have been withheld from the world at large]." When Sweden's government formally requested that the man, surnamed Gui, be released, the Chinese ambassador to Sweden said, "What, a 48 kg boxer is trying to fight a 86 kg boxer?" and booed. The Swedish expelled him from the country immediately. During the same month, Sweden took even greater steps to shut down the Confucius Institutes and classrooms within the country. In September of that year, Sweden also canceled China's use of a satellite base in its own country. All these happened as a side effect of too much Chinese arrogance.

b) Alliances with maritime powers

A continental nation, a landlocked nation, shall we say, does not know the ways of the sea. When it sees a large body of water, like the ocean, it assumes that Sea Power, or the presence of a navy, will let it conquer the seas. But for maritime nations surrounded by the sea or near the sea are different. They look at something else. If they meet a storm, they sometimes accept other countries' aid, see new worlds that they haven't seen before, experience the customs of others, and since the routes of the sea are not fixed in stone, they have a chance to see and appreciate just how large the world really is. It so follows that they naturally start to believe in getting along with their neighbors. This means they will follow a course of action stressing cooperation and alliances.

The representative maritime nation is, of course, the United Kingdom. The United Kingdom's actions serve as a type of primer for other maritime nations. Its strength lies not only in its Royal Navy. It is a friendly nation and an ally, and its military, diplomacy, economics, and culture, have close ties all over the world. Upon this cornerstone, they share harbor facilities, repair vessels, and weather intelligence, even going as far to release information about an "enemy" country. This is Maritime Power at its finest.

So a strategist will always distinguish Sea Power from Maritime Power. If the former is the hardware, then the latter is the software. Definitely, the latter is more important. Maritime Power is about a strategy of alliance. With a well-proposed alliance strategy, even a weak and small nation can survive, no matter how cruel international politics is. Otherwise, a poorly proposed alliance strategy jeopardizes even a nation with hegemony. So a good strategy means a good alliance strategy. The arrogant China of today is blind to this; alliances, I mean. Is it because it is a continental country? As for myself, I admire it for its ancient culture, and this is why I feel sorrowful when thinking about China's current trajectory.

4 Strengthen our cooperation with Japan

In the past, our country of Joseon met the unfortunate fate of losing our national sovereignty to Japan. That is why when many Koreans talk of Japan, they still dislike the country. Let us debate this viewpoint. Are all Japanese to be relegated to be our natural enemies from birth?

In Ryu Seong-ryong's *Seo-ae: a Collection of Literary Works*, there is a phrase that strikes me; it is, "The Japanese are a wide-tooth comb, while the Chinese are a fine-tooth comb." Do you understand the significance of this quote? It refers to the Japanese troops and the Ming troops of China in the Imjin War, the Japanese invasion of Korea in 1592. As said, both Japanese and Ming troops looted Joseon people, but the only difference between them was that Japanese troops looted us a little bit loosely, and Ming troops looted us severely. This is a somewhat of a different story from what we usually hear.

In the 1970s, when we started to become an industrialized country, all the technology came from Japan. Car manufacturing, steel, electronics, etc. were all copies of Japanese technology, and the Japanese closed their eyes and pretended not to see us stealing their proprietary technology. When times were hard, we complained to Japan until they gave us money. Their fathers' generation had sinned against us, so we used this leverage to get what we wanted back then. There is no eternal enemy or eternal ally in an international relationship. Historically speaking, we may have had our differences, and yet, can we turn our backs on them forever?

From my perspective, I think that in international politics, we must cooperate with them. This is similar to a couple that may argue day and night but still grow old together because they are well suited to each other, oddly enough. So what do I mean by this, exactly? I am referring to a political system. For example, freedom and dictatorships are mutually exclusive. Capitalism is incompatible with socialism.

The United States and Japan also share a partnership that strengthens them both. That is because they both stress personal freedom and capitalism.

On a more personal level, what characteristics do we seek out in friends? Honesty, diligence, and loyalty. But there is a risk here. A subtle attraction… Westerners refer to this as "chemistry." This "chemistry" surpasses reason and logic. I don't know why. You are drawn to them, and they are drawn to you. This is what you have to guard against, for it may go down in flames. The essential qualities are trust and consistency.

An extremely close friendship that we call, "Gwan Po Ji Gyo," is an idiom that originated from times long ago. While young, both did business; yet, Gwanjung would take a larger portion than the other Posuga. But Posuga did not complain. This is because Gwanjung was suffering from poverty. Gwanjung also had a history of running away from a fight. But Posuga did not call him cowardly. That is because Gwanjung had an elderly mother to care for. This is why a friend who understands my circumstances, firmly believes in me, and helps me when in need is a real and true friend.

There is not much difference between personal relationships and foreign relations. You must guard against nations who keep score and squabble about who did what, and thank the nations who silently help us when we are in need. The countries who know yet look away, and those who help us at a personal cost to themselves— these nations we must hold dear in our hearts.

On a more personal level, we must remember that there are good times as well as the bad. This is true for countries as well. Additionally, as is the case with good friends, a good country will survive accompanied by other good countries, in this bloody world of international politics. Alliances are crucial.

The very noun "Japan" may taste bitter in our mouths, yet Korea and Japan are still compatible countries. Neighbors that are compatible are rare. To live, and more importantly, live well, you must have more friends than enemies. This is Sociology 101. A country compatible with us is so rare that we can and should not turn them into enemies. Shake hands, invite them for drinks, and talk through the night, then all will be right again. When we are reasonable, at least they are willing to listen. That is why I keep reiterating the same point over and over, that Korea and Japan are the rare exception: neighbors that are compatible with one another. When discussing compatibility, one must remember some things. Inner compatibility. What do I mean by this? I mean that it is a mutually beneficial union. I need you. And you need me. You cannot live without me, and I cannot live without you. We are perfectly matched.

With countries, sometimes relationships are forged by force. One country may be so weak that it can't even squeak. This may be a forced union, but it is permissible, and sometimes necessary. But it is costly. If forging a union between countries requires force, then one party must have the necessary power to do so. There is a better method. It is talent. You have to develop a technology that no one else has, just as Maritime Power is more powerful and important than Sea Power.

National Power these days, I believe, is defined by the power of technology. An excellent firm is a conglomerate. That is why Samsung and LG are so important. Can others wrest them from our grip? No, the world is not as harsh as that. There are many such giants in the world. Let us raise our glasses to Samsung and LG.

There is a better way. Politics. Leadership. Former Korean President Park Chung-hee's leadership shaped the Republic of Korea of today. Do you remember my lamenting over the head of the UNDP, and Mr. Larzo's big regret? Leadership's power and force sometimes cause experts to misjudge. I never knew. That is why one must do well in governing a country, which requires excellent leadership. They say people in an organization matter more than anything. Some say HR is all you need, but in truth, leadership is everything.

5 The Reunification of the Korean Peninsula

A. Reunification needs to happen

Some pundits strongly oppose the reunification of the Korean Peninsula. They cite the following: costs, social unrest, conflicts, etc. They also state that reunification would not improve the current climate. They are convincing. But I still disagree. Why? Let us discuss this matter further.

Koreans have inhabited the Korean Peninsula for at least 5,000 years. We have endured many adversities, yet we have managed to forge our own language, preserve our own culture, and have been relatively homogeneous for about 5,000 years. The ethnic Korean people are unique in that, for such a long time, we have been one homogenous group for many centuries; this is not found in many countries, no matter how far and wide you seek.

But unfortunately for us, along with liberation from Japanese colonial rule in 1945, we have been as a peninsula divided with seemingly polar opposite political systems. We have been separated for over 70 years. This is a split that was caused by other nations. During this division, our Korean culture's similarities and identities have become marked by differences rather than similarities. What will happen in 100 or 200 years? We cannot stop; the time to reunify is now.

Once reunification happens, the threat of war will be quelled and our national security will be strengthened due to peace on the Korean Peninsula. We will not even have ideological conflicts. When the society becomes integrated, then ideological conflicts cease. This is why we have wasted so much time; we will be strengthened once again via an injection of new energy and new alliances to be made, all for the benefit of the Korean people. Not only this, but our greatest threat to our national security disappears. Our credit rating will increase automatically. That is why our national brand's image will receive a facelift, going from a "Korea Discount" to a "Korea Premium."

If one nation wishes to raise its voice, and voice its viewpoints as well as grievances, then it must have some bulk to it. That means that our population's national land must at least be twice the size of current Korea. Reunification will solve this problem as well. Then it means that the domestic market will grow in size, and even more importantly, with the South's capital and the North's workforce and underground resources, our newly unified country will prosper rapidly through this synergy. One economic system will also thrive by sponsoring people and materials and laying the groundwork for a strong nation.

Reunification of the Korean Peninsula will raise our geopolitical status. The closed terrain would be open and more able to spread its influence on the Asian continent, and the sea will turn unified Korea into an important transportation hub. On the mainland, we will be neighbors again with China and Siberia, for example, and the Pacific as well as the Arctic Ocean. Once a person traverses the Pacific and the northern seas, you can shrink the time needed to get to the Middle East by as much as 15 days (currently, the passage to India takes more time via sea). This is why the peninsula will become an important hub of trade for businesses, give them growth opportunities, and for the individual, more varied job opportunities and employment.

Reunification also erases the threat of war. As I have stated before, our Korean people will all love freedom and respect human dignity. This will give us a way to become a leading nation in Asia. Additionally, reunification will raise Korea's status as an economic hub that links the Pacific and continent, as a nation that leads North East Asia's peace and co-thrive.

Look at Germany! After reunification, they became the central nation of Europe. We could have the same role in Asia. Why should we refuse this role? The story I'm about to relate is from just five to six years ago. Paul Kennedy, the writer of *The Rise and Fall of Great Powers*, was asked by the University of Tokyo to give a lecture there.

> After the lecture ended, one student asked him a question.
> "For the next generation, which country will lead Asia?"
> An unexpected answer issued from his lips.
> "Never China, never Japan—maybe Korea."

Some experts lament the projected financial costs of reunification, and use this to justify why they are hesitant to reunify the two Koreas[138] This is

---

138) The costs of reunification must take into account government spending. Furthermore, upon reunification, all the necessary costs shouldered by society should also be taken into account. The British firm Eurizon SLJ Asset Management estimates that the cost of reunification will be spread over at least ten years, and cost about 2,167 trillion won. According to United States experts, it will cost at least 1,989 trillion won, and Stanford University estimates the cost to be at least 2,340 trillion to 5,850 trillion won.

typical defeatism. Won't you achieve success in fear of risk?

B. Chun Myung: A Mandate from Heaven

Man, no matter what era in which they live, is given a holy task from Heaven. This "Chun Myung" differs from obligations and actual laws passed by legislation (also called "positive laws"). It does not use force, nor are punishments used. But "Chun Myung," for an individual, means that he must take into consideration why he was born and question this miracle; this is his moral obligation as a human being.

When a person asks himself existential questions, then man becomes devout and much more moral; via this route, he realizes his own destiny. We call this "Unquestionable duty."[139] So, during these times, what is the Chun Myung for us?

Look at North Korea, for example. Our neighbors up North. Who are they? Are they not the ones who share the same bloodline as us? Are they not our comrades with whom we have a shared 5,000-year history? But what are their lives like? Are they not the worst off (from our perspective), our 25 million brothers and sisters up North?

A person must at least breathe and take in nourishment from food. He must have freedom of speech. He must be free in his movements. Our brothers in North Korea are limited in their movements. They are stripped of their right to free speech and they do not have enough to eat. The only God-

---

139) This refers to moral behaviors that God has instilled in us and our obligation to abide by these moral laws. An intellectual will take this course of action.

given right that they exercise is breathing. Their living conditions are worse than a prison. At least in prison they serve three meals a day. They easily detain people in prison or kill them.

Gentlemen! Do you now understand why I speak of reunification? Our brothers and sisters in North Korea are starving, oppressed, and unable to exercise their basic human rights. Are we really going to cross our arms and just observe these atrocities? Our moral destiny is to help save North Koreans. This is the lesson that we must learn in this time and age.

"I will make them one nation in the land, on the mountains of Israel. There will be one king over all of them and they will never again be two nations or be divided into two kingdoms." (Ezekiel 37:22)

Gentlemen! Is this not our fate? "They will never again be two nations or be divided into two kingdoms?" Let us go! Let us take the lead! Let us save our brothers and sisters!

C. How will we achieve reunification?

Reunification by absorbing North Korea is the best way. It's about kicking in the door and freeing our brothers out of prison. Vietnam did this, and Yemen too. The end is clear-cut. There are no unnecessary acts that should be fixed at the end. But we cannot do this. Who doesn't want a clear-cut ending? But as we all know, because there are no real "free" things in life, most expensive costs will follow. But a clear-cut end always ends in bloodshed. I hate bloodshed. I am a former military officer and know a little about war. War doesn't comprise of just bloodshed. We lose our humanity, and our souls become destroyed. Our shared humanity shatters.

I like water. There is a saying from the Chinese, "Great virtue has a characteristic of water." Lao-Tzu said this. It means that water's essential quality is goodness, and out of all things that are good, water ranks among the best of these elements. Water dislikes fighting, and makes everything pure. It goes where others dislike going. That is why it is so close to the good and the harmonious.[140] Water flows from above and flows below. It is modest. It always fills empty places, seeks out the shady areas, and cultivates all things. It is fair and it is wise. It does not discriminate; hot or cold, it is still water and gets along with everyone. It is generous.

Korean reunification should be as water meets water. As a small stream joins a large stream, and a large river flows towards the ocean—it must be a natural union. North Korea should flow to where South Korea is located, at an appropriate place. The Republic of Korea is about 100 times a larger river than the Democratic People's Republic of Korea. A river rushes by, and a large river avoids an islet by dividing into two, flowing around it and joining the rushing river. We speak the same language, use the same alphabet, and have the same customs; our union is soundless and will happen inevitably.

Water flows from above to below, so let us make an appropriate place. A river divided in two will naturally flow into one. We must make what is high, low, and pick the land. As two rivers meet at the lower place and become one big river, they must meet at the mouth and flow towards the ocean. We now have to end the dictatorship and suppress it. Our North Korean brothers

---

140) Water doesn't have a shape. It conforms to the vessel that contains it. It changes shape depending on the vessel that you filled it with. It doesn't change its essential quality, while adapting at the same time. This is the wisdom of Lao-Tzu.

and sisters are starving. Yet are the heavens indifferent to their suffering? The time is coming. Something is rotten. It may rot on its own. The United Nations must take the lead, and the United States, and if the Republic of Korea follows their guidance, then it may be achievable.

We must wait until our brothers and sisters hear the bells of freedom ring. We must be patient, avoid rushing, and slowly push ahead. Our brothers and sisters up North have many options to take democratic liberties that are at stake. Take issue with the humanitarian atrocities that are taking place, help the defectors to voice their concerns, and if the United States and the United Nations help, there is nothing that we cannot achieve together. Can you not see the signs? Let us be patient a little while longer. The time is coming.

I worried over the problem of the reunification of the two Koreas. Then I envisioned Hwang Jang-yop (1923-2010).[141] Aha! As Hwang has already passed from this earth, I cannot meet with him. So, I did the next best thing. I bought his book.

The first sentence was, "A dictatorship and a democratic society cannot coexist under the same sky." Then what to do? Invade? No. If you invade, then it will turn into a disaster. You dig yourself into a hole. Then it's not reunification; it's a splintering. Reunification has to be natural; it should not be forced, for otherwise problems will arise.

---

141) Hwang Jang-yup obtained a MA and Ph.D. in Philosophy from Moscow State University, also known as M.V. Lomonosov. Afterward, he served in various posts at Kim Il-sung University. He supported Kim Jong-il, and gave lectures on the philosophy of self-reliance, known as "Juche" (the underlying founding philosophy of North Korea). In 1997, he defected and sought political asylum in the Republic of Korea.

Hwang also states that a dictatorship should be suppressed and that North Koreans should become a democratic society. It is the eleventh hour. A dictatorship will collapse on its own. Hwang must have known this, as he heeded the signs of rot. Isn't this why he states that dictatorships should be suppressed? Suppose the North Korean dictatorship falls. Then, with the United Nations' help, a unitary government should be formed, and the eight provinces of old should establish local governments there. Foreign relations and national security should be the federal government's responsibility, and the local government should carry out administrative duties.

Gentlemen! If there is a fate for our time and our country, then what is it? Is there a greater calling than reunification? "Reunification" means everyone in this time and place are tasked with this great and mighty act. This is my long-cherished wish and the Chun Myung.

My beloved gentlemen! Your generation is the one that God has entrusted to reunify the two Koreas.